Intercultural Communication

Pathways to Better Interactions

David Boromisza-Habashi

University of Colorado Boulder

cognella

SAN DIEGO

Bassim Hamadeh, CEO and Publisher
Todd R. Armstrong, Publisher
Michelle Piehl, Senior Project Editor
Abbey Hastings, Production Editor
Abbie Goveia, Graphic Design Assistant
Trey Soto, Licensing Coordinator
Natalie Piccotti, Director of Marketing
Kassie Graves, Vice President of Editorial
Jamie Giganti, Director of Academic Publishing

3970 Sorrento Valley Blvd., Ste. 500. San Diego, CA 92121

Brief Contents

Contents

Preface

The experience of cultural difference in intercultural interactions between actual participants is an intensely personal experience. Participants can suddenly find themselves feeling confused, intrigued, frustrated, excited, and embarrassed, all at the same time. Students I have taught over the years often react to the onslaught of such emotions by running away from cultural difference. I wrote this book to convince them to run toward it instead.

This book was born of a desire to empower students to become competent intercultural practitioners—that is, informed communicators who can recognize when they are faced with cultural difference in communication, have strategies for making sense of cultural difference, and work toward restoring coordinated interaction with cultural others for the purpose of completing specific tasks. As a result, although the book contains a brief introduction to the field of intercultural communication in Chapter 2, its main focus is to help students chart their own pathways toward better intercultural interactions.

Given the goal of helping students become competent intercultural practitioners, I followed three principles in writing this book:

1. **Keep it interaction focused**. Throughout the book, I maintain focus on examples of actual intercultural interactions and the features of such interactions. As an ethnographer of communication working within the intellectual tradition of language and social interaction, I believe in the key role of context-bound social interaction in constituting relations in every context and at every scale of social life. Coordinated social interaction is the universal *sine qua non* of successful coexistence and collaboration among individuals in and across social groups. As Chapter 9 states: "*Communication matters*. Interacting with others creates opportunities to make the most of our interdependent lives in diverse societies. Communication is the playing field where we attempt to coordinate our interactions, our goals, and our lives. We negotiate, we persuade, we share our stories, we praise, and we hold each other accountable in social interaction." Cultural

variation in social interaction explains why many (not all!) interactions between individual speakers become uncoordinated. This book prepares students to appreciate and study differences among expressive systems that such cultural variation brings into relief. It also prepares them to avoid essentialist thinking about cultures by shifting their attention from the uniqueness of cultural groups to the uniqueness of the expressive systems social groups rely on to coordinate their everyday actions and lives. In addition, the book constantly reminds students that some elements of local expressive systems are not unique to particular groups but circulate globally.

2. **Keep it practical.** My undergraduate students tend to regard intercultural communication as a practical concern. In other words, they see it as an activity they would like to get better at. Cultural pragmatics, the approach I adopt in this book, embraces and builds on this popular orientation to intercultural communication. Cultural pragmatics is principally concerned with how speakers engaged in intercultural communication can produce knowledge about unfamiliar context-bound uses of language (including the social and cultural meanings of those uses) and how they can act on that knowledge for the sake of coordinating their communication with cultural others for the purpose of accomplishing practical tasks. This book is not designed to turn students into ethnographers of communication or discourse analysts; rather it uses theories and concepts from those research traditions to equip students to make sense of intercultural difference in communication to the extent accomplishing practical tasks (e.g., apologizing, running a meeting, asking someone out, etc.) with cultural others requires them to do so. The book also maintains focus on the moral and political dimensions of everyday communication practice and the practice of cultural investigation I call "building culture." Finally, the principle of practicality guided me to foreground interaction in Western contexts—given that most students using this book are likely to reside in the United States or other Western countries—and in interpersonal and workplace contexts, which tend to be of most interest to Western students.

3. **Keep it personal.** As anyone with firsthand experience of intercultural encounters knows, coming face-to-face with cultural difference is not a purely cognitive exercise. Rather, due to the possibility of miscommunication or the lack of time and other resources to clarify differences between culturally unique expressive systems, both the social life of the person and their sense of self are at stake. This book maintains focus on this whole-person approach to intercultural communication in two ways. First, it is written in an engaging style that appeals not only to students' intellect but also to their emotional worlds, senses of humor, and life experiences. To foster further engagement with the text, I included a

number of my students' personal narratives of encountering cultural difference. These narratives, which I have lightly edited for style and length, appear at the beginning of the chapters in Parts II to IV of the book, with the authors' names replaced with gender-neutral pseudonyms. Second, the book features a stronger authorial voice than typical textbooks. I make elements of my personal history, including my own struggles with intercultural interactions, available to students in order to emphasize that building culture is a practice in which intercultural practitioners—including the author of the textbook—engage throughout their lives, and that doesn't invariably lead to success. As the author, I take full advantage of my status as a cultural "outsider within"—that is, as a foreign-born citizen of the United States who struggles with some aspects of the local expressive system to this day.

The result of my commitment to these principles is a textbook unique in its strong focus on actual examples of intercultural interactions, the practice of (inter)cultural inquiry for the sake of improving future interactions, and the personal experience of cultural difference.

The book contains 14 chapters that can be taught in any order. The order of chapters in the book represents my own pedagogical orientation to teaching the course: begin with shorter introductory chapters that lay out the practical challenges of intercultural interaction and possible solutions offered by cultural pragmatics (Chapters 1-3), then move to the review of some (not all!) features of interaction that can lead to intercultural miscommunication (Chapters 4-11), then review the importance of cultural meaning and "normality" (Chapters 12-13), and end with a chapter that ties together the course by summarizing the process of building culture (Chapter 14).

Each chapter contains:

- learning goals to guide students' attention

- highlighted key terms (defined in the glossary)

- text boxes that address students' practical questions and link the material to principles of cultural pragmatics

- a "Barriers to Coordinated Interaction" section that creates explicit links between the material presented in individual chapters and the practice of intercultural communication

- reflection questions to aid students in their effort to process the material and link it to their personal experience

- a list of references

Supporting materials accompanying this book for adopting instructors include:

- a syllabus constructed around the structure of the book

- one PowerPoint presentation per chapter

- two to three online videos and/or activity recommendations per chapter

- a test bank featuring multiple choice, fill-in-the-blank, and essay questions

- the description of a multistage assignment (called the "Rich Point Project") designed to engage students in cultural inquiry related to their own personal experiences of cultural difference in intercultural interaction

This book would not have been possible without Nora Boromisza-Habashi, my wife, who discussed with me and accompanied me through many of the intercultural encounters I narrate in this book. I am indebted to Mike Agar, Karen Ashcraft, Benjamin Bailey, Donal Carbaugh, Bob Craig, Danielle Hodge, Tamar Katriel, Marcyliena Morgan, Karen Tracy, and Gerry Philipsen for the intellectual inspiration I have been able to draw from their research and pedagogical practices. I also owe Benjamin Broome (Arizona State University), Barbara Ruth Burke (University of Minnesota Morris), Joseph S. Caputo (Gonzaga University), Alan Hansen (Carroll College), Tabitha Hart (San José State University), Sunny Lie (California State Polytechnic University, Pomona), Trudy Milburn (Southern Connecticut State University), Kristine Muñoz (University of Iowa), Cheryl L. Nicholas (Pennsylvania State University, Berks), Max Saito (Westfield State University), and Nadezhda M. Sotirova (University of Minnesota, Morris) a debt of gratitude for their helpful comments on drafts of the book manuscript. Thanks to my research assistant, Emily Loker, for helping this book come alive with examples of intercultural interactions. I have to thank my publisher, Todd Armstrong, for believing in this project from the beginning, and my project editor, Michelle Piehl, for keeping its development on track. Last but not least, advance thanks to you, the instructor, for adopting this book and for your valiant effort to pronounce my sizable last name (*Boh-roh-mee-sah Ha-bah-she*).

David Boromisza-Habashi, Ph.D.
Department of Communication
University of Colorado Boulder

"Where Do I Look for Culture?"

A Practical Approach to Intercultural Communication

In this chapter, you will learn:

- the general approach of this book to culture

- the difference between culture as a thing and culture as a process

- the six characteristics of culture

S ometimes cultural difference unexpectedly hits you in the gut.

I (the guy who wrote this book) was born and raised in Budapest, Hungary, in the last quarter of the 20th century. I lived in my home country until I finished my undergraduate education, and then I moved to the United States (almost) permanently. In the spring of 2000, I was a young international student working on my master's degree in communication at the Albany campus of the State University of New York (SUNY). One day, while walking back to the graduate student office after grabbing lunch at the Campus Center, I saw a small gathering of students in front of the university library under the gray concrete columns of the main quad. They were listening to a smartly dressed woman in her 50s standing on a small podium. Not being in any particular hurry, I stopped to listen. It turned out the woman was representing the organization MADD (Mothers Against Drunk Driving). She was telling the story of how her young son had gotten into a drunken friend's car after a party. They died terrible deaths when they crashed into a tree in the middle of the night.

While I understood her story was intended to be a cautionary tale about drunk driving, I suddenly felt a rush of conflicting feelings. I felt sad and curious, empathetic and repulsed, glued to the spot and wanting to walk away as quickly as possible. I could no longer listen to what the speaker was saying, I was too busy sorting through these various emotions. In the end, I mustered the strength to walk back to my office. It took me a few hours to calm down and figure out why I found myself overcome by this maelstrom of emotions.

The main reason, I concluded eventually, wasn't who the speaker was or what she said, at least not directly. It wasn't even the personal connection I had to alcoholism as someone with family members who were alcoholics. I had to dig a little deeper. Growing up in Hungary during the dying days of state socialism before the country's shift to Western-style liberal democracy in 1989, I took two things for granted about public speaking. One, that it was not the job of the average citizen to speak to groups of strangers. Public speaking in my mind was tied to particular occupations. People like politicians, professors, and priests spoke publicly because it was their jobs to do so. Two, the public speakers I had listened to as a kid never spoke about the intimate details of their lives, and most certainly not about something as deeply intimate as the death of a child. In my mind, stories of birth, love, illness, and death were to be discussed in private with friends and family. From the perspective of my childhood experiences, the MADD speaker's performance seemed freakishly inappropriate.

And yet, as I stood there listening to her, I could see that the rest of the audience did not seem to be as taken aback by her words as I was. The expressions on students' faces were solemn but not disturbed. They understood the situation, and they knew precisely what to do: stand in reflective silence and wait for the speaker to finish. My brain and heart were doing cartwheels, but I could tell that my reaction was that of an uninformed outsider. It slowly dawned on me that I wanted to learn more about the communication practice called public speaking.

CULTURE AS A THING

There is no such thing as culture.

Sometimes we have to communicate with people whose culture is different from our own.

At first glance, these two statements seem contradictory. If there is no such thing as culture, how can it be possible to encounter and interact with people from other cultures? And if it is possible to do those things, how can we claim that cultures don't exist?

Actually, the two statements are less contradictory than they seem. More precisely, they are only contradictory if we view **culture as a thing**. Intuition tells us culture is a thing with certain characteristics that people have or in which they have membership.

Sometimes we think about culture as ethnic food, folk costumes, or native art. At other times, we imagine culture to be the traditions of people who live in exotic places or nations far away from ours. Some commodities, objects to be bought and sold, such as home decoration, clothing, or entertainment, are marketed to us as representative of other cultures. When people who look or speak differently from us do things that strike us as strange or morally objectionable, we often say, "Well, they did that because they are from a different culture, they have different traditions." Many of us who work or study at universities believe culture is something anthropologists study.

None of these ways of thinking about cultural differences are wrong in some abstract sense. They have been around for a very long time, or at least since the German thinker Alexander Humboldt introduced the idea of "cultural" differences among nations in the early 1800s. Humboldt believed languages were governed by cultural rules that applied to how those languages were used. Languages used according to those rules expressed the worldviews and cultural knowledge of the people who spoke those languages. Thus, the German language revealed a German culture, the French language revealed a French culture, and so on. Humboldt's thoughts influenced intercultural communication research and popular thinking about language and culture for centuries to come.

It is hard to deny this way of thinking about culture has some utility. Mainly, it helps ordinary members of societies distinguish people who can be expected to act, think, feel, or live like them from people who cannot. The question is: Do these ways of thinking about culture and cultural difference help us communicate and live together with others in our neighborhoods and around the world? And are there are other, more useful ways of thinking about culture that help us move toward these ends?

In what follows, I will first introduce you to the experience of rich points, the first step on the path toward building culture. I will then briefly address cultural pragmatics, the theoretical core of this book, and then discuss culture as a process—as opposed to a thing—with six characteristics. I leave you with the idea that culture is, in essence, communication.

INTRODUCING RICH POINTS: THE VISCERAL EXPERIENCE OF CULTURAL DIFFERENCE

In this book, you will see me share many personal anecdotes of intercultural encounters—not just my own but my students' as well—to highlight intercultural communication as a practical challenge in our everyday lives. Anecdotes are powerful things. We tend to think of anecdotes as "just" stories that make our conversations and our lives more fun. I disagree. Anecdotes entertain, but they also help us make sense of our own and each other's lives, and they model such sense making to others. When we tell anecdotes and other types of stories, we "edit" the endlessly complex world into episodes that are understandable, enjoyable, and shareable, and we show others how such editing can be done. Telling anecdotes also forces us to appreciate the contexts in which events unfold. Context is the background against which anything we say and do "means" things. Without context, there is no meaning—or at least not the kind of meaning people interacting with one another need in order to be able to move toward shared (or different) social goals. You'll read more about this later.

From Culture Shock to Rich Points

Most people in the English-speaking world describe[1] moments like these as **"culture shock"** (National Communication Association, 2019). The Canadian applied anthropologist Kalervo Oberg, who popularized the term, introduced his famous paper on the subject in this way: "Culture shock is precipitated by the anxiety that results from losing all our familiar signs and symbols of social intercourse" (1960, p. 177). He then described culture shock as a psychological state common among people who suddenly find themselves transplanted to other countries. The psychological effects of encountering cultural difference are undeniable, but what I don't like about the term "culture shock" is that it casts moments like my encounter with U.S. American public speaking in a negative light. In fact, I can't think of an encounter that led me to learn more about the United States than the one on that fateful spring day in Albany, New York.

A concept coined by another anthropologist, Michael Agar (1994), captures the productive side of the shock people experience in intercultural encounters. He called these moments "rich points." **Rich points** are moments that combine the raw and intense feelings of confusion and curiosity in roughly equal amounts. The stalling mind of the individual experiencing a rich point throws up two simultaneous questions: "Why on earth would they *do that*?" and "What did they *mean* by that?" You may point out that such moments are not exclusive to intercultural encounters, and you would be right. Sometimes our loved ones, neighbors, and acquaintances do things that throw us for a loop and make us want to figure out what they might be up to. But rich points are different in the sense that they occur in situations when the people experiencing them are inspired to seek a *cultural* explanation for the unfamiliar conduct that fails to compute. Rich points don't prompt us to explain why particular individuals did what they did: they involve us in the larger project of reconstructing the system of meanings, beliefs, and values on the basis of which their conduct apparently made sense to them and other members of their groups or communities but not to us.

---

1 You will see these in-text citations (Author Last Name, Year of Source) throughout this book. In-text citations are provided to identify key scholarly works or sources that shape and inform the ideas presented in that part of the chapter. These citations are formatted in APA (American Psychological Association), and style and format that is used throughout the social sciences. Full source information for all in-text citations is found in the References section at the back the book.

Such reconstruction means much more than trying to generalize from particular incidents to entire cultures. Once you decide to pursue a rich point, you are in it for the long haul. You are making focused observations, looking for more instances of the same confusing and intriguing conduct, identifying patterns of conduct across speakers and situations, asking questions of members of the social group you are now treating as "a culture," taking notes or keeping a diary, collecting videos and online articles, reading scholarship (if you have access to it, which I am not taking for granted), and so on and so forth.

Some Rich Points Are "Richer" Than Others

I should quickly point out that not all rich points result in such dogged pursuits of culture. Although I did all of these things after my encounter with Anglo-American–style public speaking (and continue to do them to this day), I have not pursued all of my rich points with such keen interest. To give you an example, years after my encounter with public speaking, I had another encounter with a neighbor and his ladder. By that time, I was living in the western United States and had a new family and my first house in a leafy suburban neighborhood. One day, a storm hit my town. After the storm, I noticed some broken shingles on the ground in the backyard and decided to investigate. As we had only recently moved to the neighborhood, I didn't have a ladder that was long enough for me to climb onto the roof. As I was considering various foolish plans to somehow make my way to the roof from a nearby tree, a neighbor passed by (let's call him Jay.) Jay and I chatted briefly, and I told him about the broken shingles. In a friendly and generous manner that I have come to associate with the western United States, he immediately volunteered to give me a crash course in roof maintenance. He grabbed a ladder from his house and patiently helped me replace the damaged shingles. He then told me he was going to leave his ladder next to his house, just inside the fence, and that I should feel free to grab it any time I wanted.

Long story short, a couple of days later, I did need Jay's ladder. I walked up to his house, opened the gate, grabbed the ladder, used it, and returned it the same afternoon. The following day, I ran into him in the street and thanked him for letting me use his ladder. "You got it from the house?" he asked. When I answered in the affirmative, he gave me "the look" that told me I had done something wrong. We talked for another minute and went home. Another rich point! What did I do to offend this kind man? I had simply followed his directions. I was teaching an intercultural communication course at the time and asked my students for their input. After some discussion, they suggested I should have knocked on Jay's door to let him know I was going to take the ladder, but this seemed to contradict Jay's direct offer that I should feel free to take it whenever I wanted. As intrigued and clueless as I was, and as much as I wanted to learn about the cultural rules of conduct

A Practical Question

How would you interpret Jay's conduct? Did I violate any cultural norms or expectations?

in American suburbia, I lacked the time and the energy to pursue my rich point further and eventually gave up. (Also, the pressure to address this rich point lessened considerably when Jay and his family moved away a couple of years later.)

Inevitably, our energy, attention, and curiosity are in short supply, or we get distracted and fail to follow our rich points to the stage of cultural discovery. Nevertheless, this book is based on the assumption that there will be rich points you will want to pursue with creativity and determination. My goal is to give you some conceptual and methodological tools to do just that—in other words, to put you on a path to discovery However, before we can start reviewing those tools, I need to say a few things about the approach this book takes to intercultural communication.

BUILDING CULTURE

Rich points are the starting points of cultural investigation: they are (or can be) windows on unfamiliar systems of meaningful communicative conduct. Yes, cultural investigation begins at the "gut level." What follows from this orientation to intercultural communication is that when you pursue rich points, the culture you discover will be, at least in part, built by you, for your own purposes, at a moment in your personal history and in the history of the social group or community whose culture you are busy reconstructing. Cultures don't have entirely independent existences from those who build them. I say "entirely" because it is possible to read or otherwise witness other people's accounts of a target culture. I have found plenty of articles and books on the history and practice of public speaking in the United States, and there is a lot more to read. Still, I will not be able to avoid putting these readings together with my own observations—including taking a public speaking course out of sheer curiosity and, later, teaching one—in a way that will be uniquely tied to my experiences and my identity as a White Hungarian-born cisgender heterosexual married male with three kids living in the United States in the early 21st century.

To say we build culture is not the same thing as saying culture is somehow "subjective." When we label someone's claim subjective, what we imply is that it is an expression of a unique individual's personal point of view or opinion and therefore doesn't apply to anyone else. **Building culture**, however, involves the well-informed, rigorous reconstruction of the form and local meaning of unfamiliar conduct in an unfamiliar social group or community in the process of interacting with its members. Such reconstruction involves taking all relevant blocks, bits, and scraps of information

A Practical Question

Do you have access to online or library materials for the purpose of building culture? If you do, lucky you! If you don't, there is no need to despair: you can build culture without such materials. Building culture means working with what you have.

(e.g., personal experience, observations, conversations, interviews, readings, etc.) available to the culture builder and building up a cultural interpretation of unfamiliar communication conduct.

This kind of inquiry is fundamentally **relational**: that is, it sees cultural knowledge as emerging from a process of interaction between cultural insiders and outsiders. It is also modeled on the qualitative research methodology known as **ethnography**, the rigorous study of social groups from the standpoint of an investigator who freely acknowledges their perspective is far from universal and that cultural knowledge takes shape between cultural members and the investigator. Building culture denies the possibility of seeking cultural knowledge from a "fly on the wall" external perspective. Building culture is impossible without social involvement, and social involvement is impossible without taking a perspective on life. We are, after all, humans.

Cultural Pragmatics

This is the view of culture I, adopting a term coined by communication scholar Donal Carbaugh (1993), will refer to as **cultural pragmatics** in this book. As an approach to intercultural communication, cultural pragmatics is concerned with how people who find themselves in intercultural communication encounters can produce knowledge about unfamiliar context-bound uses of language and the social and cultural meanings of those uses as well as how they can act on that knowledge for the sake of coordinating their communication with cultural others. From this perspective, building culture works a lot like what U.S. American pragmatist philosopher John Dewey (1938) called "inquiry": "Inquiry is the controlled or directed transformation of an indeterminate situation into one that is so determinate in its constituent distinctions and relations as to convert the elements of the original situation into a unified whole" (pp. 104-105). Dewey explained that this definition tied the need for inquiry to an "indeterminate situation" in which a person experiences doubt, panic, hesitation, and confusion. But these feelings should not be mistaken for a debilitating psychological condition that will keep someone from successful inquiry. In fact, these feelings are evidence that the person is *already* engaged in the process of responding to a confusing situation by recognizing they are faced with a puzzle that needs to be solved.

Culture as Process

Thus, rich points are the first step toward building culture. But what exactly is this "culture" we are building? Let's begin with what it is not: a geographic box into which one is born (Agar, 2006). In the 21st century, it is no longer viable to think about cultures

A Practical Question

Think about the neighborhood, town, or city where you live. How many cultures (or cultural traditions) coexist in these places? How do you know they are there?

as small, geographically defined communities (e.g., villages, islands) in which members learn closed systems of meanings and actions, follow those systems from birth to death, and pass them down to their children as tradition.

Instead, Agar invites us to rethink **culture as a process** with six characteristics:

1. At the beginning of the process, **culture is a *working assumption*.** Once you experience a rich point, you also assume the cultural others with whom you are communicating are not being unreasonable, misguided, or rude. Rather, you posit they are using language in a taken-for-granted manner in ways that makes good sense to them but not to you. As a result, your job is to figure out the meaning of what they said in that context.

2. **Culture is *translation*** from one system of context-bound, locally meaningful language use into another—namely, your own. It is not possible to articulate cultural understanding without reference to your own taken-for-granted communicative conduct.

3. **Culture is *relational*.** Culture is invisible from the inside. Think about it: you don't need to think about culture in order to communicate the way you regularly do. Once you start examining things you take for granted, they are no longer taken for granted. Thus, culture is only visible from an outside position, but that position is never neutral: it is always someone's position. But the culture you build will never be "theirs" or "yours": it will always be *between* you and your target speakers. To use a somewhat tired metaphor, it is a bridge between your system of communication and the other's.

4. **Culture is *partial*.** You and I are members of multiple social groups. In everyday talk, we tend to refer to these memberships as our various identities. My identities include Hungarian, a native of the capital Budapest, a U.S. academic, and a dad. What's noteworthy about these identities for the purpose of this discussion is that all of these identities come with typical ways of speaking that are sometimes inter-related, sometimes not. I speak fluent Hungarian with a standard accent after all these years of living outside the country, although my brothers who still live there sometimes have a good laugh when I use outdated slang. As a native of Budapest, I sometimes let slip a disparaging comment or two about "those people in the countryside," comments that make folks "from the countryside" (including my mother-in-law) respond with biting comments about "those people from Budapest." As a U.S. academic, I know how to participate in intellectual conversations at conferences and how to complain about the beginning of the semester with colleagues in the hallway. As a dad, I am well versed in the art form known as the "dad joke" ("Welcome to my home!" "What's upstairs?" "Stairs don't talk."). Any of these ways of speaking could be made the subject of cultural inquiry. When building culture, we must keep in mind that no person is likely to fit neatly into

one culture—in fact, most of us stand at the crossroads of multiple cultures, no matter what part of the world we are from.

5. **Culture is *plural*.** What follows from the partial nature of culture is that any culture we build will always be an element of a larger cultural mosaic. Let's do a thought experiment. Imagine you grew up in St. Louis, Missouri, with parents who immigrated to the United States from Colombia. Now imagine I went to a party your parents hosted. As I'm getting ready to go home, your dad asks me, point blank, why I'm about to leave. I tell him it's late and I have to get up early tomorrow. He says I can't leave and ushers me back to the living room. This conversation is repeated two more times. Seeing the look of mild shock on my face, you come over and explain, in a slightly embarrassed tone, that this is typical Colombian behavior, not Midwestern at all. Now, if I were to follow up on my rich point and do a bit of cultural investigation, I would find out about the Colombian leave-taking ritual the ethnographer Kristine Muñoz (Fitch, 1998) called *salsipuede* ("leave if you can"), but I would also find out about a slice of Midwestern speech culture from the perspective through which this ritual feels like an imposition. In addition, I might learn how you sometimes feel caught between two cultures when you engage in this practice yourself and that you would never think of using *salsipuede* when there are no Colombians around. I would be making a mistake if I were to assume that because you have Colombian parents you would act Colombian across contexts, all the time, without any uncertainty or self-doubt. This doesn't call the existence of *salsipuede* into question, but we do need to be mindful of the extent to which the cultures we build explain the context-bound conduct of our cultural others—in other words, the explanatory power of culture.

6. **Culture is the *product* of the process of inquiry.** Culture, again, is not a thing that exists independently of those who observe it. Culture is one of those dual terms that Dewey (1925/1958) called double-barreled: they point to processes *and* the products of those processes. (Other examples of such terms include "communication," "dialogue," "experience," "performance," "expression," "conflict," and "illustration.") Think about culture as a verb and a noun, two sides of the same coin. When we "culture" (verb), we make a decision to treat someone's seemingly odd communicative conduct as an expression of culture, and we view that someone as a cultural other. Then, once we reconstruct the taken-for-granted forms and meanings of a cultural other's communicative conduct, we produce an account of "culture" (noun). To put it simply, *when you build culture, you get culture.* (I like this formulation better than "when you culture, you get culture"—this sentence sounds odd even to my non-native speaker's ear.)

The Disadvantages of Viewing Culture as a Thing

Let's turn to summarizing some of the disadvantages of conceiving of *culture as a thing other people have or do* from the perspective of everyday practitioners engaged in intercultural communication. First, such a view is *essentialist* in the sense that it imagines people being born with, or into, one culture and living with that same culture throughout their lives. Culture is their essence, their very nature. Members of cultures, in this view, run culture almost like an operating system. They can neither look beyond their cultures nor change them on their own. Their ways change only when their whole cultures change.

Second, this view is *anachronistic,* or outdated. Very few people live their lives today in neatly identifiable "cultures" isolated from the rest of the world. As finance, trade, politics, entertainment, and social media go global, our lives are touched by events that happen elsewhere, products made elsewhere, thoughts first thought elsewhere. This is not to say the world is becoming homogenous: this view of globalization is almost as outdated as the notion of discrete cultures. The truth is somewhere in the middle: people around the world live lives that are in some respects different from, and in other respects similar to, the lives of others elsewhere.

Third, viewing culture as a thing can be socially *alienating.* Because culture can seem too big, too complex, too unwieldy, too exotic, or too far away, it is easy to conclude the average person cannot possibly make sense of it. It is even easier to conclude other people's cultures are inferior to one's own. This type of alienation can breed stereotyping, prejudice, and a general attitude of dismissal toward other cultures.

Finally, the culture-as-thing view tends to produce *simplistic* ways of thinking about cultural difference. Often, those who approach culture as a discrete object quickly overgeneralize their observations about the conduct of individuals to the conduct (or ways of thinking) of entire social groups across speakers and contexts. It is also easy to fall into the trap of overstating the significance of cultural differences at the cost of other types of difference. Cultural difference is not the only reason for communication breakdowns among those who see themselves as members of different cultures—the cause can also be different interests or differences based on gender, class, race, ethnicity, or political opinions, among others. Reducing all social difference to cultural difference is a simple but erroneous solution.

CULTURE IS COMMUNICATION

By now, you have probably picked up on an underlying assumption of this book: culture and communication are indistinguishable. Communication expresses culture to outsiders, and outsiders can draw on observable acts of communication to identify cultural ways of speaking. Outsiders can observe unfamiliar acts of communication, ask questions, and read communication research, social media posts, and comments. They can listen to recordings and watch videos and build up an account of a different cultural system of communication little by little, observation by observation, mistake by mistake, and speculation by speculation. (This is the research process known as **abduction**.)

The culture they build will capture the taken-for-granted system of communicative means and the meanings members of a cultural group draw on to take care of the business of everyday life. This insight helps them align their own ways of speaking with those of cultural others and strive to improve intercultural communication with them.

A Practical Question

What is your image of "research"? Do you imagine scientists in lab coats? A professor with glasses and a beard, wearing a jacket with elbow patches, writing complicated equations on a whiteboard? Students sitting among piles of books in a library? In this book, we take a more practical view of research as a process of inquiry anyone can engage in, even if they don't have access to all the resources of a professional scientist.

Notice that thinking of communication and culture in these ways implies you can try to treat any system of communicative means (consisting of words, phrases, idioms, stories, apologies, genres, rituals, etc.) and their local meanings as cultures. You don't even have to leave your neighborhood. This books invites you to cast a cultural look at any social group distinguished by ethnicity, race, gender, political affiliation, sexuality, religious belief, region, ability, fandom, occupation, or nation whose members surprise you with their distinctive unfamiliar communicative conduct.

Let me end this chapter by coming full circle to the two statements with which I started out: *"There is no such thing as culture"* and *"Sometimes we have to communicate with people whose culture is different from our own."* In light of the discussion so far, these statements should seem less contradictory than they did at the outset. You should be able to recognize there are no such things as self-contained cultures whose distinctiveness is evident independently from an outside observer's perspective. We build cultures when we need them for groups or communities whose members communicate with us in unfamiliar ways. Cultures are explanations of difference between people who depend on one another, who would like to get something done with one another but cannot succeed in their efforts because they rely on different communication systems. Successful intercultural communicators can build cultures that capture the reasons why members of some groups communicate in seemingly odd ways and why they can translate those reasons into their own communication systems and use cultural knowledge to communicate in ways that are recognizable and agreeable to both parties.

REFLECTION QUESTIONS

1. Think back on the rich point involving Anglo-American public speaking. Are you familiar with this practice? If you are, how would you explain why U.S. public speakers often tell personal stories to cultural outsiders? If you aren't, how would you begin building culture for this practice?

2. When was the last time you experienced culture shock that did not turn into a rich point? Why did you decide not to pursue understanding the conduct that shocked you from the perspective of cultural insiders? Did you make a conscious decision, or were there other reasons you moved on to other things?

3. When was the last time you experienced a rich point? How far did you pursue trying to understand the local meanings of the cultural conduct that caused your rich point?

4. Recall a time when you managed to figure out a puzzle. (Think of any kind of puzzle, such as figuring out how to operate a machine, how to cook a complicated dish for the first time, or why someone you care about was angry with you one day.) Try to reconstruct the process you went through. How did your process of inquiry start? What kind of information did you gather, and how did you gather it? Did you encounter dead ends? Did you make, and correct, mistakes? How did your inquiry end?

5. Think of the identities you call yours and that come with membership in particular social groups. Do any of those identities require you to speak in particular ways?

2

"What Does Communication Have to Do With Culture?"

Introducing Cultural Pragmatics

AN INTERCULTURAL ENCOUNTER IN SOUTH CENTRAL LOS ANGELES

In this chapter, you will learn:

- various approaches to intercultural communication

- the view of intercultural communication as social interaction

- the main principles of studying intercultural communication

Have you ever read something that fundamentally changed how you thought about the world? One such reading in my life was anthropologist Benjamin Bailey's article, "Communicative Behavior and Conflict Between African American Customers and Korean Immigrant Retailers in Los Angeles" (2000), which I read way back in graduate school. Bailey was living in Los Angeles around the time an immigrant South Korean shopkeeper, Soon Ja Du, shot unarmed African American teenager Latasha Harlins inside her store because she (wrongly) suspected the teen had stolen a bottle of orange juice. Along with the beating of Rodney King by LAPD police officers, Harlins's death was one of the events that sparked the 1992 Los Angeles riots (also sometimes referred to as the "1992 Los Angeles uprising").

Bailey, who studies audio and video recordings of how people of different ethnicities manage conversations with one another, wanted to understand how communication among

African American customers and Korean shopkeepers in South Central Los Angeles fed into the long history of tension between the two communities. While analyzing video recordings of regular mundane interactions between customers and shopkeepers in Korean-owned convenience stores in the Crenshaw neighborhood, Bailey noticed that when Korean customers walked up to the counters to purchase items, their interaction was short, task oriented, and lacking in social niceties. By contrast, when African American customers approached the counters, they tried to engage the storekeepers in sociable small talk. When Bailey interviewed some of the customers, they told him they found the storekeepers' responses rude: they did not greet them with smiles, they did not maintain eye contact, and they refused (or were reluctant) to engage in small talk. These customers interpreted Koreans' way of participating in service encounters as evidence of their lack of respect for African Americans. When he described African Americans' perception of their actions, Koreans responded to Bailey that they saw unsolicited small talk as a sign of bad manners and a lack of personal restraint.

A Practical Question

What are your expectations regarding polite service encounters? How much do you talk? What do you say? What kind of response do you expect? What do you think might go wrong if these expectations are violated?

This is a classic example of cultural miscommunication. Bailey masterfully painted an image of crossed lines of communication and mismatched cultural expectations, both of which reinforced the two sides' stereotypes about the other. But—and here is the kicker that caught me off guard—he also showed that despite experiencing the same frustrating service encounters with one another, African American customers and Korean shopkeepers *kept at it*. In his paper, Bailey presented a transcript of a recording from 1995 in which a customer keeps trying to engage shopkeepers in small talk even after he turns to leave, and the storekeepers grow more and more reticent. The exchange begins when the customer walks up to the cashier with the intent to pay for beer. (I have omitted some of Bailey's transcription symbols to make the transcript easier to read.)

EXCERPT 2.1. (from Bailey, 2000, p. 97, simplified)

Cashier	Two fifty. [*Cashier rings up purchase and bags beer.*]
Customer	I just moved in the area. I talked to you the other day. You remember me?
Cashier	Oh yesterday, last night ...
Customer	Yeah.
Cashier	Oooh yeah! [*Cashier smiles and nods.*]
Customer	Goddamn, shit, then you don't ...

Owner	New neighbor, huh? *[Customer turns toward owner.]*
Customer	Then you don't *know* me.
Cashier	I know you. *[Cashier gets change at register.]*
Customer	I want you to *know* me so when I walk in here you'll know me. I smoke Winstons. Your son knows me …

Although the cashier clearly recognizes the customer, the customer wants to be recognized without prompting the cashier to do so. After all, from his perspective, they already share an interpersonal history. The conversation continues with the customer beginning to share personal details and even cracks a joke.

EXCERPT 2.2. (from Bailey, 2000, p. 97, simplified)

Customer	I had a total knee so my company is retiring my old black ass at 54 … *[Customer smiles and gazes at owner.]*
Owner	Mmh. *[Owner shakes his head and gazes away from the customer.]*
Customer	… and they gave me some money …
Cashier	Huh. *[Cashier smiles briefly.]*
Customer	… so I'm spending my money at your store on liquor! Heh heh heh heh hah hah hah hah hah *[Customer laughs animatedly, turning toward the owner, who does not smile but who continues to shake his head as he takes a few steps to the side.]*
Owner	You can still work?

This is not going well. The customer's joke is not received as a joke. In fact, the owner responds to it as a factual report on the customer's condition. Nevertheless, the customer doesn't give up and explains how his company is making him retire and, in order to avoid further injury, he is now being retrained.

EXCERPT 2.3. (from Bailey, 2000, p. 97, simplified)

| Customer | … so I gotta go get another trade for them to pay me the money. So I'm gonna get another trade. But then like, after I get another trade they pay me a lump sum of money, and I'm gonna do what I wanna do. *[Pause.]* They only gonna give me about 60 or 70 thousand. *[Pause.]* Plus my schooling. *[Pause.]* So I got to take it easy for a little bit. *[Customer moves toward exit.]* That's why I'm gonna buy enough of your liquor, so I can take it. |
| Owner | Alright, take care. |

Although the customer pauses three times during his turn in order to give the cashier and the owner a chance to respond, they don't do so. Still, the customer doesn't give up. He walks back into the store, introduces himself by name, asks and learns the names of the owner and the cashier, and shakes their hands. He then talks about riots in Chicago and offers to protect the cashier and the owner if such riots were to happen again in their neighborhood. He then talks about how people are the same everywhere and how wrong racists are. Finally, he again heads toward the exit, but as he gets there, he turns around and begins to talk again in an animated, almost angry tone. He is so agitated, Bailey reports, that his sunglasses, which he had pushed to the top of his head, almost fall off as he speaks.

EXCERPT 2.4. (from Bailey, 2000, p. 98–99, simplified)

Customer	Okay, what I'm saying is if you throw five kids in the middle of the floor and don't tell them what they are nothing like that they just grow up to be people. They don't even know that they Black. They don't even know they Korean, they don't know that they White, they don't know this and that. It has to be an old person like you or me, George Washington and all these motherfuckers. Martin Luther King and all these motherfuckers. *[Customer gazes first at owner, then cashier, switches to a dispassionate tone.]* Anyway, have a good day.
Owner	Later. *[Customer turns and exits.]*

Here we are, at the end of a lengthy service encounter, with two sides that could not be more socially distant from one another. As the customer says more, the cashier and the owner say less. Bailey points out that this is not simply a matter of the two sides not understanding what the other is doing. Instead, we see both African American and Korean participants digging in their heels, acting along the lines of their own cultural and communicative expectations, trying to compel the other to act according to those same expectations. What is at stake is no longer the buying and selling of convenience store items: it is *identity*. Both sides are suggesting, implicitly, "I will not talk like you because I am not like you." Yes, members of different social groups often *cannot* communicate in compatible ways, but sometimes they will *refuse* to match their communication patterns to those of others for the sake of enacting and reinforcing social boundaries. In the case of Korean retailers and African American customers, their mismatched communication patterns become a handy resource for highlighting the division between the two ethnicities in Los Angeles.

CULTURAL PRAGMATICS SAYS

To interpret encounters between Koreans and African Americans as an example of racism is only a part of the story. Cultural pragmatics calls on us to try to understand these encounters as intercultural encounters as well.

It was Bailey's ability to capture the nuances of observable interaction and their meanings in a larger historical context that finally convinced me to pursue a doctoral degree in communication.

For our purposes here, the greatest takeaway from this study is that Bailey treats culture and communication as two sides of the same coin. Korean and African American cultures are expressed when Koreans and African Americans use language in the context of social interaction with others, including Bailey during research interviews. Of course, Bailey does not deny the usefulness of reading scholarship about Korean and African American ways of speaking, but his primary source of cultural information (or data, as scholars like to put it) is the words spoken by members of the social groups whose cultures he is reconstructing.

My main goal in this chapter is to help you understand that this book and Bailey's compelling study represent one approach among other possible approaches to intercultural communication. In other words, understanding what this book is trying to teach you includes understanding what ground it is *not* designed to cover. First, we will review three main research paradigms in order to locate this book on the map of intercultural communication research. Then we explore the roots and main principles of our approach through a review of Edward T. Hall's pioneering work. Finally, we develop an interpretation of intercultural communication as social interaction.

APPROACHES TO INTERCULTURAL COMMUNICATION

Bailey's approach to communication among members of two cultural groups falls within a particular research paradigm in intercultural communication research. **Research paradigms** are systems of basic theoretical assumptions about how the world works (including intercultural communication) and about how the way the world works (including intercultural communication) should be studied. In the field of intercultural communication, we can distinguish three main research paradigms: postpositivist, interpretivist, and critical (Martin, Nakayama, & Carbaugh, 2012).

The Postpositivist Paradigm

Following the research logic of the natural sciences (such as physics, chemistry, and astronomy), postpositivists study intercultural communication as a set of independent phenomena that can be observed from an objective external perspective. Postpositivists tend to treat culture as one independent variable that causes people to communicate in certain ways. They tend to view culture as national cultures (the cultures of the United States, Ghana, Poland, and so on), and they view people as members of national cultures. The preferred modes of research among postpositivists are survey research and structured interviewing. Their main research goal is to predict how (national) cultures will influence communication behavior and what is going to happen when members of different (national) cultures come into contact.

A recent example of such a study is one by communication scholars James Neuliep and Morgan Johnson (2016). They wanted to understand different conflict styles in the United States and Ecuador for the purpose of helping speakers from both countries better manage intercultural conflict situations. They used a theoretical model called Conflict Style Dimensions (CSD) to contrast conflict styles in these two countries. CSD distinguishes eight styles: dominating (using one's authority to win the conflict), integrating (collaborating with others to reach a solution), obliging (putting the other's needs before one's own), avoiding (not discussing the conflict), compromising (finding middle ground), emotional expression (acting on one's feelings), third-party help (finding an outsider to act as a go-between), and neglect (ignoring the conflict, getting a preferred response through aggressive acts). They gave questionnaires to 114 U.S. and 132 Ecuadorian students and asked them to share information about how they manage conflict in relationships. The analysis of the questionnaires led them to predict that Ecuadorians are more likely to use an avoiding conflict style, whereas U.S. speakers are more likely to opt for dominating and emotional expression styles.

A Practical Question

Do you think the ability to predict people's behavior is useful? I certainly do. Nevertheless, be careful as you try to act on predictions about the communication conduct of entire nations. Such large-scale generalizations hide from you the cultural and communicative diversity within nations.

The Interpretivist Paradigm

Unlike postpositivists, interpretivist intercultural communication scholars are principally influenced by the social sciences, including sociology, anthropology, and linguistics. Interpretivists view intercultural communication as the site of people engaged in meaningful social activity in context. Because they place emphasis on the meaning and interpretation of communication, interpretivists freely admit that the meaning of the communication phenomena they study will be shaped, in part, by their own interpretations. This does not mean that interpretivists simply interpret communication as they please—they use a set of qualitative research methods (such as ethnography and discourse analysis) to understand how speakers from various cultures expect to participate in intercultural communication encounters and how they make sense of what happens when they do. Interpretivists view culture as a set of practices people engage in, cultivate, transform, and pass on to others. They see culture as shaping communication but also as shaped by communication. They seek to understand how members of cultures communicate and why they communicate in those ways on members' terms.

An example of the interpretivist approach to intercultural communication is communication scholar Saskia Witteborn's (2010) study of the work of the transnational nongovernmental organization (NGO) Save the Children (STC) in northwestern China. Like many other transnational NGOs, STC brought a liberal, humanistic, and individualistic approach to childhood education. As Witteborn found out from visits to STC's local headquarters and their website, STC encouraged children to take themselves seriously, to express themselves, and to participate in the lives of their communities by, for example, making decisions, speaking up at children's forums, and presenting recommendations to policy makers. This approach seemed entirely alien to local semi-nomadic herders whose children participated in STC's programs. When spending time with the herders, Witteborn learned they loved their children as much as any parents, but they had a radically different view of children and childhood than STC does.

> I was told that children are not involved in many decision-making processes that affect their lives, such as when to move to the winter quarters or when to do their daily household duties. They are also not supposed to ask too many questions, disagree with their parents, or critique them or other adults. For the people, the extended family and its needs were more important than individual wishes in order to survive (p. 10).

Despite their good intentions, Witteborn warned, transnational NGOs' development work and advocacy rooted in supposedly universal values often runs up against cultural conceptions of family life and communication. This incompatibility can, in turn, limit the amount of good NGOs can do at the community level.

A Practical Question

What practical advice would you give to STC in light of Witteborn's findings? What practical advice would you give to the herders? Why?

The Critical Paradigm

Critical intercultural communication scholars have more in common with interpretivists than with postpositivists. They, too, view intercultural communication as a site of active, meaningful, context-bound engagement between speakers, and they often rely on qualitative methods for studying such engagement. However, they criticize interpretivists and postpositivists for disregarding the fact that intercultural contact hardly ever takes place on a level playing field. Most intercultural communication, they argue, involves participants with different political interests, degrees of power and influence, and access to economic and communication resources. These differences become more apparent when we examine the historical contexts in which intercultural communication takes place, including not only the historical moment of communication but also the historical processes that shaped participants' views of the cultural "other." Critical scholars squarely reject the notion that the boundaries of cultures are the boundaries of nations, and they promote viewing culture as a site of struggle for dominance between various ideologies and their beneficiaries. For them, culture is not a benign and innocent object of study but a battlefield where participants leverage their cultural resources (e.g., language, education, prestige, wealth, etc.) to cast themselves and their ways of speaking as more valuable and more authoritative than others' and, by doing so, amass more resources and power.

College can be such a battlefield, as communication scholar Patricia Covarrubias (2008) claims in a study of American Indian students' reactions to White students' silence after someone makes a discriminatory statement about American Indians. Covarrubias, who interviewed 35 American Indian undergraduate and graduate students from various tribes at a university in the western United States, shows that although American Indians tend to value silence in general, they can't help interpreting these silences against the background of centuries of oppression. White students' silences affirmed White privilege and the second-class citizen status of American Indians.

> **A Practical Question**
>
> Fewer Native American students finish college in four years than White American students (23% vs 44%; "Native American Students," 2018). Do you think the experiences of Native American students Covarrubias describes may be one explanation for why this is happening?

THE GENERAL APPROACH OF THIS BOOK TO INTERCULTURAL COMMUNICATION

Bailey's study of service encounters between African Americans and Koreans in Los Angeles is a good example of scholarship that stands somewhere between the interpretivist and critical paradigms. In his discussion of miscommunication between customers and shopkeepers with different cultural backgrounds, he leans toward interpretivism. However, when he looks at the intercultural communication that takes place between the two sides through the lens of historical context and participants' forceful assertion of ethnic boundaries, his analysis takes on a critical flavor.

Cultural pragmatics, the view of intercultural communication I rely on in this book, also takes a position between the interpretivist and critical paradigms. I approach ethical considerations in the practice of intercultural communication from the critical paradigm. The rest of the book, which is dedicated to the discussion of the practice of intercultural communication ("building culture") leans toward interpretivism.

Edward T. Hall

The three basic principles of this book, which I discuss below, come from the work of a scholar who was thinking about intercultural communication before these paradigms even existed. Actually, he came up with the term "intercultural communication." The person I am talking about is American anthropologist Edward Twitchell Hall (1914–2009). Hall was not a typical anthropologist. During the time when his career took off in the 1940s and 1950s, anthropologists were expected to dedicate their professional lives to the study of particular cultural groups and to compare cultures. Early on in his career, Hall did study Navajo and Hopi cultures in Arizona, but his interest in culture changed when he was hired to work for the U.S. State Department after World War II. He was recruited in 1950 (just 5 years after the end of the war) to work at the Foreign Service Institute (FSI), where diplomats and technicians were trained to carry out President Truman's foreign policy. A key element of the Truman administration's goal was to win over the hearts and minds of citizens of other countries for democracy and the capitalist economic order. Hall's job at the FSI was to oversee the training of technicians in "intercultural relations"—that is, to make sure they could communicate in culturally appropriate ways in developing countries where they provided technical assistance in agriculture, industry, and healthcare in exchange for goodwill toward the United States.

At the FSI, Hall had to invent a new way to teach culture. His students were not curious anthropology students but hard-nosed technicians and diplomats required by the government to carry out a limited range of practical tasks in target countries while avoiding being confused by local ways of behavior. And confused they were! Many technicians and diplomats returned from the field frustrated by the odd manners of the locals and their own inability to make sense of those manners. Their personal frustration was, of course, only one side of the story: the cultural ignorance they exhibited abroad reflected badly on the United States as well. Just read the first few sentences of Hall's 1959 bestseller, *The Silent Language*:

> Though the United States has spent billions of dollars on foreign aid programs, it has captured neither the affection nor esteem of the rest of the world. In many countries today Americans are cordially disliked; in others merely tolerated. The reasons for this sad state of affairs are many and varied, and some of them are beyond the control of anything this country might do to try to correct them. But harsh as it may seem to the ordinary citizen, filled as he is with good intentions and natural generosity, much of the foreigners' animosity has been

generated by the way Americans behave. As a country we are apt to be guilty of great ethnocentrism (p. 9).

Ethnocentric conduct, as you can imagine, is hardly the best way to win the hearts and minds of people in faraway countries. It was clear that Hall's cultural expertise was needed at the FSI, but, as he discovered quickly, he could not teach culture the same way as he had during his years as a college professor. He could not organize the material around deep dives into the cultures of specific peoples and then compare those peoples along cultural features of interest to anthropologists, such as kinship systems and material culture. His students at FSI were dissatisfied with such an approach. They wanted to get better at communicating with locals and figuring out the puzzling conduct of cultural others they encountered in the field.

In light of their interests, Hall changed his curriculum. Instead of concentrating on particular cultures and their observable features he switched to a culture-general approach that highlighted the hidden taken-for-granted features of cultural systems and how those features shaped the ways people communicated. Together with a linguist, George Trager, who taught foreign languages at the FSI, Hall set out to build what he called a "cultural interface" (Hall, 1992, p. 221) for his students, a system of cultural categories they could use to make sense of surprising moments in intercultural communication and to adjust their own communication to local ways of speaking and behaving. These cultural categories included such areas of everyday life as "language and technology, social organization and all defensive activities, work and play, two sexes and what they learn, and time and space" (p. 214).

THREE PRINCIPLES OF CULTURAL PRAGMATICS

Intercultural communication as a field has come a long way since Hall's time, and what he called his "map of culture" is not used any more, as far as I know (although some elements of it are), in intercultural communication research and training. In this book, I will use different categories, the categories of communication resources and meanings, as an intercultural interface you can rely on for the purpose of intercultural communication. Nevertheless, Hall's work at the FSI and afterwards teaches us three fundamental principles that serve as the intellectual foundations of cultural pragmatics, the intellectual heart of this book.

Principle 1: Culture Is Communication

Culture, the taken-for-granted norms, beliefs, expectations, and assumptions speakers bring to communication, are not immediately observable. Speakers of any culture are usually unable to tell you what they are taking for granted about the way they communicate. As you make culture, you are looking across instances of unfamiliar, sur-prising communication to identify local forms (or patterns) of communication and their meanings, translate those into your own communication system of forms and meanings, and devise ways to communicate in ways that are recognizable and appropriate to other participants of your intercultural encounter. To put it more bluntly, communication is the material out of which you can make culture. In Bailey's example, African American and Korean participants could have reconstructed one another's cultural preferences for respect and restraint from the ways these two groups communicated and could have acted according to those preferences for the purpose of coordinating their ways of speaking. They, however, had different goals.

Culture is communication in a different way as well. When Koreans communicated with what they saw as restraint. they were following the cultural expectations of their community *and* they were reinforcing those expectations. The same with African Amer-ican customers' attempts to elicit respect from Korean shopkeepers: they were following and reinforcing expectations. Culture and communication are mutually constitutive.

Principle 2: Intercultural Communication Is a Practical Exercise

Hall, whose approach to intercultural communication falls squarely into the interpre-tivist paradigm, taught intercultural communication at the FSI in a way that responded to his students' practical needs. With human communication being a complex and a largely unpredictable activity, Hall knew he would not be able to prepare his students for every possible communication encounter abroad. Instead, he devised an approach to culture and cultural difference in communication that allowed his students to think on their feet after experiencing rich points and to reconstruct what a baffling bit of communicative action meant from the perspective of local speakers.

This way of teaching intercultural communication implies that understanding cultural differences cannot be achieved without direct involvement in communicating with cultural others. No one is going to be able to produce a manual that will tell you how to communicate with members of a target culture across all possible contexts of interaction. You have to make culture in the process of intercultural communication from your own perspective, translating one communication system into another by trial and error as you go. Some of the tools you bring to this exercise (such as basic theories about how communication works in context) are universally applicable, but they are no more than tools you need to use in intercultural encounters. Then, once you have accomplished culture, once you can articulate the taken-for-granted ways in which the other is communicating, you can begin to work toward coordinating your ways of speaking with the other's—once again, through a process of trial and error. Learning intercultural communication is learning by doing.

Principle 3: The Goal of Intercultural Communication Is Coordinated Interaction

Michael Agar and Edward T. Hall would agree that intercultural communication becomes necessary when we become aware of a communication problem. Suddenly, in the middle of a conversation, you and a conversational partner are no longer on the same page, not because you disagree about something or because you discover that you are pursuing different goals or interests but because you simply don't understand what the other is *doing*. You fail to comprehend what they are trying to accomplish by saying "*X*"—even though you are speaking the same language!

This realization doesn't come easily to those who are not used to reflecting on cultural difference. Humans are famously quick to rush to judgment about speakers' internal qualities (e.g., personality, moral character, level of education, etc.) based on the words they speak. Especially in moments of communication breakdown, we tend to regard the words of others as windows into their souls, their essence, who they really are. As a result, when communication derails, we grasp for stereotypes or personality categories to explain what it was about the other *person* that led to the breakdown.

Instead, what I hope you will take away from this book is an ability to *shift your attention from people to actions* in moments when you experience a rich point while you are communicating with someone. Hall teaches us that in moments of communication confusion, we ought to halt the ongoing flow of communication, step back, and examine how our actions ended up being mismatched. To imagine uncoordinated interaction, imagine trying to ask an actor the time during a Shakespeare play, attempting to discuss current affairs with a woman in the throes of childbirth, or trying to sell something to a cashier at a grocery store. The two sides' actions and expectations about appropriate actions don't match: they are uncoordinated, like the awkward movements of inexperienced ballroom dancers. In some (not all!) situations in which participants are engaged in uncoordinated communicative actions, building culture can help because it helps participants alter their habitual communication actions and speak in ways that make sense to their conversational partners and allows both of them to work toward their shared or individual social goals.

I will have to add two caveats here. First, as you could see in Bailey's example at the beginning of this chapter, coordinated interaction is not always in the interest of the participants in intercultural encounters. In fact, from participants' perspectives, in some cases the breakdown of coordinated interaction is the ideal outcome. Second, intercultural communication can lead to coordinated communicative action without participants having a clear holistic understanding of each other's cultural perspective. Because intercultural communication is a practical exercise, it is closely tied to contexts of actual exchanges. Developing a holistic account of a social group or community's cultural perspective takes more than figuring out how to successfully communicate with members of that group in one particular context.

INTERCULTURAL COMMUNICATION AS SOCIAL INTERACTION

I realize that I have been throwing around terms such as "social interaction," "context," "communication resources," and "meaning" throughout this chapter. Let's end with a clarification of these terms, drawing on the example of the exchange between the African American customer and the Korean shopkeepers from Bailey's study.

Defining Social Interaction

The kind of communication we are focusing on here is social interaction. **Social interaction** is the sequence of meaningful communicative actions between two or more participants that are meaningful relative to a set of contexts. Let's take this somewhat complicated definition apart. It is possible to communicate without engaging in social interaction. When you talk to yourself out loud or when you leave a Post-it Note on the fridge, you are of course communicating, but you are not necessarily engaged in social interaction—unless someone responds to you. **Communicative actions** are the things we do with words, phrases, syntax, pauses, intonation, and so on. We perform these actions (or **communication practices,** if we perform them regularly in culturally meaningful ways) in order to make some kind of change in the state of affairs around us. We ask questions, reproach people, complain, tell stories, and keep silent around others because we would like to accomplish something. We are working toward some kind of outcome that our conversational partners can recognize and (hopefully) find appropriate and to which they can respond. For example, when the African American customer says to the cashier, "I want you to *know* me so when I walk in here you'll know me," he is making a request. When the Korean shopkeepers don't respond to the customer's account of his workplace injury, even though he noticeably pauses to offer the shopkeepers opportunities to respond, what they are saying to him is that he has outstayed his welcome.

Communication Resources

Speakers assemble their communicative actions and communication practices from locally available **communication resources.** Such resources include, but are not limited to, the words and grammar of a language. Lacking the ability to speak the language of your conversational partner or to construct grammatically correct sentences can contribute to communication breakdowns. But not being able to construct grammatically pristine sentences doesn't mean that you will not be able to communicate! It wasn't until I moved to the United States from Hungary for a year at the age of 12 that I came to realize the accuracy of this statement. Even though I could only speak a few words of English, I could *do* things: introduce myself, ask someone to repeat what they said, recognize when another kid said something silly and laugh, ask for the football during recess, and so on. Sharing a language with others is helpful, but it is not the be-all and end-all of intercultural communication. What matters more is knowing what to do with the communicative resources you have at your disposal. Those resources include the words and the grammar of the English language or any other language, but they also include verbal genres such as jokes and greetings, the ability to take turns in a conversation (for example, to appropriately take, hold, and yield the conversational floor), and to produce and recognize ambiguity.

Participants

Participants of social interaction include everyone present in the immediate situation who are implicated in the ongoing communication activity. Presence can be physical or virtual. Following Goffman (1981), we can distinguish three kinds of participant roles: speakers, addressed recipients (hearers whom the speaker is overtly addressing), and bystanders (hearers whom the speaker is not addressing overtly). These roles shift constantly as the conversation progresses. In Bailey's example, the customer is always in a speaker or addressed recipient role, but the storekeepers take on all three roles. Some communities of speakers have culturally specific ways of using these participation roles to communicate in meaningful ways. For example, Morgan (2014) reports the African American practice of pointed indirectness, which involves criticizing an overhearing individual or a group indirectly by complaining about them to a conversational partner. In Morgan's example, a woman says to another woman in the presence of teenage girls: "When I was young I wore too much makeup and looked like a fool" (p. 60). The girls know exactly who she is talking about.

Meaning in Context

In my intercultural communication class, I often find myself discussing meaning with my students. In particular, we talk about how we know what a particular communicative action means. Like clockwork, one of them always says, "That depends on the context." They are not wrong! The **meaning** of actions, its function for the participants in the moment of interaction, is inseparable from the contexts in which those actions are performed. **Context** is any feature of the situation that acts as a background to the communicative actions, a background against which those actions take on functions for the participants. Now, that's as broad and abstract a definition as it gets. Let's make context a bit more concrete. We can distinguish four kinds of contexts (Goodwin & Duranti, 1992):

1. **Setting.** Interaction always takes place in some kind of physical or virtual setting and involves a set of participants. In the Bailey example, the setting is a Korean convenience store, and the participants are a customer, a cashier, and the owner. (Note, however, that participants make different sense of the relationships among themselves. The customer sees the three of them primarily as members of the same neighborhood; the storekeepers see themselves primarily as providing a service to the customer.) Just outside the door is the Crenshaw neighborhood of Los Angeles.

2. **Behavioral environment.** Behavior here is anything participants do that is nonvocal (e.g., gesture, posture, gaze, attention, etc.). Bailey's analysis doesn't delve very deeply into the behavioral environment, but we find some interesting clues in the transcript about elements of this context that may be relevant to the participants. Notice how the cashier smiles but the owner doesn't. What might this say about their relationship to one another and the customer? What about the owner directing his gaze away from the customer as the customer gazes directly at him? What are we to make of the fact that the customer's jerky gestures indicate he is slightly drunk? What is the significance of the fact that the customer headed for the exit, turned back, and headed out again?

3. **Language as context.** In the course of social interaction (except at the very beginning and the very end of an exchange), what we say points back to what has just been said and points forward to what might be said. Consider, for example, when the owner says to the customer, "You can still work?" This is a request for information that is designed to accomplish two additional things: to shut down the customer's joking and friendly advances and to reframe the conversation as a serious one that takes place between people who are decidedly not friends. The customer, as we find out, is not willing to play into this definition of the situation, which is one of the reasons why the conversation becomes more and more uncoordinated.

4. **Extrasituational context.** This context contains all background knowledge and frames of reference outside the immediate interaction that are necessary for participants to carry on interacting with one another. Participants' interpersonal history; their race; the history of interethnic tension between Korean immigrants and African Americans in South Central Los Angeles; the very recent memory of the Latasha Harlins killing, the Rodney King beating, and the riots in Los Angeles; the string of shoplifting and robberies in Korean convenience stores; the histories of African American slavery and Korean migration patterns; and the history of racism in the United States are all elements of the extrasituational

context in which the interaction between the customer and the storekeepers falls apart. Also, consider an element of this context we haven't addressed before: the owner and the cashier were both middle class (the owner had an undergraduate degree from UCLA, and the cashier attended college and graduate school in South Korea), and the customer was working class, according to Bailey's African American informants. Besides racial difference, could class difference have something to do with how this interaction unfolded?

Intercultural communication that aims at forging or restoring coordinated interaction requires building culture. Building culture, in turn, requires that you identify communicative actions and their meanings on the terms of cultural others with whom you are interacting. Part III of this book will guide you through the process of identifying meanings, including cultural rules and norms, values, and the making of community.

REFLECTION QUESTIONS

1. As you read the transcript of the service encounter between the Korean shopkeepers and the African American customer, what impression do these speakers make on you? What do their styles of communication tell you about them as people? After answering these questions, describe specific characteristics of their speech that made you interpret their words in these ways.

2. Can you recall a time when you found yourself persistently using a particular style of communication to make a point or to force someone to accept, and maybe even adopt, your chosen style of communication?

3. Hall was inspired to think about intercultural communication, in part, by the perception of Americans abroad. How do you think the rest of the world sees Americans today? Why?

4. Recall a conversation you have recently had. Take one particular thing you said during that conversation and describe what that communicative action meant relative to the four contexts discussed in this chapter.

3

"How Do I Do This Well? How Do I Do It Right?"

Practical and Ethical Reflections on Building Culture

C anadian American psychoeconomist Sheena S. IYENGAR is recognized for her research on choices and their consequences. In 2010, she gave a TED Talk in which she began with an account of a **rich point** she experienced in Kyoto, Japan, while she was living there working on her dissertation.

> On my first day, I went to a restaurant, and I ordered a cup of green tea with sugar. After a pause, the waiter said, "One does not put sugar in green tea." "I know," I said. "I'm aware of this custom, but I really like my tea sweet." In response, he gave me an even more courteous version of the same explanation: one does not put sugar in green tea. "I understand," I said, "that the Japanese do not put sugar in *their* green tea, but I'd like to put some sugar in *my* green tea." Surprised by my insistence, the waiter took up the issue with the manager. Pretty soon a lengthy discussion ensued, and finally the manager came over to me and said, "I am very sorry. We do not have sugar." Well, since I couldn't have my tea the

In this chapter, you will learn:

- a healthy dose of skepticism toward others' claims about cultural difference

- how cultural inquiry (building culture) works and what its outcomes are

- some of the ethical implications of cultural inquiry

way I wanted it, I ordered a cup of coffee, which the waiter brought over promptly. Resting on the saucer were two packets of sugar.

What happened here? The waiter and the manager were refusing Iyengar service *and* lying about the availability of the condiment she requested. Anyone in the United States with a passing familiarity with restaurants knows these are major violations of some of the basic rules in the customer service rule book. But was that the meaning of what they were doing *for them*? Iyengar offered a cultural explanation for the waiter's and the manager's odd behavior:

> My failure to procure myself a cup of sweet green tea was not due to a simple misunderstanding. This was due to a fundamental difference in our ideas about choice. From my American perspective, when a paying customer makes a reasonable request based on her preferences, she has every right to have that request met. The American way, to quote Burger King, is to have it your way because, as Starbucks says, happiness is in your choices. But from the Japanese perspective, it's their duty to protect those who don't know any better, in this case, the ignorant *gaijin* [foreigner], from making the wrong choice. Let's face it: the way I wanted my tea was inappropriate according to cultural standards, and they were doing their best to help me save face. (Iyengar, 2010)

Although I thought Iyengar's explanation of American assumptions about choice in the rest of her talk was fascinating, I have to admit that when I heard her interpretation of the events at the restaurant from a Japanese perspective, I was skeptical. Sure, her explanation sounds plausible enough in the sense that it resonates with our cultural expectations: Americans value individual choice, and the Japanese value tradition and **face**. She is a world-renowned academic whose credibility and international experience is unquestionable. Also, the focus of her TED Talk was the psychology of how we make choices, so how could we hold her accountable for not giving us a well-researched survey of Japanese culture and customs? Yet I had some nagging questions about this anecdote and Iyengar's interpretation. Did she base her claims about Japanese culture on a single occurrence, or did she witness multiple instances of such behavior? Could it be that she just happened to walk into a restaurant that prided itself on serving tea strictly according to custom? How did she find out about Japanese concern with **face**, and how did she know the waiter and the manager

CULTURAL PRAGMATICS SAYS

Should Iyengar have enjoyed a cup of unsweetened tea just to have that experience? I'm not sure. From the perspective of cultural pragmatics, a better question to ask is "In the context of this interaction, would trying a cup of unsweetened tea have helped Iyengar accomplish her communicative (and social) goals, including coordinating her interaction with the Japanese staff?"

were attending to face at the cost of angering a clearly non-Japanese customer? Did she confirm her explanation of their conduct with Japanese friends and acquaintances? And finally, did she change the way she consumed tea at Japanese restaurants after this incident in order to avoid similar situations?

It is of course quite likely that Iyengar, as a discerning scientist, did all of these things, but that's beside the point. In this chapter, I invite you to think critically about claims about cultural difference. In the first part of the chapter, we will review the methods and resources at your disposal for building culture in a way that is as rigorous and valid as possible, given your circumstances ("doing it well"). The second part of the chapter addresses some important ethical issues you may face as you pursue rich points ("doing it right").

DOING IT WELL: THE PROCESS OF BUILDING CULTURE

Building culture is a set of practices modeled on qualitative research methods, particularly **ethnography**. Unlike qualitative researchers, practitioners engaged in building culture don't strive to produce published research articles about the unfamiliar social group in which they experienced rich points. This does *not* mean there are no standards of quality for building culture. There are better and worse ways of thinking about, studying, and acting upon cultural difference. However, the ultimate test of the culture you build is *whether it works* in intercultural encounters, not whether a scientific community accepts your claims and arguments or whether a scientific journal publishes a research report you wrote.

At this point, you might ask, "How do I know I have succeeded? How do I know intercultural communication worked as a result of my efforts to build culture?" These are some indications the culture you have built is helping you engage in coordinated interaction:

- You and your conversational partners seem to have a shared sense of the situation (what is going on) and how you are supposed to be communicating in that situation.

- Throughout the interaction, you and your conversational partners seem to have a shared sense of what everyone is doing communicatively.

- You feel reasonably certain you are accomplishing what you are trying to accomplish (e.g., present an identity; attend to your and others' **face** needs; begin, transform, or end a relationship, etc.).

- You experience the interaction as flowing smoothly—and when it is not, you can be reasonably sure the "rough patch" in your conversation is not there because you lack a relevant piece of cultural knowledge.

- A particular feature of interaction that used to confuse you is no longer confusing.

- When you make a mistake, you are aware of it and know how to do better next time.

- You are able to use language in ways your partners find creative (funny, moving, memorable, etc.).

The processes of building culture (which this book prepares you to do) and conducting cultural research overlap in significant ways. For example, cultural research often begins with the researcher responding with simultaneous feelings of confusion and intrigue to something surprising a member of an unfamiliar social group says or does—in other words, a **rich point**. Building culture borrows research methods from cultural research, such as participant observation, interviewing, field notes, document analysis, and reviewing relevant scholarship. Cultural researchers also test their findings about the language and culture of a social group or community by using language with community members in what they think are culturally appropriate ways. If the coordination of social interaction with group members fails repeatedly, it is likely that the researcher drew the wrong conclusions from their observations of local communicative conduct. But while building culture is grounded in an individual's practical need for coordinated interaction across cultural boundaries (say, to manage a relationship with someone from a different cultural background), the aim of cultural research tends to be the holistic representation of an entire cultural system (or as much of it as possible). To accomplish that, cultural researchers must spend more time interacting with more members of a social group than the average intercultural practitioner. They need to collect more data across a wide variety of social contexts and institutions, and they need to document and analyze that data in greater depth.

In an important sense, the cultural researcher is a professional culture builder. This is precisely why published cultural research—if you have access to it—can aid you in your efforts to build culture for the purpose of accomplishing coordinated social interaction. Published research may not address precisely the type of communication you are trying to understand from the cultural perspective of another community, but it will either teach you about the community and its unique history, social structure, or communication system in general or help you identify and label the various types and elements of communitive action and the contexts in which they become meaningful.

The Practical Goal

Let's turn to the process and outcome of building culture. As Michael Agar (1994) explains, the final goal of building culture is the construction of intercultural frames. In the context of intercultural communication, coordinated interaction becomes problematic due to misaligned **interactional frames**—that is, participants' mismatched sense of (a) the situation in which the interaction is happening and (b) how that interaction should unfold. This latter element of frames is called a **script**. Scripts are expectations toward, rather than descriptions of, how interaction occurs in actual social interaction. As interpretive devices, frames help us edit and simplify complex reality, define situations, and act meaningfully and strategically in them. In order to create **intercultural frames**—that is, frames that borrow elements of both mismatched frames and allow participants to act in ways that are meaningful to all parties—participants have to step back from the interaction, recognize they are dealing with a case of mismatched frames, identify the type of communication that is causing the problem, and coordinate their interaction in a way that responds to at least one or a combination of both frames.

In the example above, we see Iyengar making some important moves toward building an intercultural frame. She notices a communication breakdown, and she identifies misaligned interactional frames. In her words, from her American perspective, she sees herself as a "paying customer [making] a reasonable request based on her preferences [who] has every right to have that request met." On the Japanese side, she sees two people protecting an "ignorant *gaijin* from making the wrong choice" and violating "cultural standards." They are also helping her "save face." The communication issue here is that her request (a speech act) is met not with a fulfillment of the request but with a refusal (another speech act) motivated by a concern for face (positive self-presentation). Iyengar's story shows her grasping all of this, but it doesn't give us evidence that she made the critical final move toward coordinated interaction. The coordination of interaction could have happened in at least two ways. The next time, she could have deferred to the Japanese frame and ordered green tea with no sugar. Or she could have found a cultural middle ground by acknowledging that, because she was in violation of a local custom, she had to go out of her way to find a restaurant where she would have been served green tea with sugar. (I am not sure if such restaurants exist in Japan, but from the perspective of building intercultural frames, it's the effort that matters.)

> ### CULTURAL PRAGMATICS SAYS
>
> In this process, you are using culture as a working assumption. What that means is that instead of assuming your conversational partner is unreasonable, misguided, or rude, you *assume* they are using communication resources in an unfamiliar way.

The Process of Building Culture

As I mentioned earlier, another missing piece of Iyengar's story is how she figured out the Japanese waiter and manager were, in fact, trying to protect her from embarrassment. Let's turn to a closer examination of how the process of cultural inquiry progresses in eight stages as we strive for coordinated interaction with cultural others. Let's pop the hood, so to speak, and take a look at the engine that drives a practical approach to intercultural communication.

> **Stage 1. Experiencing a rich point.** No one can warn you about rich points. Like it or not, they happen, and they tend to happen when you least expect them. The trick is to know when you have experienced one—when you feel a combination of confusion ("What just happened?") and intrigue ("Why did they say that?")—and not to panic, knowing that you have just taken an unexpected step toward building culture. Rich points might occur when someone does something you simply don't understand, when they do the opposite of what you expected, when you think you've figured out how things work in the target group and something a member says proves you wrong, when group members keep saying something and you don't know why, when they say familiar things in unfamiliar ways or unfamiliar things in familiar ways, or when they say something that just rubs you the wrong way or makes you downright angry (Agar, 1999). Rich points aren't always singular events: sometimes you only learn you are experiencing one after witnessing the same strange communicative conduct multiple times.

> **Stage 2. Suspending interaction.** The second critical step in the process is the conscious decision to stop the flow of communication as soon as possible. Sometimes you can get away with disengaging from an ongoing communicative encounter right away, while sometimes you have to muddle through the interaction to the best of your ability and then stop to get your bearings. Disengaging from the normal business of social interaction is a necessary step toward trying to figure out whether you are dealing with a communication issue or something else. It is entirely possible that the speaker who was the source of your rich point was simply being difficult or downright obnoxious. But it is equally possible that you are dealing with misaligned frames. It is worth stopping to investigate in order to mitigate the potential social threat resulting from misinterpreting someone else's actions.

A Practical Question

"Does disengaging from the normal business of interaction mean stopping the conversation right then and there?"

Not necessarily. You may be involved in an interaction over which you don't have that type of control (e.g., in a service encounter or while talking to your boss). In such cases, complete the interaction as best as you can and review what happened later.

Stage 3. Establishing a communication pattern. Cultural investigation begins with the attempt to decide whether the odd bit of communication at the heart of your rich point is an element of a pattern. The popular saying "One is an accident, two is a coincidence, three is a pattern" is a useful rule of thumb you can follow as you search for patterns. If you can see the same odd communication conduct—ideally, across different speakers who belong to the same social group or community—you've got a pattern on the basis of which you can start working toward making claims about cultural difference. Your quest for patterns can, of course, lead you to reexperience the sting of your original rich point at a higher or lower intensity. If you can't see the odd communication occur across speakers, or if the speaker (or speakers) involved in your original rich point doesn't repeat it, you are free to conclude the speaker was either having a bad day or you are not socially compatible, to put it mildly.

Stage 4. Labeling the relevant communication pattern. The next challenge is to identify the communicative act (or acts) at the core of your rich point. Your investigation at this point will run on two parallel tracks. On the one hand, listen for local labels members of your target community apply to the odd bit of communication you are investigating. If they have a word for it, you are in luck because you can ask them about it. On the other hand, you can tap into existing communication research to label your pattern. This book is designed to introduce you to such useful research. The communication scholarship you will read about here—or that you may be able to identify with the help of your instructor—will help you navigate such specialized vocabularies and teach you about the possible social meanings of communicative actions in context.

Stage 5. Reconstructing relevant context(s). Once you have identified a pattern across speakers and labeled it, it's time to turn your attention to the context (or contexts) in which the target communication pattern tends to occur and take on meaning. You can ask questions like these: Does the pattern typically occur before or after group members say or do something else? Does it occur in specific physical places or at specific times of the day/month/year/life cycle? Do particular types of people tend to be there when the pattern occurs? What is the relationship among them? Do speakers and their audiences tend to be pursuing specific goals (e.g., social, material, political, esthetic, spiritual, etc.) when the pattern is used? What form does the pattern take (e.g., spoken, written)? Are other media used? Is silence the relevant channel of communication? Do participants have a local term for what they are saying or doing or the kind of situation in which the pattern occurs? Not all of these questions will yield relevant information, but all of them can be potential leads.

Stage 6. Establishing connections to a local system of meanings. Once you figure out the "how" of communication ("How does this type of communication get done appropriately?") you can begin asking "why" questions ("Why do they communicate in this way?" "Why do they believe this is an appropriate way to say X?"). Besides the immediate context in which they tend to occur, communicative actions also take on meaning relative to the cultural system of meanings the community draws on as they produce and evaluate their own and others' communication. In order to understand the communicative act you are investigating, as a communication *practice,* you will need to capture as much of its cultural meaning as possible, given your circumstances and practical needs. Your early rich points in an unfamiliar social group will most likely occur because you are still using your own cultural perspective and system of meaning to make sense of the group's conduct. The more rich points you experience and the more patterns you identify, the better sense of the local system of meanings (including norms, beliefs, and value assigned to communication practices) you will develop. Each pattern and its meanings will become the pieces of a larger puzzle. As more pieces fall into place—that is, as you build culture—the easier it will be for you to interpret the communication patterns that confuse you and to build intercultural frames.

A Practical Question

"What do norms, beliefs, and value look like?"

Norms can be formulated as statements like this: "In the context of a breakup, in order to not come across as a rude or weak person, one should break up with another person face-to-face." Beliefs capture basic assumptions about how the world works. Here is one: "Diversity in the workplace fosters creative thinking." Value captures what communication practices speech community members find desirable. When you hear someone say, "Express yourself!" they are assigning value to statements that highlight individual uniqueness and creativity. Norms, beliefs, and value are ways in which speech communities express the "why" of communication.

Stage 7. Attempting coordinated interaction. The final test of the culture you have built and the communication practices you have reconstructed is whether they allow you to successfully (appropriately, or even creatively) participate in social interaction. Use the culture you have built to try to accomplish a social task or goal in a coordinated manner: ask someone out on a date, ask for someone's forgiveness, or place an order in a restaurant. If you are not immediately able to succeed at coordinated interaction in the ways I describe at the beginning of this section, don't despair. The worst that can happen is that you experience more rich points that inspire (or force) you to go back to the drawing board and engage in more culture building.

Although cultural inquiry begins with, and remains rooted in, personal experiences, *building culture is not the same as inventing culture.* You are not making up the information you use to build culture. The process is not entirely predictable, but you can infuse it with rigor by carefully attending to people's actual communication practices and always being prepared to revise your interpretations of what those practices mean to members of the

target community in light of new observations that don't fit your interpretations. Also, the process of cultural inquiry is not linear: you don't simply proceed from Stage 1 to 7 and call it a day. The process is **iterative** in the sense that you might have to repeat certain stages before you can move on to the next. You may have to experience some rich points before you can identify patterns, identify a number of patterns before you get an inkling of relevant cultural systems, rethink cultural systems in light of new rich points, and so on. The process is also **cyclical**: even if you succeed in understanding and using a local communication practice and you build a relevant intercultural frame, you may experience new rich points that require you to start the process all over again. It is quite likely that you will never stop building culture for a target community, although it is equally likely that the more familiar you become with the community, the less frequently you will experience your rich points.

Resources for Building Culture

As you build culture, you transform observations and existing knowledge into information you can use to manage coordinated interaction. But where do these observations and existing knowledge come from? Fortunately, you don't have to reinvent the wheel: there are time-honored resources on which you can rely. Let me list a few here.

Participant observation. Cultural inquiry requires you to always keep an ear and eye open for new observations that can help you establish communication patterns and practices. The best way to accomplish this is by becoming directly involved with the social group you are studying: spend time with them, interact with them, and learn their ways of social interaction through trial and error. You will find it valuable to keep a **field journal** in which you write down a day's events and surprises and begin to keep track of communication patterns in response to rich points.

Interviewing. Your interaction with group members can include more focused conversations in which you can ask your trusted informants about communication practices and their local meanings. Your interviews don't have to follow a set structure. Rather, you should ask questions that prompt your informant to reflect on how a particular practice is used well or badly in context. As much as possible, try to get your informant to share stories or anecdotes about actual events that illustrate a practice and its use. Try to interview more than one group member in order to establish patterns of observations and anecdotes across interviews. You can also reach out to your informants for feedback on your interpretations of local communication and its meanings. (This is called a **member check** in ethnographic research.) The advantage of interviews over participant observation is that you can talk to group members from a distance using phones or online audio or video conferencing. The advantage of participant observation is that the secondhand information you gather from informants can be unreliable. Just like you, community members very rarely think about their own communication practices and can therefore have a skewed understanding of how they actually use them in context.

Collecting materials. Whether or not you are physically present in the target community, you can collect written materials (e.g., newspaper or magazine articles) or audio and video materials online that help you make sense of the community's ways of communicating. Use your web searching savvy to find representations of the communication acts or practices at the core of your rich points or to find out more about the community's relevant norms and beliefs.

Reading scholarship. If practitioners of intercultural communication have easy access to academic journals and books about a target group, these materials can be a treasure trove of information. However, these resources are difficult to access if you are not affiliated with a university or other institution that subscribes to journals or purchases books. If you aren't, you can still refer to open access journals or books available through a public library. If you are, you should take full advantage of academic databases (e.g., *Communication & Mass Media Complete, ComAbstracts, Sociological Abstracts, AnthroSource*, etc.) and scholarly journals that regularly publish articles addressing the relationship between language and culture (e.g., *American Anthropologist, American Ethnologist, Current Anthropology, Journal of Intercultural Communication Research, Journal of International and Intercultural Communication, Journal of Linguistic Anthropology, Journal of Sociolinguistics, Language & Communication, Language in Society, Research on Language and Social Interaction, Text & Talk*, etc.). Search terms you can combine with either the name of your target community or with local labels for recognized types of communication (or both) to find relevant articles and books include "language" (or "linguistic"), "discourse" (or "discursive"), "talk," "speech," "communication," "culture" (or "cultural"), "ethnography," and "anthropology."

I am not assuming you will have access to all of these resources. Limited access, however, shouldn't stop you from building culture. But it is also true that relying on a wider range of resources in the process of your cultural inquiry will help you develop more accurate and comprehensive intercultural frames and make fewer interactional mistakes. A useful rule of thumb is the one cultural researchers interested in the lived experiences and communication practices of other people follow: *Use what you can.*

This Book as a Resource

As you can probably tell by now, building culture is a complicated and somewhat unpredictable endeavor. Much depends on your circumstances, the amount of time and other resources at your disposal, community members' willingness to cooperate with you, and so on. This book will not tell you what the communication practice at the heart of one of your rich points means. But it helps you in two important ways: it gives you a strategy for moving toward more coordinated interactions across cultural differences in an ethically informed way, and it gives you resources for labeling some communication patterns and investigating their local meanings. Some of the chapters will introduce you to communication practices that my students most commonly experienced in the past as rich points (such as words, language, personal address, interpersonal relations, speech acts, humor, topic selection, gender/political/racial identity, the amount of talk, and silence), while others will help you reflect on cultural meanings (such as norms, rules, beliefs, value, and community). The rest you will need to figure out on your own by trial and error in a process of learning by doing.

DOING IT RIGHT: ETHICAL REFLECTIONS ON THE PROCESS OF BUILDING CULTURE

Note that the process of cultural inquiry and the project of restoring coordinated interaction rest on three key assumptions:

1. You and members of the target community are on equal footing in terms of privilege.

2. You are relatively free to study local communication practices.

3. You will find the communication practices you discover morally acceptable.

A Practical Question

"How do you know if you are on equal footing with your conversational partners in terms of privilege?"

Ask the questions listed at the beginning of the subsection titled "Equal Footing."

It is important to remember that you can't take any of these assumptions for granted. In terms of relative privilege, you may be in a higher or lower position in relation to members of the target social group; your cultural curiosity may be dampened by the group's unwillingness to accommodate you; you may find local communication practices morally unacceptable. When you reflect on relative privilege, the freedom of cultural inquiry, and your moral commitments, you are exercising **reflexivity** (systematic reflection on social interaction with cultural others, including the process of building culture). Reflexivity matters not only because it allows for a moral evaluation of your interactions with members of your target community but also because, as you can see below, a lack of reflexivity can undermine coordinated interaction.

Equal Footing

In interaction with members of the target community, do you have control over who you are and your actions, or do the group's members have control over you? Are you in a position to influence their lives with your communicative actions, or are they more likely to influence yours with theirs? These are some of the questions you will need to ask as you interact with people for whom you are building culture. Keep in mind, though, that these relationships of power can shift from interaction to interaction: you may be in a one-up or one-down position depending on the identity of your interactional partner(s).

A Japanese international student found himself in a one-down position of privilege during a discussion of his internship arrangements with an academic adviser at the university he was attending in the United States. The adviser thought the internship the student found in an international dormitory was not "academic enough" to merit a grade. Later, in an interview with a Japanese intercultural communication researcher, Mariko Kotani, the student reported the American adviser was angry with him and told him to find a better internship, which he did. He gave a cultural explanation for the adviser's conduct:

EXCERPT 3.1. (from Kotani, 2017, p. 469)

Student	After all, it was a cultural difference. ... You have to make an action in [U.S.] society, whereas in Japanese society, you behave as your surrounding circumstances let you do. I grasped it when I had that incident with the adviser. Like, "Oh I see. He wouldn't accept what I think." In Japan, I would say, "If you give me some ideas, I'll do as you say," but it doesn't work here because it's totally different.
Interviewer	Will you explain to me what you mean by totally different?
Student	You have to take care of what you have to do here, right? But I expected my teachers and adviser to take care of me in a lot of ways. But it turned out to be wrong, I realized.

Interviewer	Like, if the international dormitory is not good, then "How about this?" You expected something like that?
Student	Yeah. I expected him to look for a better place for me and say, "There is a place like this," showing me a concrete place and saying, "Why don't you go there?" or "I'll talk to the manager." I was stupid to have expected something like that.

The Japanese international student and the American adviser were not on equal footing in terms of privilege. An important consequence of this is that the student was forced to come up with a cultural explanation for the adviser's conduct and play by the cultural rules the adviser was observing. He also had to deal with the shame of feeling "stupid" for thinking he knew where the adviser was coming from. The relatively more privileged adviser didn't have to build culture for the student.

Acting on relative privilege doesn't automatically make someone a bad person. I am not even sure if the adviser was aware of his relative privilege or if he enjoyed the same privilege across all of his conversations with international students. The problem is that acting on privilege can lead to worse social consequences. For example, the Japanese student also reported that, following the conversation in which the adviser got angry with him, he found an internship he thought the adviser would like more and routinely exaggerated the work he was doing to make the adviser happy. His fear of the adviser's anger may have cost him some very important learning opportunities.

Acting on privilege can lead to serious social injustice. The intercultural communication researcher Michael Meeuwis (1994) studied English-language training sessions between Flemish engineers and South Korean and Tanzanian students in Belgium. He noticed the engineers who harbored negative stereotypes toward the Tanzanian students were much less tolerant toward them than they were toward the South Korean students in cases of communication breakdown, even though the Tanzanian students spoke better English than the Koreans. Because the engineers were in a position of privilege, they could simply disregard the breakdowns and Tanzanian students' frustration. "Intercultural encounters," Meeuwis reminds us, "do not occur in 'neutral territory'" (p. 402).

The Freedom of Cultural Inquiry

The lack of privilege can also lead to, and be reinforced by, access to cultural information you may need to build culture. In intercultural encounters, ask yourself: "Does relative privilege keep me from gathering information I need to achieve coordinated interaction with someone? Does my identity (e.g., racial, ethnic, national, sexual, gender, religious, etc.) get in the way? Is my conversational partner withholding information from me that I might find useful, or are they giving me less useful information just to please me? Conversely, is it possible that I feel less compelled to include a conversational partner's odd communicative conduct in my inquiry because I am in a relatively higher position of privilege?"

Lack of access to cultural information leads to the failure to accomplish coordinated intercultural interaction, which, in turn, can have important material consequences—in some cases, it can be a matter of life or death. The Belgian sociolinguist Jan Blommaert and his research team studied the kinds of communicative challenges asylum seekers in Belgium have to deal with as they are interviewed by local bureaucrats. The bureaucrats' decision to grant someone asylum depended to a large extent on how convincingly interviewees could narrate their plights in their home countries in English. Blommaert (2001) reported refugees' stories were often negatively evaluated because they were told with hesitation, with lots of self-corrections, in grammatically incorrect English, and in ways that violated Belgian bureaucrats' norms and expectations regarding refugee storytelling. How, Blommaert asks, could asylum seekers with limited education, limited English, and limited familiarity with Belgian cultural expectations be expected to tell the kinds of stories the bureaucrats wanted to hear? They simply lacked the information necessary to even attempt to coordinate their interaction with those who decided their fates.

A Practical Question

"What are you supposed to do when you encounter a cultural communication practice you find morally unacceptable?"

The answer to this question depends on who you are, what you are trying to accomplish, and the social consequences of refusing or condemning the practice. Taking the example of *piropos* and *catcalls*, you have the option not to engage in these practices as a man or to call out other men when you see them giving *piropos* or catcalling. As a woman, you can ignore these practices, call them out, encourage men not to engage in them, and so on. Whenever you think about your response to morally unacceptable practices, always think about your safety, too.

Moral Commitments

After you unravel the cultural uses and meanings of a local communication practice, you may find it distasteful or morally unacceptable. I would like to argue against the misguided notion that just because a communication practice is "cultural" (that is, widely accepted and practiced in a community you treat as culturally different from yours), you have to accept it as appropriate. Certainly, I would encourage you not to judge a communication practice without making any attempt to understand it in terms of the people who use it regularly. Doing so may lead you to make mistakes in interpreting its local meanings and in coordinating interaction with community members. However, you do not have to give up your moral commitments in the process of building culture. *You don't have to conflate understanding with acceptance.*

For example, I see no reason to convince my female students in the United States not to be offended by the practice of *piropo* in many Spanish-speaking countries from Spain to the Caribbean. *Piropo* is a form of flirty flattery that consists of men making vaguely sexual remarks in public toward women whose ages can range from adolescence to about 40 (Bailey, 2017). No matter how "cultural" this practice may be, my female students experience it as harassment, plain and simple. For them, *piropo* is a strong reminder "of their subordinate position and vulnerability to violence" (p. 203) in societies where this type of communication is practiced. As culturally sensitive and tolerant as they are, they can't help seeing a resemblance between *piropos* and *catcalling*, an U.S. American practice they also find morally unacceptable.

Nevertheless, try to balance having a strong moral compass with maintaining a curiosity about moral systems different from yours. A local system of action and morality, or **localized ethic** (Kovats-Bernat, 2002), may make good sense to those who observe it in the context of local systems of meaning and local material, social, historical, and political circumstances. I am not advocating moral relativism. What I am advocating is openness to the possibility of coordinated interaction, to the extent that such interaction doesn't violate your moral commitments.

REFLECTION QUESTIONS

1. Recall a claim you have recently made about cultural difference. What sort of evidence did you have to support your claim? What sort of evidence could have strengthened your claim?

2. How does Iyengar's story about ordering tea illustrate the stages of building culture? Does it illustrate all stages?

3. In the anecdote about the Japanese exchange student, do you think the academic adviser should have behaved differently? Why? If you think he should have, what would have been a better course of action?

4. Have you ever come across a communication practice you thought you understood but rejected on moral grounds? What did you do after you rejected that practice? Did you refrain from doing it? Did you call it out? Did you do something else?

5. Can you think of a localized ethic that is unique to a social group you call yours or with which you are familiar?

4

"What Does That Word Mean to Them?"

Words and Key Terms

MORGAN: My mom used to work with a woman who was from South Africa. They became close friends, and she had daughters close in age to my sister and me. One day my mom said that we were all going to go to the beach and that we were going to go to her friend's house first. When we got to their house, the moms were getting all the stuff together for our trip to the beach. Right before we were ready to go, my mom's friend told us all to go put our "costumes" on. My sister and I looked at each other, confused. We even laughed. How could she be telling us to put costumes on? Did she not know we were going to the beach? Why would we need a costume for that? After she saw the look on our faces and heard us laugh, she caught herself right away and began to laugh as well. She forgot that she was talking to us, who would not understand what she meant. Then she told us that where she and her family were from in South Africa, they called bathing suits "costumes."

PEYTON: For my first couple years of college, I had a significant other who lived in a town called Peterborough in England. When we first met, we noticed many differences in how we expressed

In this chapter, you will learn:

- the difference between misunderstanding and cultural miscommunication

- the importance of studying the meaning in use, and not only the dictionary meaning, of words

- the different ways in which words can be used for making culture

ourselves. In particular, I noticed a difference in the way we would react when we did not understand something or could not hear what someone was saying in a social setting. In those situations, I always respond by saying "What?" The first time I reacted using the word "what" around my significant other, he responded with confusion and offense. Eventually, after he became more accustomed to this reaction, he began to mock my word usage and laugh when I would respond that way. I asked him why he found the word "what" so funny. He told me that when he or other people from his culture respond with "what," it is often out of disrespect or disregard for the other person. Therefore, my casual use of the word in everyday conversation was shocking and confusing to him. Generally, in UK culture, I know that people interact in a more proper manner than in the U.S.

Word-based rich points vary considerably in their degree of richness. Consider Morgan's rich point narrative about "costume" and "bathing suit." The confusion she felt was genuine, but the rich point was resolved immediately after the South African woman explained what she meant by "costume." There was no need to delve further into this difference once Morgan and her conversational partner clarified the local meanings of the words they used for the same object. This was a case of simple **misunderstanding**, a failure to understand language use in context.

FROM MISUNDERSTANDING TO MISCOMMUNICATION

Compare Morgan's narrative to Peyton's about "What?" in the US and in the UK. The stakes are higher; we are no longer dealing with a simple misunderstanding but inter-cultural **miscommunication**. Intercultural miscommunication happens when a misunderstanding has a cultural basis and social consequences for participants and participants recognize the combination of these three features (misunderstanding + cultural basis + social consequences) in the history of their communication with one another (Banks, Ge, & Baker, 1991). Participants tend to recognize intercultural mis-communication only after they have been misunderstanding one another for some time and have started to misinterpret other participants' motives and intentions. Usually, participants name problems first (e.g., feeling mistreated or stereotyped, noticing interaction is not going smoothly), and only then do they recognize miscommunication has occurred. Sometimes participants themselves don't recognize they are dealing with intercultural miscommunication—only that there is some kind of strain on their rela-tionship—but others to whom they turn for help do.

Peyton's rich point narrative is an example of intercultural miscommunication with the use of a word at its center. She notices her significant other's repeated "confusion and offense"—and, later, mockery—in response to what she intended to be a simple request for clarification. Although both of them seem to recognize their interaction is uncoordinated, she continues using "What?" and he continues responding with confusion and derision. She finally has enough and takes issue with being made fun of. They clarify to each other their different interpretations of "What?" and it turns out they attributed the wrong kinds of motives to one another: she thought he was making fun of her, whereas he wanted to call her attention to a *faux pas*; he thought she was being rude, whereas she was signaling her need for clarification. Peyton, an American student, succeeded in identifying differences between "U.S. culture" and "UK culture" as the source of miscommunication, although, as we will see later, her conclusion that British ways of communicating are somehow superior to U.S. ways is mistaken.

A Practical Question

"Is there a reliable method for detecting miscommunication as it is happening?"

Unfortunately, there is not. In our day-to-day interactions, we like to believe we understand what our conversational partners mean by what they say. As a result, we are slow to pick up on mismatched meanings. This is why outsiders who can help us retrace our meaning making can be so helpful.

DOING THINGS WITH WORDS

In my experience teaching intercultural communication, words and their meanings are the most frequent sources of rich points for students. In intercultural encounters, words can cause confusion in two ways. First, different groups of speakers can attribute different referential meanings to the same word. **Referential meaning** is the meaning of a word you find in a dictionary. Dictionaries provide you with meaning(s) most commonly attributed to particular words that have been abstracted from their everyday use. Such abstractions tend to capture word-to-object relations: word X stands for object Y. (The referential meaning of *"costume"* in U.S. English is something you would wear on Halloween; for some South African speakers, the same word refers to a bathing suit.)

A Practical Question

"What is the practical value of linguistic taxonomies?"

Taxonomies can help you map unfamiliar social settings or unfamiliar relationships among objects. A particularly useful taxonomy is the organizational chart that captures formal roles in an organization and the relationships among them. You can also create taxonomies for different types of food if you are working in an ethnic restaurant (think maki vs. sashimi vs. nigiri as types of sushi) or the types of relationships your significant references in conversation (e.g., parents, aunts, second cousins, friends, close friends, neighbors, etc.).

For the intercultural practitioner, the value of knowing the referential meaning of words is that it allows them to construct **linguistic taxonomies.** Taxonomies are systematic classifications of words and concepts that map relationships among their referential meanings. For example, "costume" would be equally classified as a type of garment in South African and U.S. English, but in South African English, it would be further classified as a type of swimwear, while in U.S. English, it would fall into the category of outfits people wear to pretend to be particular characters from pop culture, legends, plays, and so on.

But words can also confuse speakers with their **pragmatic meanings**, that is, with those meanings they typically take on in social interaction (Bailey, 2004). Pragmatic meanings capture what speakers in a speech community tend to *do* with particular words. (The word "pragmatic" derives from the Greek word *pragma* "deed.") The second rich point narrative (Peyton's) centered on a pragmatic meaning of the word *"what."*

Example 1: "Ass"

The same word can cause referential and pragmatic confusion for language learners. Consider the below excerpt from a stand-up comedy performance by the Finnish comedian Ismo Leikola. Ismo appeared on *Conan*, a late-night talk show hosted by Conan O'Brien, in early 2018. In his brief performance, he discussed his experiences with the English language after moving to the United States from Finland. In the excerpt below, he talks about his struggles with one particular English word. (If you want to get a sense of his hysterically deadpan, thoroughly Finnish delivery, find the video on YouTube.)

> I studied English for years, and I thought, *"I know English."* But then I move to America. Turns out, no. Like I didn't *really* know it, like all the things. ... I think the hardest word to truly master has been the word "ass." "Ass." I thought *"It's really easy. It means a butt."* But no. Like yeah, sometimes it can mean a butt, but that's just the tip of the assberg. Like there are so many meanings of the word "ass," I think it's the most complicated word in English. I've been trying to write a whole dictionary about just "ass." There's so many ... like, for example, "lazy-ass." That means "lazy." Like "my lazy-ass husband." It's the same sentence without the "ass." The "ass" is just optional there. And "long-ass" means long. Like "a long-ass flight." It's a long flight. But if you want to make it longer, you can add "ass." And my definite favorite one, "a grown-ass man." It turns out it means "a grown man." The entire man has grown, not only his ass. [...] But you have to be careful, because sometimes if you add "ass" to something, it can actually reverse the meaning of the original word. Like, for example "badass." That's good. Bad is bad, badass is good. But not always. Like "dumbass" is still dumb! So how can you know? You have to know specifically which ones are flipped. And then there is the concept of "your ass." "Your ass"—that means like,

yourself. Like "Move your ass!" That's like, everything. Like move your ass, and the rest of your body. If you have a car, that's included in the ass. All of them, same direction, just move. So "your ass" means yourself plus all that you have, but "my ass," that means "no." Like if I say, "This car is really fast!" and you say, "Ah, fast my ass." So it means like, "No, it's not fast." And to make it even more complicated, "ass" can be divided! Like if you're "an ass," that means you're being stupid. But if you're "half-assed," then it means you're not concentrating properly. (Team Coco, 2018)

Explaining humor sucks the life out of it, but given our discussion here, let me point out that one reason why this comedy routine works is that Ismo is able to capture the wide gap between a word's referential meaning—"ass" is a mildly inappropriate word for the gluteus; I don't think too many people in the English-speaking world refer regularly to a donkey as an "ass" these days—and the diverse referential and pragmatic meanings it can take on in combination with other words ("badass," "dumbass") or as an element of formulaic expressions ("your ass," "my ass"). Or consider the use of "ass" as an **upgrader** ("lazy-ass husband," "long-ass flight"). Upgraders intensify an utterance and make it more direct.

Example 2: "Dude"

An equally versatile word I encountered as a non-native speaker of English was "dude." During the first year of my master's studies, I was able to stay at the house of one of my father's childhood friends for free. At the time, most, if not all, of my friends were European international students. Towards the end of the first year of my graduate program, I had to realize that, although not having to pay rent was great, if I were to make any American friends at all, I had to change something about my lifestyle. The student leader of an on-campus club to which I belonged was looking for an apartment mate, so I moved in with him and another American student. Living with Bradford and Nelson taught me a lot about American friendship, the meaning of "hanging out" as a social activity, and the difference between the undergraduate and graduate student experience (both of them were undergrads), but I also learned to appreciate the seemingly insignificant word "dude." At first, I experienced "dude" as a mild rich point—not overly confusing but intriguing regardless. I quickly figured out that "dude" referred to particular categories of people. When my apartment mates referred to someone as "dude," they were signaling a relationship of equality with, and relatively small social distance from, that person. The people to whom they referred as "dude" also tended to be young males, although they sometimes used "dude" with young females as well. But they also did a range of other things with "dude": they used it to grab someone's attention ("Dude!"), to reprimand others ("DUDE!"), to indicate surprise ("Duuuuuuude ..."), and to emphasize a point or start a serious discussion

("Dude ..."). Their proud awareness of the word's many pragmatic meanings was on full display when they introduced me to the 1998 movie *BASEketball*, in which two climactic dialogues between the characters played by Trey Parker and Matt Stone consisted mainly of the two saying "dude" to one another.

Years later, I found out about a study by the sociolinguist Scott F. Kiesling (2004) that confirmed many of my casual observations about the social life of "dude" and added depth to my understanding of the type of relationship "dude" signals. Kiesling, who studied the language of White fraternity brothers at the University of Pittsburgh, noticed that "dude" could be used in such communication activities as reacting positively or negatively to news or a situation, participating in mock confrontations, expressing affiliation and connection, and signaling agreement. But perhaps most importantly for me as someone invested in making culture for America, "dude" is also an index of what Kiesling called "cool solidarity." **Indexicality** is the concept "that undergirds the pragmatic assumption that in order to understand the meaning of any communicative act, one must understand how it functions in context" (Hughes & Tracy, 2015). Words and other bits and pieces of language index (point to) elements of the context in which social interaction is taking place. We understand what others are *doing* communicatively when we understand the indexical properties of what they are saying and when those others are *doing* things communicatively in ways that make the best use of the indexical properties of language. When used according to cultural expectations, "dude" is an efficient way of signaling and affirming a particular type of relationship between males that walks the fine line between a desire for solidarity (intimacy, "male bonding") and heterosexuality (which is seen as the polar opposite of homosexuality and is thought of as "normal" male sexuality). The cool solidarity that "dude" indexes is a cultural ideal for male-to-male relationships that are close but casual. The use of "dude" among fraternity brothers activated and confirmed the existence of such a relationship and affirmed the community of "dudes" and the "normalcy" of those involved in interaction.

VARIATIONS ON A LANGUAGE: U.S. vs. BRITISH ENGLISH

Intercultural communication gets complicated when different words have the same referential meaning in different varieties of the same language. Consider the difference between American and British English as national varieties of English. Americans wear "sneakers," while the British put on "trainers." Americans eat "potato chips" and "eggplants," while Brits enjoy "crisps" and "aubergines." An American would ride the "elevator" to the floor where their "apartment" is located, while in Britain, you take the "lift" to get to your "flat." Countless lists of lexical differences between the two varieties of English are available online.

Are Different Vocabularies Evidence of Cultural Difference?

It is possible to observe more subtle differences beyond the different-word-for-the-same-thing type. The American-born linguist Lynne Murphy, who currently teaches in the United Kingdom, is an expert on differences between British and American English. She notes (2018), for example, that what Brits call "bacon" is "ham" by American standards. (The British have a word for what Americans consider "bacon": "streaky bacon.") This is due to the fact that the British and Americans operate with different prototypes of what counts as ham and bacon. Or, when Americans refer to someone as "middle class," they generally mean that person is like most people. In Britain, by contrast, referring to someone as "middle class" has a much less egalitarian ring to it. In fact, Brits often use "middle class" to refer to someone who thinks they are above everyone else. While in America, "middle class" is associated with an average, unremarkable lifestyle, in Britain, "middle class" invokes a life of prosperity and conspicuous consumption.

However, before you conclude that differences between British and American vocabularies are clear evidence of cultural differences between the two countries, think again. For one thing, when we put some differences in a historical context, it turns out that words we thought were of American origin were in fact first used in Britain. Today, we think of "soccer" as an American word for what the British call "football." As Murphy explains, the word "soccer" was born in the United Kingdom. The British, who like to give nicknames to sports, shortened "rugby football" to "rugger" and "association football" to "soccer." What about the American "sidewalk," which the British love to hate? As it happens, the first documented use of "sidewalk" occurred in Britain in the 17th century. To make matters more complicated, some words we in the United States firmly associate with British English are of U.S. origin, such as "bumbershoot" meaning "umbrella." (A bona fide British word for "umbrella" is "brolly.") Others come from outside the English language entirely, such as "poppycock," which is of Dutch origin. Everyday speakers, Murphy cautions, lack the knowledge to correctly identify the national and historical origin of words.

On its own, lexical variation is not a reliable window on culture. A better place to look for culture is moments of intercultural encounter in which participants don't understand the indexical properties of what cultural others say or when they try to say something without fully understanding the indexical properties of the language they are using for a particular community of speakers.

Words in Intercultural Encounters

Consider this exchange between American tourists and a British guard the linguist Lynne Murphy overheard in the National Gallery in London.

Tourist	Could you tell us where the restroom is?
Guard	Do you need a rest?
Tourist	Oh no—I mean the bathroom.
Guard	Why? Do you want to have a bath?
Tourists	[*Gasping for another word*]
Guard	I can direct you to the ladies' toilets.

Did the guard really not understand what the words "restroom" and "bathroom" meant? He most definitely did, Murphy explains; he was only having a bit of (macho) fun at the female tourists' expense. Many in the United Kingdom believe Americans are unnecessarily prudish when it comes to, well, using the bathroom. Why don't they just call it what it is: going to the toilet? What the guard doesn't understand is that in the United States, the word "toilet" tends to be used to refer to the object ("We should replace the toilet. It's cracked.") But in the United Kingdom. it refers to the location where people retire to exercise their bodily functions.

Language Ideologies

Why is this exchange not a case of simple misunderstanding? Why does the guard make fun of American usage with such confidence? And why are the tourists so caught off guard and embarrassed? To answer these questions, we have to look beyond the word "toilet" to **language ideology**, deeply held cultural beliefs about the function and value of various languages and linguistic varieties and the value (social standing, prestige) of those who speak them (Woolard, 1998). We all make distinctions between "better" and "worse" forms of languages we know and "better" and "worse" people who use those forms regularly. Murphy highlights two relevant language ideologies she calls American Verbal Inferiority Complex (AVIC) and British Verbal Superiority Complex (BVSC). AVIC holds that American forms and usages of English will always be inferior to more "proper" and "correct" British uses; BVSC is the belief that American English is inherently flawed. An extreme version of BVSC maintains that *any* kind of English that looks or sounds wrong *must* be of American origin and thus a sign of sneaking globalization corrupting "correct" (British) English. These sets of linguistic beliefs are just that: beliefs. "Despite ample evidence that (a) Americans did not invent various 'wrong' things said in Britain today, and (b) the British are no better at using 'proper' grammar than Americans are, the 'British is more correct' stereotype lives on. In the United Kingdom, it is a symptom of British Verbal Superiority Complex. In the United States, it's a symptom of American Inferiority Complex" (p. 49).

AVIC and BVSC are, of course, not the only language ideologies out there. For example, different generations have very different ideas about the language of texting (Thurlow, 2006) or the internet (McCulloch, 2019).

Let's take insights about AVIC and BVSC back to the exchange between the British guard and the American tourists. The guard does something interesting with the tourists' descriptions of what they are looking for ("restroom," "bathroom"): he takes their descriptions literally ("room where one rests," "room where one bathes") and feigns misunderstanding. The tourists buy into his performance and accept that misunderstanding is occurring; what they miss is that, in fact, they are being schooled for misusing the English language. The guard is indexing a distinction between U.S. and British English and casts the former as "incorrect" and the latter as "correct." He is also indexing his status as a speaker of British English and the status of the tourists as speakers of American English. Indexing these distinctions as relevant elements of the ongoing interaction's context allows him to do three things simultaneously. First, he toys with the tourists by taking advantage of AVIC and making them doubt their own communicative competence. Second, he calls out and reprimands their prudish use of "incorrect" English ("Why can't Americans just call a toilet a toilet? What's the big deal?"). Third, he exercises what the sociolinguist Deborah Cameron (1995) called "verbal hygiene." **Verbal hygiene** is an umbrella term for a complex set of practices directed at preserving the "purity" of a language (particularly vocabulary and grammar) from external corruption and thereby affirming the value and unity of the community that calls that language its own. Under the influence of BVSC ideology, the guard takes it upon himself to protect "correct" British English from the corrupting influence of "incorrect" American English. Unfortunately for Americans, what the guard is doing is not all that uncommon. Murphy explains that provoking the linguistic insecurities of Americans is a favorite British pastime.

Pointing out differences between national or regional versions of languages for the purpose of highlighting differences between different types of people is, of course, not a unique feature of interactions between British and American speakers. For example, I can always count on my students from California when I ask my class to name regional differences in U.S. English. Students from Southern California proudly list surfer terms such as "gnarly" ("extreme, cool"), "stoked" ("excited, exhilarated"), and "brah" (the local version of the address term "bro") that have spilled over from beach talk into mainstream slang. Students from Northern California counter that it's not just words from "SoCal" that have become national phenomena: the commonly used "hella" ("very") started out in the Bay Area. Southern California students are quick to point

CULTURAL PRAGMATICS SAYS

The culture you build for a social group is always *plural*. When you encounter speakers of British English, don't assume their speech represents the speech of all British speakers. British English varies considerably by region, just as U.S. English does.

out that the term "SoCal" is a Northern creation and therefore they wouldn't claim it as their own, but they would certainly claim referring to major California highways as "the 101" and "the 5" as opposed to "101" or "I-5." They continue excitedly listing and laughing at regional terms among themselves long after the rest of the class has moved on to another topic of discussion. It is clear that, for them, regional variation is a source of communal pride and identity thousands of miles away from home—even though many of the words they claim as their own have been disseminated in the media and appropriated by other speech communities.

Fortunately for intercultural practitioners, words and phrases are well within speakers' limits of conscious awareness, unlike most other communicative resources they use on a regular basis. As a result, you will have no trouble hearing people talk about their words, the words of others, and why their words are better than those of others. But don't take these statements at face value: try to look beyond words to actions (pragmatic meaning) and the beliefs that render those actions sensible and recognizable to speech community members. Differences between national and regional vocabularies within the same language can be interesting and fun to talk about, but they serve you better as windows on culture once you see what speakers do with them and the differences among them.

CULTURAL KEY TERMS

There is a specific class of words that you will absolutely want to see in action and use in making culture for the group or community that uses them regularly. These words are called cultural **key terms** or **key words**. These words are "key" (i.e., more important than other, more regular words) to the cultural investigator such as yourself because they help you "unlock" large, complex, and unfamiliar systems of meaningful communicative action. Key terms are referentially and pragmatically connected to many other words, actions, and relationships that are important to the group for which you are building culture. Therefore, if you pursue their uses and meanings, you will discover a number of cultural threads you can follow on your quest toward coordinated action.

It takes a while to determine whether a term is a key term or not. They might just be words you hear spoken more often than others. Or they might be words you don't immediately understand, and when you ask for clarification the group member you're talking to stops, thinks, and says, "I don't

A Practical Question

"How do you know that a term is *not* a key term?"

It takes time to make this determination. Initially, you may assume a term is a key term but then later realize it is used less than you thought, speech community members don't think of it as a key term, or it doesn't help you build culture for a target social group.

know, it's complicated" or gives you a hesitant translation but adds, "It means that, but it means a bunch of other things, too." Likely, you will experience a rich point when you realize this word either doesn't have an equivalent term in your own language or its meanings are too contested or fractured to be captured by a single definition. Let's have a look at an example of each of these possibilities: Japanese *amae* and Hungarian *gyűlöletbeszéd* ("hate speech," pronounced roughly as *dyoo-lo-let-beh-said*).

Amae in Japan

The noun *amae* refers to a uniquely Japanese emotion. English-speaking scholars have been trying to identify the English equivalent of *amae* and its verb form *amaeru* for decades, but no single word seems to do justice to the term's Japanese meanings (Wierzbicka, 1997). *Amaeru* has been variously translated as "to depend on another's affection," "to presume another's love" "to take advantage of," "to behave like a spoiled child," "to encroach on one's kindness," and "to be coquettish." All of these translations elucidate some, but not all, meanings of *amae* as an emotion. Wierzbicka explains that reconstructing the term's meanings is difficult for a Western observer but the effort pays off in the long run because it takes us into the heart of Japanese culture. To understand *amae*, conjure in your mind the classical image of a mother's unconditional love for her child. What do we know about such a relationship? Well, we know that since her love is unconditional, the child can't do anything that would make the mother revoke it. We also know the mother is in a one-up position: her safety and survival don't depend on the child, but the child's do depend on her. This unidirectional dependence creates a hierarchical relationship between the two. This hierarchical arrangement is not one that implies oppression or exploitation: it is simply a natural consequence of biological differences between mothers and children. Now, in order to get to the meaning of *amae*, let's take this image and superimpose it onto a romantic relationship. A romantic partner experiences *amae* toward another when they feel so unconditionally loved by, and dependent on, that person that they exist in a state of complete abandon and can afford to act like a spoiled child. They know nothing they can do will disrupt the love and nurturing of the other person, and therefore they have the liberty to relax and act toward them on impulse. What would normally seem like an imposition—or "encroaching on one's kindness" by taking their love and goodwill for granted—is actually a key feature of *amae*. A female singer in a Japanese pop song put this type of relationship into words in this way:

> On the day
>
> we are finally one
>
> hug me,
>
> hug me,
>
> and you'll let me play baby, won't you? (p. 239)

Amae, however, is not exclusive to romantic relations. It can exist in any kind of relationship in which one participant is dependent on the other who is in the position of a superior. Inside the family, one can enact *amaeru* toward a parent or an older sibling. Beyond the family, bosses and leaders can also be objects of *amae*. According to Japanese expectations, *amae*-seniors (i.e., those in superior positions) can and will arrange the lives of *amae*-juniors. *Amae*-juniors submit to *amae*-seniors in the assurance that seniors' actions are motivated by (motherly) love juniors will never be required to earn.

If all of this sounds vaguely suspect to you, you are having a cultural reaction. By Western cultural standards, *amae* goes against the model of the independent self and the preference for individual autonomy. The Western ideal of romantic love conceives of romantic partners as equals who maintain some, if not all, of their autonomy and their capacity to make independent choices about their lives and selves. This is the ideal that makes the title of *The Onion* article "Woman Who Changed Self to Please Boyfriend Enjoying Happy Long-Term Relationship" (2012, June 13) sound so creepy. Westerners tend to believe changing the self for the sake of someone else endangers the health of the self and, potentially, the entire relationship in the long run. By contrast, *amae* makes sense in a social context in which there is a shared cultural preference for interdependence across the full range of possible relationships. This type of cultural orientation challenges us to understand the negative connotation of terms such as "dependence," "obedience," and "hierarchy" as distinctively cultural.

"Hate Speech" in Hungary

Unlike *amae*, the Hungarian term for "hate speech" (*gyűlöletbeszéd*) is easily translatable into English. In fact, the Hungarian term is the direct translation of the English term ("hate" = *gyűlölet*, "speech" = *beszéd*). The term appeared in Hungarian public discourse in the 1990s around the time when Hungarians suddenly found themselves having to deal with the consequences of allowing free speech after decades of communism. As in many other Western countries, White supremacist and neo-Nazi groups were taking full advantage of laws protecting freedom of expression and were making racist statements in public the political mainstream found unacceptable. The term "hate speech" serves as useful shorthand for all manners of unacceptable, though legal, public expression. However, by the mid-2000s, "hate speech" could be used to describe any kind of public expression one found unacceptable, including the expression of one's political opponents. As someone educated in the United States, where "hate speech" is still quite strongly associated with racist expression, I experienced the Hungarian use of "hate speech" as a rich point, so much so that later I wrote a book about the term (Boromisza-Habashi, 2013).

The deeper I delved into the local meaning(s) of "hate speech" in Hungary, the more I recognized it allowed me to see some deep rifts in Hungarian society. One such rift opened up at the height of political debates surrounding hate speech in 2003 around competing interpretations of the limits the Hungarian constitution placed on free expression. The constitution in effect at the time—mind you, this was Hungary's third constitution, only to be replaced in 2011—contained a contradiction between the right to free expression and the right to human dignity. Politicians agreed that hate speech violated human dignity, but they couldn't agree if hate speech qualified as free speech. Center-left liberals and conservatives made this argument:

> Hate speech violates the human dignity of others. Human dignity is protected by the constitution. The freedom of expression is also protected by the constitution. Since the right to human dignity and the right to free expression are both within the constitution, one cannot be compromised for the sake of the other. Therefore, hate speech is a mode of expression protected by the constitution.

Socialists, who at the time were left of the liberals on the political spectrum, countered with the following interpretation:

> Hate speech violates the human dignity of others. Human dignity is protected by the constitution. The freedom of expression is also protected by the constitution. Since the right to human dignity and the right to free expression are both within the constitution, one can serve as the limit to the other. Therefore, hate speech is a mode of expression not protected by the constitution.

Both interpretations were reasonable readings of the constitution. However, in the context of heated debates surrounding hate speech, both became dogma for the political groups supporting one over the other. And then I haven't even mentioned the Hungarian far right, which interpreted public discourse about "hate speech" as a propaganda tool created by the left for the purpose of silencing opinions they didn't like. All of these political groups tried to exercise verbal hygiene by claiming that only their interpretations of hate speech captured the true meaning of the term.

Following "hate speech" as a key term showed me that translating it (back) into English or trying to craft a precise English-language definition of the term shed very little light on its conflicting local meanings. In fact, from a cultural perspective, any attempt to define "hate speech" would have been beside the point. "Hate speech" in Hungary, as it turned out, was an **essentially contested term** (Boromisza-Habashi, 2010). Its meaning *was* its contestation: every time someone used or defined the term in public, they inevitably conjured up competing interpretations. They also identified themselves as a member of a social or political group, and they positioned themselves against other groups that tended to advocate competing interpretations. In the end, although I had to realize that finding a single definition or translation of Hungarian "hate speech" was an exercise in futility, I learned a lot about what you could and couldn't *do* with the term in the Hungarian context and about a culture I call my own.

BARRIERS TO COORDINATED INTERACTION

1. **Rushing to judgment about a group's social characteristics based on local vocabularies.** Have you ever found yourself thinking British words (not to mention their pronunciations!) were somehow more "refined" than American words? Did you think Japanese *amae* was evidence that the Japanese were a people who lacked self-confidence and were incapable of autonomous action and thought? These thoughts say more about you as an American/Westerner than the people whose ways of using language you are describing—and, as such, they are important steps toward making culture! Remember, when you are making culture, you are building up a system of differences and similarities between yourself and cultural others. You cannot not reflect on the ideas, assumptions, and ideologies you are bringing to this encounter. Your attitude toward the British and their words may be informed by the belief that American English is somehow inferior to British English, a belief that is not grounded in linguistic fact. Your feelings about *amae* may speak to your own cultural preference for individual autonomy in relationships. A keen awareness of your own cultural orientation is important, but using that orientation to evaluate the lives and characteristics of entire peoples is simply counterproductive.

2. **Missing the meaning of situated word choice or key term use.** Often, when you encounter a word you don't recognize, you will need to figure out its referential meaning quickly in order to continue a conversation. But always remain open to two possibilities: (1) the word may mean different things to different people in different types of situations (see the examples of "dude" and Hungarian "hate speech"), and (2) speakers may be telling you or each other something important by using a particular term and not others (recall the British museum guard purposely "misunderstanding" "bathroom" and "restroom"). Speakers (including you!) *do* a wide variety of things with words: yes, they point to things in the words, but they also correct others, present identities, manage relationships, and so on. Of course, grasping these pragmatic meanings takes quite a bit of immersion in a local communication system.

REFLECTION QUESTIONS

1. Can you recall a time when you experienced miscommunication? If you can, think about whether it had a cultural basis.

2. Can you think of language ideologies associated with languages or linguistic varieties other than British English?

3. Do you think cultural outsiders could see "dude" as a cultural key term in the U.S. context? Why or why not?

4. Where have you encountered examples of California English mentioned in this chapter?

5. Verbal hygiene is exercised in countries around the world. Can you think of a form of language use that is often the target of verbal hygiene in the United States?

5

"What Happens if I Don't Speak Their Language?"

Different Languages, Different Codes

DEVIN: Being of Filipino heritage, I have experienced aspects of the culture, including the language, food, and basic customs, through my family connections. My grandmother lived in Manila, the capital of the Philippines, for the majority of her life and is a speaker of Tagalog, the native language of the country. As a native speaker of English, I had trouble understanding her accent growing up but have come more accustomed to it over time. I visited the Philippines for the first time during my senior year of high school. During my time in the Philippines, I met many people who had grown up and lived in various parts of the island chain, including Manila. Some locals we met spoke English to varying degrees, but most spoke only Tagalog. The difficulty I have had throughout my life with interpreting accents combined with the language barrier made the communication process difficult to navigate throughout the 3-week trip. When I found myself in situations where I couldn't understand the people I was communicating with, I would often respond by asking "What?" or "Excuse me?" I felt uncomfortable and incompetent having to ask people to repeat themselves because of my lack of comprehension. There would often be an awkward moment in these

In this chapter, you will learn:

- about the difference between knowing and speaking a language

- about the relationship between language choice and identity

- about various language selection practices in multilingual societies

interactions where I would be trying to decipher what the person was saying, which they often notice because of my confused body language and facial expressions.

LEE: One very distinct memory I have was walking around downtown Denver on a weekend and seeing a large crowd of people dressed in sharp, bold, out-of-the-norm clothes and costumes heading somewhere. I walk up to a guy around my age, maybe a little younger, and ask him what he's doing in costume. He informs me that Nan Desu Kan is happening right now. I ask him what that is, and he says it's the annual anime convention in Denver. He then goes on to say that I should definitely dress up and gives me a suggestion stating that I would be a perfect character from a certain anime, I don't remember which one. He then said something in what sounded like broken Japanese (he was White) and then told me to have a good day. I was very confused that this guy would tell a random stranger to don a costume and come to this anime convention.

I f you are reading this book, chances are you have a good command of the English language. You can certainly read a text written in the English language, and it's probably safe to assume you speak the language as well. But I can't tell if you are a native speaker of the language or if you, like myself, learned to speak the language later in life. I also can't tell how fluently you speak English, just as you can't tell how "good" my spoken English is. As you probably know, there are lots of people in the world who can understand and even write English-language texts but have very little practice speaking English. Fortunately, as someone who lives in the United States, I have had plenty of opportunities to improve my English-speaking skills.

Since childhood, we are taught that if we want to communicate with people from other parts of the world, we have to learn their language. In the United States, the educational system encourages young people to learn other languages, including Spanish, French, Mandarin, and Japanese, and many competitive colleges and universities have a second-language requirement. Knowing a second language is generally considered the sign of a well-rounded, educated person. As the first account of a rich point above illustrates, it can be quite an awkward experience to communicate with people in another country where one doesn't speak the local language. (There is much more to this rich point, but more about that later.)

However, the relationship between language and intercultural communication is more complicated. There are two reasons this statement is inaccurate: "If you want to communicate with someone from X culture, you have to learn their native language." First, knowledge of another speaker's language is not a prerequisite for, nor does it guarantee, coordinated interaction in the context of intercultural communication. Second, if you are a competent speaker of the English language, it is quite possible that you can get by in the world without ever learning another language. In this chapter, we will first take a look at these two counterarguments one by one. Then we will examine how language selection in the context of social interaction is a useful resource for presenting social identities.

LANGUAGE vs. COMMUNICATION

Most people learn a second language in language courses offered by schools, colleges, universities, or through cultural institutes like the British Council, the Goethe-Institut, or Confucius Institutes. You can also purchase language-teaching software or download language apps designed for your mobile devices. The languages you learn in this way are versions of languages spoken in the world abstracted from the context of their everyday use, even when the courses claim to teach you "conversation skills." As the anthropologist Mike Agar explained in his book *Language Shock* (1994), our common conception of language—which is also the basis for designing second-language courses—draws an imaginary circle around grammar books and dictionaries and calls those "language." I am not arguing that knowledge of this abstract version of languages will not come in handy when you enter into conversations with speakers of those languages. However, because of its abstract nature, the language you learn in a second-language course will not automatically help you *communicate*. Communication, Agar argues, is possible even when you are only partially aware of a language's grammar and vocabulary. You can use bits and pieces of grammar and some words to get by in an unfamiliar country if you learn how to use them in locally recognizable—that is, *cultural*—ways. The practical challenge of intercultural communication is putting language to use, an exercise that takes you into the realm of culture.

A Practical Question

"Does this mean that we can communicate with cultural others without any knowledge of their language?"

Yes, that is possible. In a very limited range of social situations (e.g., service encounters, asking for directions, warning someone of danger, etc.) you can get by with others using only gestures, silences, and your own language. To accomplish more complicated communication tasks, you will need to know some (or a lot) of the other's language.

Culture, Agar says, erases the circle around language and brings your identity into play.

> Culture happens when you learn to use a second language. ... Culture starts when you realize that you've got a problem with language, and the problem has to do with who you are. Culture happens in language, but the consciousness it inspires goes well beyond it. (pp. 20-21)

We need culture in order to communicate in ways that allow us to get what we want while being seen the way we want to be seen. Let me give you an example. I can barely put together a grammatically correct sentence in Egyptian Arabic, but I can order a glass of lemonade with mint in Cairo in a culturally appropriate manner. Yes, taking Arabic lessons at the International Language Institute in Cairo helped: I learned words (*lemoon* "lemon"/ "lemonade") and politeness formulas (*law samaht* "please"/ "excuse me"). However, I learned how to actually place an order in cafes from my Egyptian wife. Watching her order and listening to her reactions to my initially feeble attempts taught me three things: (1) servers understood that when I asked for a lemon I wanted a lemonade, and (2) I could get away with making grammatical mistakes and speaking with a strong foreign accent, mainly because (3) I would always be seen as a foreigner, and foreigners are not expected to speak Arabic but at least I should make an effort to sound a tad more polite than an average Egyptian in order not to be seen as standoffish.

The notion that linguistic competence equals communication competence can also paralyze speakers who try to speak a second (third, fourth, etc.) language. The equation suggests that better knowledge of (abstract) language means greater success at communication. This leads some speakers to believe their limited mastery of an unfamiliar language's grammar and vocabulary will prevent interaction with native speakers. This could not be further from the truth. Think about it: Do you speak your native language well because you have extensive knowledge of its grammar and vocabulary? Or do all speakers of your native language with extensive knowledge of grammar and vocabulary excel at social interaction? I will wager that your answer to both of these questions is "no."

A Practical Question

"Will native speakers judge me for not speaking their language perfectly?"

Probably. Most (not all!) speakers will, however, be more invested in accomplishing a shared task with you than in letting you know how badly you speak the local language.

Communication Accommodation

Also, we are quite good at accommodating speakers who are non-native speakers of the language we are speaking at the moment, whether that language is our native language or not. The applied linguist Pamela Rogerson-Revell (2010) studied how members of a group of European financial experts managed using English as the common language for their meetings. Meeting participants included native and non-native speakers of English. Both groups made a clear effort to smooth over their colleagues' occasional struggles with the English language. Rogerson-Revell found meeting participants responded to their colleagues' linguistic errors or struggles in accordance with **Communication Accommodation Theory** (CAT; Giles & Ogay, 2007). CAT predicts that speakers will adjust their speech patterns according to whether they seek to increase, decrease, or maintain social distance between themselves and others. This type of social distance is not the physical distance of 6 feet in the context of the COVID-19 pandemic; rather, it is symbolic distance that captures whether participants see one another as socially similar (close) or different (distant). Speakers manage such perceived distance through communication. For example, in order to decrease social distance, speakers tend to rely on the strategy of convergence—that is, matching their communication patterns (word choice, style, dialect, etc.) to the patterns of others. Rogerson-Revell observed two types of accommodation strategies in the European meetings: *normalization* (e.g., ignoring mistakes, avoiding correcting other speakers, using self-deprecating humor, etc.) and *convergence* (e.g., using a "careful" speech style marked by slow, clear speech and the avoidance of jargon, etc.). In this way, participants not only created a linguistically inclusive social environment but also signaled their desire for decreasing—or at least not increasing—social distance between themselves and others in the meeting regardless of their national origin or linguistic abilities.

Gatekeeping Encounters

However, speakers can't always take such accommodation for granted. Some intercultural communication takes place in **gatekeeping encounters**, interaction where there is a clear distinction between participants who possess the authority to set conversational rules and expectations and participants who are required to conform to them (Gumperz, 1982). Consider, for example, the job interview where the interviewer is in the gatekeeper position. In the excerpt below, a native speaker employee of an Australian business is interviewing a Balinese job applicant. Although the applicant speaks English quite well, the interview takes an unfortunate turn.

The Balinese interviewee misunderstands the interviewer's questions about his travel plans. He thinks the interviewer is taking an interest in his plans for leisure travel, while the interviewer wants to find out if the interviewee plans to commit to the position for the long run. As a result of the misunderstanding, the interviewee inadvertently creates the impression that he is looking for a temporary position that will allow him to make enough money to move to Europe. In the position of the gatekeeper, the interviewer is not required to make an additional effort to ascertain whether her interpretation of the interviewee's words is correct. She can simply deny the interviewee the position, which is precisely what she did.

EXCERPT 5.1. (from Williams, 1985, pp. 173–174)

Interviewer	Erm … this place that you have now in Fremantle [city in Western Australia] … this is a permanent address? You're staying there permanently, are you?
Interviewee	Yes.
Interviewer	And you are over in Australia to stay, or would you like to travel later on … ? Or …
Interviewee	I think I would like to travel.
Interviewer	You would like to travel. Er, where would you like to go?
Interviewee	Europe.
Interviewer	Europe … mm …. Any idea when … when you would like to go?
Interviewee	Erm … depend when I get the job, you know.
Interviewer	Good, okay.
Interviewee	After I'm … getting … after I get a job, I think, then earn some money, and then …
Interviewer	So how long would you like to work for us for? If we gave you a job, how long do you think you'd be working for us before you wanted to travel?
Interviewee	Mm. Until enough money to … until enough money to go to travel.
Interviewer	Right, okay. So that's really why you want the job is to get some money for travelling.
Interviewee	Yeah, for travelling. I love travelling.

Gatekeepers' expectations regarding the appropriate use and interpretation of language use in intercultural encounters are often shaped by so-called **centering institutions**, institutions with the authority to decide what meanings of communicative conduct will be considered normative (Blommaert, 2005). Perhaps the most powerful centering institution is the state. The court system, for example, regularly disadvantages speakers who don't speak the standard variety of the local language in institutionally recognized ways. Members of Western Desert Aboriginal groups in Australia who are competent English speakers find themselves flustered by Anglo courtroom communication norms and sentenced for misdemeanors they had not committed. "Embarrassed by being personally exposed in a public setting and faced with highly assertive courtroom personnel,

A Practical Question

"Is there anything I can do to influence a gatekeeper's (negative) evaluation of my communication skills?"

There is not much you can do to that end. Being in a position of power, gatekeepers usually don't feel obligated to carefully evaluate your abilities to communicate. What you can do is anticipate and play into their expectations and preferences, closely monitor their responses to what you are saying, clear up mistakes and misunderstandings in the moment, and hope for the best.

Aboriginal people find it difficult to articulate a defense, and very frequently concur with any matter that is proposed to them" (Liberman, 1990, p. 179) in order to escape the bewildering courtroom setting. Similarly, English-speaking Native American students in the U.S. American education system often struggle with the expectation to speak to teachers in front of their peers (Philips, 1972) or to deliver speeches in the public speaking classroom (Carbaugh, 2005). Their difficulties have a cultural foundation: young people in these communities are not expected to be heard in public. Anglo teachers who are unaware of this often conclude such students are either not properly motivated or lack basic communication skills necessary for academic success.

ENGLISH AS GLOBAL LANGUAGE

The phenomenon of multilingual speakers is becoming more and more common around the world. (Keep in mind, though, that in countries like India, Luxembourg, South Africa, and Singapore, multilingualism is the norm rather than the exception!) The British linguist Tom McArthur (2005) describes his family's linguistic life in this way:

> English is a vast language, whereas Scottish Gaelic now has about 70,000 speakers left. A thousand years ago, Gaelic was the primary language of Scotland, accumulating a strong tradition of orature and literature that only a few can now access. I was born into a family whose last Gaelic speaker died in the 1930s. My children know only a few words (such as *slainte* "health," and also a toast which few know, and *glen*, which many know because it became an English word). Both my father and I wanted to acquire it, but life got in the way. However, all three of my children know English, and also French, from living in Quebec; my older daughter is fluent in Japanese, and my son is competent in Italian. Alas, however, none speaks Persian, their mother's language, because she chose not to use it with them. Crucially, however, neither set of grandparents when young could have predicted the languages their grandchildren would know, and this seems increasingly to be the way of the world. (pp. 57–58)

The presence of multiple languages within families and larger social groups (including nations) doesn't change the fact that today English is the most widely used language around the world in intercultural communication encounters. English is also widely regarded as the language of modernity and upward social mobility, and it is often used as a **lingua franca**, a shared communication resource among speakers who speak different languages.

World Englishes

There are two models that illustrate the global dominance of the English language quite well. The first one of these is the three circles model of **World Englishes** (Sharifian, 2014). This model was designed to capture how the norms of standard English are disseminated from *inner circle countries* (the United States, the United Kingdom, Australia, and Canada) toward *outer circle countries* (such as India and Singapore) where English is routinely learned as a second language and toward *expanding circle countries* (such as China, Japan, Korea, and Egypt) where English is learned as a foreign language. Although inner circle countries set the norms of standard English, outer circle countries develop their own norms for using the language and produce local varieties—hence the term "World *Englishes.*" Expanding circle countries tend to adopt the linguistic norms set by norm-providing countries, norms that cover not only grammar and vocabulary but also expectations regarding "native speech." Non-native speakers of English learn the norms of "native speech" through a variety of training platforms, including online training sessions where they can regularly communicate with "native speakers"—that is, speakers of preferably American or British origin who speak standard varieties of English. Communication scholar Tabitha Hart (2016) identified six rules of "native speech" online language trainers used to evaluate the linguistic abilities of Chinese students who were preparing for the International English Language Testing System (IELTS) speaking test:

1. Speak in an organized fashion.
2. Speak succinctly; don't ramble.
3. Speak spontaneously; don't produce "canned" speech.
4. Be original and honest.
5. Take initiative; be proactive.
6. Be supportive and positive.

These rules had three functions. First, they helped Chinese students develop a sense of the standards IELTS could be expected to apply to their performance as language learners. For example, language testers tended to evaluate "canned" speech as inauthentic, memorized, or plagiarized, and thus instructors tried to steer students away from producing such talk. Second, they confirmed American cultural expectations about what counts as native (spontaneous) speech. For example, these rules invoke the American communication ideal of passionate, extemporaneous, original, honest, supportive speech and the Anglo-American cultural logic of reasoning. Finally, they affirmed the social function of IELTS as a centering institution with the authority to control the communication norms of "native speech."

Language Death

The second model classifies languages based on the degree to which they are likely to suffer **language death**—that is, the passing of a language's last speaker. McArthur (2005) argued that the size (dissemination) and influence of languages increased their chance of survival. Based on this assumption, he identified seven levels of linguistic longevity:

Level 1: English

Level 2: Chinese, Spanish, Hindi-Urdu

Level 3: Arabic, French, German, Japanese, Malay

Level 4: Languages that are significant nationally and/or regionally (e.g., Amharic, Swahili, Persian, etc.)

Level 5: Languages that are locally and socially strong (e.g., Catalan, Danish, Tagalog, Quechua, etc.)

Level 6: Small languages still likely to survive (e.g., Faroese, Maori, Welsh)

Level 7: Extremely small and endangered languages (e.g., Aboriginal Australian languages, Cherokee, Mohawk, Scottish Gaelic, etc.)

As you can see, for now, the English language is in virtually no danger of dying out. But what is this "English language" we are discussing here? McArthur notes the English language and other Level 2 and 3 languages are best described as language complexes rather than singular languages. The description of English as a **language complex** "retains the tradition of *English* as a single entity while allowing for both the *Englishes* and *the English languages* as terms for handling a multiplicity that includes *African English, African American English, American English, British English, China English, Indian English*, and *Nigerian English*" (p. 56). In addition, consider the fact that today it is possible to identify *Business English* and its national varieties, *United Nations English*, and *Euro-English*, a variety of English spoken throughout the institutions of the European Union. The longevity of the English language derives from its frequent use in, and constant adaptation to, a broad range of social and institutional contexts.

English: A Thief or a Resource?

Not everyone around the world welcomes the growing influence of the English language. The Māori poet and writer Vaughan Rapatahana doesn't mince his words when he calls the English language a thief. He argued (2017) that due to the history of colonialism and the contemporary interest in the English language fueled by language teaching and examination institutes, the publishing industry, and the international network of International Baccalaureate (IB) schools and cultural institutions like the British Council, English invades and corrupts indigenous languages and carries with it Western cultural biases that undermine native worldviews. As a former teacher of English as a second language, he writes about his students in this way:

> ... the English language has been force-fed to them and disseminated as somehow vital to their life chances as a neutral and value-free panacea for everything, when in fact, it is all too often a thief of their time, their money, their own tongues, and thus their cultural identities, their existential well-being. (p. 64)

The survival of the Māori language, however, should serve as evidence that local languages can be kept alive "with support, legal backing, indigenous pride, and persistence" (p. 71). Others, including the Ethiopian applied linguist Nigussie Negash Yadete, take the opposite view. Yadete (2017) says the value of the English language ought to be separated from the dark history of European colonialization. English as a global language connects people around the world, including learners and producers of knowledge, and it is the only truly pan-African language that facilitated the local overthrow of colonial powers. English doesn't colonialize minds, he argues: it liberates them.

> In today's global world, multilingualism is the order of the day. Living in this era compels us to give due value to our indigenous languages, but at the same time, all citizens of the world should have the right and opportunity to become proficient users of English, the de facto global lingua franca. Learning English cannot be a luxury or a privilege given only to the selected few (i.e., the privileged social class). (pp. 60–61)

Is the English language a global thief or a global resource? As you communicate with non-native speakers of English, keep in mind that their attitudes toward English can shape how they interact with you in the context of intercultural communication.

LANGUAGE SELECTION AND IDENTITY

The languages you select for the purpose of communication **index** identities—your inability to speak a language—can prevent you from indexing an identity you would like to claim as your own. Consider the rich point anecdotes at the beginning of this chapter. The first student, Devin, reports that although he had grown up in a Filipino family, his command of Tagalog (the native language) and Filipino-accented English was limited. As he details his difficulties communicating with native-born Filipinos in Manila, you can sense he is struggling with the challenge of presenting a Filipino identity without sufficient knowledge of local ways of speaking. By contrast, in Lee's rich point narrative, the Denver cosplayer was able to use a "Japanese-sounding" phrase to present the identity of an anime fan, given that U.S. popular culture closely associates anime with the Japanese language. He managed to accomplish this identity presentation even though he failed to convince Lee to dress up and participate in the convention.

Speaking a language can help you claim an identity, as can the ability to strategically switch between languages or varieties of languages. In this section, we will look at some of the ways in which **multilingual** speakers (speakers who speak more than one language or linguistic variety) use language selection to do identity work. The communication practices we will look at fall into the larger category of **heteroglossia** (the use of two or more languages or varieties of languages in a speech community, where the use of each language is considered appropriate for particular social functions, occasions, or institutions), which includes **code-switching** (speakers switching between codes as they switch between audiences or interactional partners in order to index meanings, hierarchies, values) and **code-mixing** (the fusion of formerly distinct codes into a new code, used without changing audiences or interactional partners). **Codes** here refer to systems of locally recognized, meaningful communicative conduct. Notice that codes and languages are not (necessarily) the same thing. Codes are defined by how people *use* languages or elements of languages, while languages are systems that comprise grammar and vocabulary abstracted from actual language use.

A Practical Question

"Is it possible to present identities to cultural others without speaking their language?"

It is. Language choice is only one way to present identities. Consciously or unconsciously, you begin presenting identities the moment you appear in someone's field of vision. If you don't speak the local language, you can get creative with other resources available to you (appearance, gaze, movements, proximity to others, etc.) in your effort to present identities you want to claim.

Code-Switching

In a spoken work performance presented at a TED event, the professor and poet Jamila Lyiscott (2014) described an encounter with a White woman who referred to her as "articulate." The use of this adjective, one that is commonly applied in the United States to Black speakers who speak Standard American English (SAE), made her reflect on the fact that SAE was only one of her languages. Besides SAE, she also spoke Trinidadian

English in her home with her family and African American English in her neighbor-hood of Crown Heights in Brooklyn, New York. These latter two varieties of English are of course less valued outside the speech communities in which they are spoken than SAE, a variety of English highly valued throughout the United States and beyond. Nonetheless, she had come to regard these three varieties as three languages. As she explained to her (predominantly White) audience:

> So I may not always come before you with excellency of speech
>
> But do not judge me by my language and assume that I'm too ignorant to teach
>
> 'Cause I speak three tongues. One for each:
>
> Home, school and friends. I'm a trilingual orator
>
> Sometimes I'm consistent with my language now, then switch it up so I don't bore later
>
> Sometimes I fight back two tongues while I use the other one in the classroom
>
> And when I mistakenly mix them up I feel crazy like I'm cooking in the bathroom

Lyiscott's use of language is heteroglossic: she reserves each variety she speaks competently for different social situations—namely, the home, the neighborhood, and academic settings. In intercultural interactions, including interracial and interethnic encounters, heteroglossic speakers who engage in communication accommodation often find that as they mute other varieties or languages they speak, they also "mute" the identities those other varieties and languages index and lead their conversational partners to conclude that they no longer possess those identities. In Lyiscott's case, the White woman concluded that because Lyiscott was "articulate"—that is, she spoke SAE—she had successfully left behind her "inarticulate" ethnic identities.

Speakers who practice heteroglossia sometimes switch between the languages or varieties they speak within the same social situation in order to signal their membership in various social groups or speech communities. These switches show how, in the con-text of use, speakers turn languages and linguistic differences into locally meaningful codes—that is, resources for meaning-making. Such meaning-making includes, but isn't limited to, enacting ethnic or other kinds of group identities. Dominican American speakers, for example, can use Dominican Spanish to flirt with other Spanish speakers, then switch to African American English to signal a non-White identity and solidarity with African American friends, and then switch to SAE to perform polite speech—all within the same social situation and in a matter of seconds (Bailey, 2000).

Code-Mixing

In the prior example, speakers switch between codes as they switch between audiences or conversational partners. However, sometimes speakers exercise code-switching without changing partners. Consider this example of Moroccan immigrant girls in Spain switching between Arabic and Spanish while playing with dolls (García-Sanchez, 2010). In this scene, two girls imagine two women (their dolls) running into each other in the street.

EXCERPT 5.2. (from García-Sanchez, 2010, p. 533)

Wafiya [Arabic]	Salam.	Hello.
Worda [Arabic]	Kiraki sayra?	How are you?
Wafiya [Arabic]	Labas.	Fine.
Worda [Arabic]	Hadri asbanyouliya hadri!	Speak Spanish, speak!
Wafiya [Spanish]	Hola.	Hello.
Worda [Spanish]	Qué tal?	How are you?
Salma	[Indicates that Wafiya's doll dropped her purse]	
Worda [Spanish]	Se te ha caído el bolso?	Did you drop the purse?
Wafiya [Spanish]	Y yo también.	And me too.
Worda [Spanish]	Te vas a la playa?	Are you going to the beach?
Wafiya [Spanish]	Sí, vamos.	Yes, let's go.
Worda [Spanish]	Vale.	Okay.

There is more going on here than meets the eye. As the girls switch to Spanish in the middle of their game, they are indicating that their dolls are grown-up Spanish women who have the liberty to go to the beach, where they are likely to wear bikinis, when they please. Through the use of Spanish, the girls are expressing fascination with, and a desire for, a type of liberated femininity that is denied to them both by their conservative, male-dominated families and by Spanish society, which treats them as social and economic outsiders.

Code-mixing also does identity work by creating a new code from elements of other codes (languages) that indexes a particular type of identity. In Zimbabwe, for example, there is a type of person called the *masalad* ("the one who eats salads"; Veit-Wild, 2009). *Masalads* are young people who imitate Western culture to appear cool. This includes wearing hip hop clothing, mixing English with the local language (Shona), and, yes, eating salad. Mixing English and Shona resulted in an urban dialect that indexes a claim to social status (wealth, influence, trendiness) and that many Zimbabweans find inauthentic and make fun of. The novelist and playwright Aaron Chiundura Moyo, for example, puts the following words into the mouth of an urban upstart *masalad* who wants to show off to some higher-status young women in his company by bossing around his driver, Tops, over the phone:

EXCERPT 5.3. (from Veit-Wild, 2009, p. 695)

Iwe Tops! *Ah! Are you sick* he-e? *Shut up*, kurumidza kuunza *order* yandakupa vana*madam* ava vave nenzara. He-e, kana mota yako isina mafuta, *use mine but don't overspeed* nokuti haisi *car* yenhando.

Hey, Tops! Ah! Are you sick or what? Shut up, hurry and bring the order I have given for these ladies, they are hungry. Yeah, if your car does not have petrol, use mine but don't overspeed because this is not an ordinary car.

A Practical Question

"Wait, isn't this just broken English, or broken Shona?"

When you say "broken," you are implying that the way this *masalad* speaks is somehow insufficient or substandard. From the perspective of cultural pragmatics, the ability to speak in locally recognizable ways—and present locally recognizable identities—is more important than speaking distinct languages in grammatically correct ways.

Marking particular types of identities with code-mixing is, of course, not unique to Zimbabwe: rather, it is becoming increasingly frequent, particularly in multilingual urban environments. Rap, for example, thrives on code-mixing. Rappers in Quebec, for example, mix together varieties of French (Standard Quebec French, Nonstandard Quebec French, European French), English (Standard North American English, African American Vernacular English, and hip hop terms), Caribbean Creoles (Haitian Creole, Jamaican Creole), and Spanish in their lyrics to catch the attention of other rappers, to signal their own ethnic backgrounds, to challenge dominant language standards, and so on (Sarkar & Winer, 2006). Stand-up comedy is another cultural scene where performers routinely rely on code-mixing to present identity types. The Hong Kong comedian C. W. Wong, for example, mixes English into his Cantonese to signal a unique Hong King identity that stands in an uneasy relationship with a Chinese identity being imposed on citizens of Hong Kong by mainland China (Tsang & Wong, 2004).

Monolingualism

Although the use of multiple languages and codes may sound like a communication "superpower," in fact, it can invite negative judgment from within and outside one's speech community. In a classic study of 20 Puerto Rican families living in a single New York City block, the linguistic anthropologist Ana Celia Zentella found some inhabitants of *el bloque* frowned upon Spanish and English code-mixing, or what many today would call "Spanglish," and encouraged other speakers to keep the two languages separate (Zentella, 1997). In countries with one dominant language, such as the United States, heteroglossia can cause confusion and prompt criticism in inter-cultural communication encounters. **Monolingualism**, the ability to speak only one language, can become naturalized (taken for granted) over the course of decades and centuries as citizens imagine, discuss, and reinforce a strong relationship between the dominant language and national unity. Monolingualism can eventually become a **language ideology** that holds that

- language reflects the objective world ("objective" in the sense that the world exists independently from how we apply language to it);

- the goal of "good" (standard, accent-free, correct) communication is the successful transfer of information about the world;

- the social use of language (that is, the use of language whose goal is not to transfer information about the world) is not important;

- language variation is noise that prevents "good" communication; and

- multilingualism (including heteroglossia, code-switching, and code-mixing) is marked (out of the ordinary), whereas monolingual, standard speech is unmarked (normal). (Bailey, 2007)

Motivated by this language ideology, many monolingual speakers respond to the communication practices I described in this chapter with "Why do they have to talk like that?" or "Why can't they talk normally?" instead of trying to learn about the many social functions of multilingualism, including identity work. They may also worry about language variation's effects on national unity and ask, "How can we be a strong nation if we don't speak the same language?" The language ideology that gives rise to these questions tends to devalue the nondominant language varieties and communication practices of social groups that are often in a marginal position relative to dominant monolingual social groups.

Members of speech communities in which heteroglossia is regularly practiced have been forcefully pushing back against monolingual ideology, particularly because they can easily appreciate how nonstandard, nondominant varieties and practices allow them to live rich and fulfilling social lives. The writer Juliana Delgado Lopera captures the value of "Spanglish" vividly in their (Lopera's preferred gender pronouns are "they," "them," and "their") gender reflections on growing up in Miami:

> Here, English and Spanish were not mutually exclusive; they were not two sep-
> arate languages, but rather open circles touching each other. We didn't know
> where one ended and the other began. It didn't matter. Here we *lived* and *spoke*

in Spanglish. Because it made sense for us. Our lived experience did not take shape in White English or in standard Spanish: it was a mix and match of the sounds we heard around us from the different Latin American immigrant groups. (Lopera, 2020)

Growing up speaking the language of their home, Spanglish, Lopera later struggled to succeed in U.S. literary circles where, to this day, standard English is valued over Spanglish. To Lopera, these struggles were not simply career obstacles but a question of whose identity and life experience is valued over others': "If Spanglish is wrong and standard White English is 'correct,' then who's being understood? Whose world is called into life?" Monolingualism as language ideology creates and sustains hierarchies of speech *and* speakers.

BARRIERS TO COORDINATED INTERACTION

1. **Failing to understand the social meaning of languages and linguistic varieties and their use.** As you communicate with others who seem to regularly use two or more languages—or two or more varieties of the same language—keep in mind that, more likely than not, the selection of one language (or variety) as opposed to another, or switching from one to another, carries social meaning for them. That is to say, they use these languages or varieties as codes. They are not making mistakes, and they are not being lazy or uneducated: they are telling you something about their social worlds, who they are in those worlds, and what they are trying to accomplish in interaction with you. These meanings will not be immediately obvious to you, so take your time and observe these practices before you interpret or evaluate them.

2. **Missing the connection between hierarchies of languages and social identities.** It is polite (or politically progressive) to say that all languages are created equal. Unfortunately, not everyone in the world subscribes to this principle. Dominant social groups are deeply invested in instituting their variety of a language as the standard language, and the global domination of English gives it value above many (if not all) other languages. The relative value of languages and linguistic varieties is shaped by politics, policy, and markets. The resulting language hierarchies translate into hierarchies of speakers: those who speak more valued varieties (or languages) will be regarded as more valuable people. If you are a (native) speaker of English, you might walk into social situations with built-in credibility in countries where English is considered a high-prestige language. Conversely, your intelligence, sincerity, or competence may be questioned in countries or social groups where your linguistic variety holds relatively low prestige. Keep in mind that such value hierarchies are part and parcel of the social life of any

human language, and know that they can undermine coordinated interaction in spite of the good intentions of participants.

3. **Monolingualism as language ideology.** If you are from a country or community that attaches a great amount of value to the knowledge and use of a standard language, be aware of your possible monolingual biases. For example, when you find yourself evaluating the "correctness" of someone's speech performance in an intercultural communication encounter, it is quite likely that you are formulating an evaluation based on a monolingual bias. Instead of assessing how "correct" someone's use of a language may be, try to focus on what they are *doing* as they use a nonstandard variety or they mix standard and nonstandard varieties. It is of course possible that their ability to speak a language (your language) is limited. In that case, make sure you don't automatically translate their substandard performance into a negative evaluation of various facets of their identity (education, cognitive abilities, professional competence, motivations, etc.).

REFLECTION QUESTIONS

1. To what extent do you think native speakers of English follow the six rules of "native speech"?

2. Would you agree with Rapatahana's view of global English as a thief or Yadete's view of it as a resource? Why?

3. In what gatekeeping encounters have you participated in the course of your life? Which centering institutions lent those gatekeepers their authority?

4. Have you ever been in a situation in which you needed to be able to speak a language or a linguistic variety in order to enact an identity? Did you succeed or did you fail? Why?

5. Can you think of a favorite entertainer who uses multiple codes in their performances? How do they juxtapose those codes, and what do those juxtapositions mean?

6

"Why Do They Call Each Other That?"

Personal Address

DYLAN: Having studied German for a while, I was aware of the distinction between the formal and the informal "you." *Du* is very informal and a type of address reserved almost exclusively for friends and family. *Sie* is deemed as the respectful "you" and is used much more often in everyday talk, even among people who have gotten to know each other quite well. But I did not really learn the importance of this distinction until I made the mistake of addressing someone as *du* (informal) instead of *Sie* (formal). This person was my German professor here in the U.S. I had gotten to know this professor quite well, and we had spoken quite colloquially in German together many times after class. Initially, I addressed this professor as *Sie*, but after getting better acquainted with her, I switched to *du*. The first (and the last) time I did this, she immediately snapped back at me and said: "*Benutzen Sie 'Sie'!*" ("Use '*Sie*'!") I was shocked by her response and felt like a child as a result. I promptly said: "*Entschuldigung*" ("Sorry") and left the conversation feeling like I wasn't as close to this professor as I had hoped. To have her respond to my use of *du* in the way she did immediately made me step back and reevaluate the friendship I thought we were beginning to forge.

In this chapter, you will learn:

- to distinguish various types of personal address

- about second-person pronouns, proper names, and kinship terms as forms of personal address

- to reflect on the importance of personal address in building and maintaining identities and relationships

AZUL: As a Mexican American, I am amazed by how much of the Latin community consistently and frequently uses terms of endearment with people they have just met or barely know. I have encountered this practice in Latin America and the U.S. as well. Salesclerks, waitresses, friends, elders, family members, workers—the majority of people I encounter in these scenarios will always use terms such as *preciosa*, *mihija*, *mi amor*, *linda*, *corazon*, *quierdo*, *carino* … the list goes on! This is a rich point to me because most of the American culture I've grown up in has saved terms of endearment for people who are very special and close to their hearts. It is rare for me to go out to public spaces and have a random person call me "darling" or "sweetie," and if they do, it is always something I notice. With my first boyfriend, it was a huge deal when we began using pet names with each other. It was a landmark in our relationship, so to hear the nicknames that took me so long to comfortably use with a loved one being used so casually definitely catches me off guard and intrigues me!

I would wager that, at some point in your life, you have struggled with choosing an appropriate term of address in conversation with someone you knew. I certainly have. In Hungary, it is customary to address aunts and uncles using a combination of their first names with *néni* ("auntie") or *bácsi* ("uncle"). "Auntie" and "uncle" are **kinship terms**, terms that mark one's family relation with the addressee. One of the many social challenges of Hungarian teenage years is deciding when you can get away with addressing aunts and uncles using only their first names. I have two rather imposing uncles with whom I still hesitate to be on a first-name basis.

Later, while working on my master's degree in communication in the United States, I met a professor whom I greatly admired—and had no idea how to address. "Professor Sanders" sounded too formal, "Dr. Sanders" didn't do justice to his academic rank (he was a full professor, and "Dr." is usually reserved for assistant and associate professors), and "Bob" felt too informal. I felt quite awkward around him as a result until a fellow grad student revealed that she addressed him as "Dr. Bob," and he hadn't minded. What a relief! This address term allowed us to strike a perfect balance between professional respect and interpersonal closeness. The use of "Dr." instead of "Professor" brought him closer to our level in the academic hierarchy by a rank or two but elevated "Bob" above the purely first-name-based form of address I used with fellow grad students.

The two accounts of rich points at the beginning of this chapter point to an important feature of personal address terms: they don't only express and affirm relationships that exist between speakers, but they can also be used to alter relationships. Dylan made an attempt to affirm a different type of relationship with a professor by switching from a formal to an informal pronoun, but his attempt failed when the professor resisted affirming the relationship by rejecting the pronoun he used to address her. Azul experienced a series of rich points as she tried to come to terms with the different meanings of **terms of endearment** (terms of address one uses with intimate others) in the two **speech communities** in which she had membership: Latino and Anglo-American.

Personal address refers to a type of communicative action when speakers use locally available terms to refer to other persons in interaction with them. Personal address is a subcategory of **person referencing**, or communication practices designed to identify persons, whether or not they are present in the interaction. This distinction is important because speech communities make some but not all forms of person referencing available to speakers for the purpose of personal address. To give you an example, speakers of the indigenous Mayan language Tzoltzil in the Mexican state of Chiapas use a complex system of nicknames to identify nonpresent others as they gossip about them (Haviland, 2007). Using people's official names is not always helpful—there are lots of people in the community whose "official" Spanish name is Domingo Pérez Gómez. However, when people refer to *ch'aj Romin* ("Lazy Domingo"), everyone knows who they are talking about. All members of the speech community get a nickname; eventually, some have more than one. However, using such nicknames to address the person to their face is off-limits. Speakers' options for personal address are much more limited. Men of equal age, for example, will address one another by first name, as *ompre* (from the Spanish *hombre* ["man"]) or as *kumpa* (from the Spanish *compadre*) if they had previously entered into a coparenthood (*compadrazgo*) relationship by sponsoring one another's children in a rite of passage (e.g., baptism, first communion, marriage, etc.).

In this chapter, we will explore various categories of personal address and their functions in managing relationships, both of which are culturally variable. We will also review some of the interactional problems the use of personal address terms can cause in intercultural communication.

TYPES OF ADDRESS TERMS

The most commonly used personal address terms in the English language are the following:

- **second-person pronouns** (the singular and plural "you")

- **proper names** (such as "Anna," diminutive forms like "Tommy," or marital names such as "Mrs. Martinez")

- **kinship terms** (such as "Mom," "Pops," or "Abuela")

- **titles** (official titles such as "Doctor" plus last name, "Professor" plus last name, or honorifics such as "Madame Speaker" and "Your Excellency")

- **nicknames** (such as "Missy" and "Peanut" or ones derived from personal characteristics, such as "Chubs" or "Carrot Top")

- **terms of endearment** (such as "babe," "sweetie," and "snookums," including terms derived from nonhuman entities such as "tiger" or "Honey Bunches" [of Oats])

- **terms of derogation** (such as "moron," "redneck," and racial and ethnic slurs)

In the remainder of the chapter, we will focus on the first three categories: second-person pronouns, proper names, and kinship terms.

Some categories of address terms allow for more creativity and innovation than others. For example, the number of second-person pronouns you can use in any language will be restricted. However, there is virtually no limit to how many nicknames or terms of endearment or derogation you can invent and apply to others in conversation. (Just ask my kids—they hear me come up with new nicknames for them almost every week.)

Some widely used address terms don't fit neatly into any of the above categories. For example, the African American English term "nigga" and its variants, "my nigga"/"ma nigga"/"manigga," sound like terms of derogation to those English speakers who are not members of or aren't familiar with ways of speaking in the African American speech community. This is not surprising: "nigga" sounds a lot like the "n-word" ("n****r"), which is considered a racial slur and is therefore a **cultural taboo** in the United States. (Cultural taboos are actions social groups forbid of their members on the basis of cultural beliefs and values. Some taboos, such as incest, apply across social groups, while others are more group specific.) In African American usage, however, "nigga" has developed a wide variety of functions, including personal address (Jones & Hall, 2019). African American speakers use "nigga" as opposed to "my nigga"/"ma nigga"/"manigga" to express social distance or solidarity with others. Consider these two examples:

A Practical Question

"I am not African American, but I understand the meaning of 'nigga' and 'manigga.' Why am I not allowed to use these address terms in conversation with African American speakers?"

Understanding the meaning of an address term doesn't automatically entitle you to use freely it in interaction. Building culture includes developing an understanding of what types of personal address terms a speech community makes available to what range of speakers. As an intercultural practitioner, you have to be mindful of the social consequences of violating a speech community's communication norms.

Don't play me, nigga. I will end you. [spoken to the suspected cheating husband of a friend; Dina (Tiffany Haddish), *Girls Trip*] (p. 493),

Manigga, it wasn't even like that, manigga. [man to a friend, 145th Street and St. Nicholas, Harlem, May 24, 2014] (p. 494)

In the first example, "nigga" signals that the speaker is angry at the addressee. In the second example, "manigga" marks closeness and friendship. Although both terms function as address terms (or what linguists call vocatives) in these examples, they aren't pronouns, kinship terms, terms of endearment, or any of the other types of personal address listed above. Although the meanings of the n-word have shifted over the years, one thing has not changed: *only African Americans are welcome to use it, as an address term or otherwise.*

SECOND-PERSON PRONOUNS

The main difference between second-person pronoun use in English and other languages is that, on the surface, the English system is quite simple: "you" does double duty as the singular and plural form of this pronoun. There is, however, considerable regional variation in the form of this humble pronoun. In England, a popular version of the second person plural is "you lot." Using "y'all" to address individuals or groups (and "all y'all" to address groups) can be frequently heard in the American South. You and your group may be addressed as "you'uns" in Appalachia, "yinz" in the Pittsburgh area, and "youse" or "youse guys" in New York City. The use of these terms may signal regional pride, especially when used to address outsiders.

In addition to regional variation, you can also notice political variation in the use of second-person pronouns. An increasing number of English speakers hold, for example, that using "guys" or "you guys" to address two or more participants in a conversation is not an inclusive way to address those who don't identify as male. Such speakers are likely to train themselves to replace "you guys" with one of many gender-neutral options, such as "you all" or "y'all," "folks," "friends," "team," "colleagues," and so on, depending on the context in which the interaction takes place.

An Example: Colombian Spanish

Other languages present speakers with a rich set of resources for second-person address. Consider, for example, the intricate system of second-person pronouns in Colombian Spanish (Fitch, 1998) in Table 6.1.

These address forms allow speakers to present identities relative to their conversational partners ("Who am I to you? Who are you to me?") and affirm or comment on the relationship (social distance) that exists between them. As Dylan's touch point narrative illustrates, switching from one pronoun to another can be used to (try to) switch from one type of relation to another. In Mexican Spanish, for example, the switch from *tú* (informal) to *usted* (formal) can signal anger with another person and the disruption of a friendly relationship. Below, a Mexican construction manager is expressing strong disappointment with a contractor who failed to do his job:

TABLE 6.1. Second-person pronouns in Colombian Spanish

Term	Literal translation	Grammatical function
tú	you	informal, singular
usted	you	formal, singular
vis	you	informal, singular
su merced	your mercy	formal, singular, affectionate
su mercedita	your little mercy	formal, diminutive, affectionate
su persona	your person	formal, singular, affectionate
su personita	your little person	formal, diminutive, affectionate
ustedes	you	formal, plural
vosotros	you	informal, plural

Fitch, 1998, p. 36

¡El que no entiende eres tú porque yo ya entendí perfectamente bien! ... ¡El que no entiende es usted! ... ¡Quiero cumplimientos, quiero resultados!

You (using "*tú*") are the one who doesn't understand because I understood perfectly well! ... The one who doesn't understand is you (using "*usted*")! ... I want follow-through! I want results! (Covarrubias, Kvam, & Saito, 2019, p. 179)

The Effects of Globalization

Globalization can shape the use of second-person pronouns. Western corporations, for example, often expect their employees in non-English speaking countries to conform to their norms of friendly customer service. As a result, in countries where the use of the informal pronoun signals closeness and the formal pronoun social distance, employees are required to shift to the use of the informal pronoun from the more commonly used formal pronoun. This shift was particularly noticeable in Hungary, where Western corporations like McDonald's appeared almost overnight after the fall of state socialism (Cameron, 2003). I recall the widespread confusion caused by retailers and advertisers suddenly addressing customers as "*te*"/"*ti*" (informal) instead of "*ön*"/"*önök*" (formal). The matter of which form of address is appropriate for customer service encounters is not settled to this day.

The opposite of this can happen as well, particularly when speakers try to break into globally dominant markets where different languages are spoken. For example, English translations of Japanese cookbooks replace the use of gendered third-person pronouns ("he"/ "she") in instructions and address the reader with the second-person singular pronoun ("you"). This switch accomplishes two things: the authors avoid appearing sexist by eliminating the use of the generic "he" for both sexes and the generic "she," which suggests that cooking is the woman's job, and they play into the cultural expectation of English-speaking audiences that addressing individual readers as "you" sounds friendlier (Matwick & Matwick, 2015).

Misuse of Second-Person Pronouns

If you are feeling bewildered by the systems of second-person pronoun use in languages you don't (yet) speak, I encourage you not to despair. In intercultural encounters with speakers of such languages, you can learn a lot from careful observation and from helpful native speakers. The linguist Roel Vismans (2009) interviewed German and British study-abroad students in the Netherlands about their experiences learning the proper use of formal ("u") and informal ("jij/"je") second-person pronouns in personal address. Students reported they could rely on observation and helpful bystanders.

> I think in the beginning I was more likely to use "u" than Dutch people seemed to be, and I think I reduced that with time 'cause I noticed that other people if they were in a pizzeria or something if it was quite informal like the waitress was probably a student or something similar, they all used "jij." And at first I used "u" but then I changed. And when the other students told me what to say, they said we don't use "u" anywhere near as much as Germans use it, so therefore they noticed. (Martin, German student; p. 223)

In addition, when students made mistakes, they could usually count on the leniency of native speakers.

> I wrote an email to a lecturer once, using "je" all the time, and then she wrote back saying because I'm one of your teachers it should be "u." That was when I first arrived in Belgium as well, so I thought "oh, brilliant start there." [laughter] That was really horrible, I thought I had really offended her. But she was ok. (Rudy, British student; p. 222)

A Practical Question

"Can I always count on the leniency of native speakers?"

The answer depends on who you and your conversational partners are. It is not surprising that European study-abroad students in another European country can get away with using a wrong personal address term. Unfortunately, research (Meeuwis, 1994) has shown that racist attitudes can lead speakers to withhold such leniency.

In fact, you can learn a lot about how members of a speech community see their shared identity from listening to their explanations of second-person pronoun use. Vismans also reported that Dutch students took pride in using the informal "you" more often than German speakers because they saw the prevalence of the informal form as the mark of a modern and egalitarian society. In this way, Dutch students' explanation for their pronoun preference reveals a fundamental **language ideology** that posits language use is the expression of national character.

PROPER NAMES

The sociolinguists Ron Scollon and Suzie Wong Scollon (2001) imagined the following encounter on a plane between a businessman from Hong Kong called Chu Hon-fai and another businessman from the United States named Andrew Richardson (Scollon & Scollon, 2001, p. 135) to illustrate how the use of proper names can lead to intercultural **miscommunication.**

EXCERPT 6.1. (Scollon & Scollon, 2001, p. 135)

Mr. Richardson	By the way, I'm Andrew Richardson. My friends call me Andy. This is my business card.
Mr. Chu	I'm David Chu. Pleased to meet you, Mr. Richardson. This is my card.
Mr. Richardson	No, no. Call me Andy. I think we'll be doing a lot of business together.
Mr. Chu	Yes, I hope so.
Mr. Richardson	*[Reading Mr. Chu's card]* "Chu, Hon-fai." Hon-fai, I'll give you a call tomorrow as soon as I get settled in my hotel.
Mr. Chu	*[Smiling]* Yes. I'll expect your call.

In the Scollons's example, although it seems the two men departed on amicable terms, they actually had rather different interpretations of what happened. Andy Richardson thought he was off to a great start toward building a friendly and lucrative relationship with a fellow businessman. He insisted that Mr. Chu use his first name, and he also called Mr. Chu "Hon-fai," which he saw not only as a friendly gesture but also as the culturally sensitive choice. He assumed he was using Mr. Chu's "real" first name, Hon-fai, as opposed to his Western name, David, which he surely adopted because of the pressure to use English names in the cultural environment of global business. Mr. Richardson, however, misunderstood Mr. Chu's smile. His Hong Kong counterpart was actually feeling quite awkward. As someone who had studied abroad in the United States, he understood Americans' preference for quickly signaling close egalitarian relationships and by going on a first-name basis. In the name of cultural sensitivity, he accepted Mr. Richardson's friendly advances. However, as someone from a culture that preferred maintaining some degree of social distance in professional relationships, he would have preferred that Mr. Richardson use either his more formal name (Mr. Chu) or his English name (David), which he had chosen precisely to help English speakers like Andy Richardson address him informally. For Mr. Chu, having an English name did not mean succumbing to Western cultural imperialism—he was simply drawing on a Chinese **expressive system** that tied name use to types of situations and relationships. From his cultural perspective, David was an appropriate name for interacting with an American stranger, as was Mr. Chu, while Hon-fai was not.

I hope you don't read this (made-up, though quite plausible) anecdote as an argument against cultural sensitivity. Cultural sensitivity is certainly valuable, but it does not prevent miscommunication. Avoiding miscommunication requires sensitivity, yes, but also observation and, in this case, an appreciation for culturally variable, intricate systems of naming.

Naming Decision Points

Our names shape the identities we can present in interaction, just as they shape the identities others assign to us. As a result, when we have a chance to make decisions about our names or the names of others, we tread carefully and try to anticipate the social consequences of our choices as best as we can. In the United States, there are five life events when many Americans find themselves weighing naming options:

1. birth
2. adoption
3. marriage
4. divorce
5. gender identity transition

Such life events are, of course, present in other cultures besides the United States, but speakers in those cultures often have a different range of names available to them, and the choices they make have different social consequences in interaction and beyond.

Naming Children

The Unites States has a relatively liberal approach to names. By contrast, Hungarian parents are required to choose names from a list of officially accepted first names. In both countries, however, there is a strong cultural preference for sex-specific first names. Just think about the Johnny Cash song *A Boy Named Sue*. The narrator tells the story of his absent father, who called him Sue at birth. After years of ridicule and fights he had to endure as a result, he runs into his father in a bar and decides to take revenge. As they brawl, his father reveals he gave the narrator the name anticipating he would be picked on: "I knew you'd have to get tough or die/And it's the name that helped to make you strong." The narrator says he'd "come away with a different point of view," but he adds: "And if I ever have a son, I think I'm gonna name him … Bill or George! Any damn thing but Sue!" By contrast, Tibetan exiles whose children are named by lamas often bear the name of the 14th Dalai Lama (whose first name is Tenzin), regardless of their sex. This is not to say that androgynous (non-sex-specific) names are not available to new parents in the United States, but they are used far less often than sex-specific ones.

In terms of children's last names, the majority of U.S. children born into heterosexual marriages are given their fathers' names. The same goes for adopted children of heterosexual couples. This **patronymic convention** is less strictly followed by same-sex couples who adopt children. The dominant trend among such couples is to hyphenate their last names and use that name as their children's last name (Patterson & Farr, 2017).

Marital Naming

At the time of marriage, the cultural expectations that apply to heterosexual couples is that the woman would make the decision regarding changing her own name and that she would choose her husband's last name. To this day, the vast majority (94%) of American woman take their husbands' names in marriage (Pilcher, 2017). (My wife's and my decision to create a new last name for ourselves by hyphenating our premarital last names is exceedingly rare.) This strong pattern, however, hides two important facts: women have different reasons for choosing to adopt their husbands' last names, as do the few who choose not to. A study of college-aged heterosexual women (Keels & Powers, 2013) showed women had a variety of reasons for adopting or rejecting their husbands' last names in marriage:

Pro:

- a marriage practice that families expect

- a traditional act that should be honored

- a good way to build family unity

- easier than having different names

- important if the couple is going to have children

- showing respect toward the husband

- gaining social status through name change

Con:

- a bad idea if she wants to keep her family name going

- a disadvantage if she has already built a career

- giving up the woman's identity

- giving the husband power over the wife

Neutral:

- a personal choice based on how the name sounds

- not an important issue (accepting the social norm of changing last name)

Some of these interpretations of various choices have direct implications for personal address. For example, the social status some women expect to gain from a name change is realized in particular interactions, such as when a woman is addressed as "Mrs. Anderson" as opposed to "Miss Beauregard." The same thing with family unity: introducing a couple as "Mr. and Mrs. King" portrays people as the heads of a traditional family. A woman's choice to revert to her pre-marriage last name after a divorce takes on interactional meaning is well ("Hello, Mrs. Cross!" "Oh, it's 'Ms. Cope' now.")

Gender Identity Transition

In the case of gender identity transitions, we can observe two dominant patterns in the U.S. context: individuals either switch to another sex-specific first name (from male to female, or vice versa), or they choose a gender-neutral name. The first choice often results in interactional problems in which first names are used as address terms. In a study conducted by sociologist Catherine Connell (2010), a Latina trans woman named Julie reported that, when working as a customer service representative, customers often "misheard" her name due to her masculine-sounding voice: "When I said 'This is Julie' on the phone, they would repeat it back to me as 'Julian?' So I started saying 'Juliette,' but they still changed it into a guy's name, even less related sounding—'George?' 'Jake?'" (p. 41). A White trans woman who did not find the "girly girl" mode of gender presentation satisfactory chose the gender-neutral name Agape (Greek for "love"), which highlighted her opposition to the gender binary.

A Practical Question

"I am sure Covarrubias's teacher meant no offense by shortening her name to Pat. Pat is a common way to shorten Patricia. Why was she offended?"

In intercultural encounters, a rule of thumb is not to assume that a cultural other will consider shortening their name acceptable or preferable. Always ask how someone likes to be called and/or if you can refer to someone by the shortened form of their name. (For example, I will tell you that I detest "Dave.")

Local Varieties of Proper Names

Proper names (particularly first names) have local varieties that are sometimes unrecognizable to speakers from other speech communities, and their use in intercultural encounters can cause and entrench struggles with identity. The communication scholar Patricia Covarrubias (2000) was born and lived in Mexico until she was 8 years old. Then she moved to the United States with her brother and their parents. During the first 8 years of her life, most speakers around her addressed her using Spanish diminutive forms of her first name ("Pati," "Patricita," "Paty," or "Patty"), nicknames ("Pato" ["duck"], "Patita" ["little duck"]), or terms of endearment ("*mi rosita de Castilla*" ["my rose of Castille"], "*mi orquídea*" ["my orchid"]). But on the first day of third grade in the United States, her teacher introduced her by saying "Class, this is Pat." Covarrubias recalls being shocked by hearing this name she didn't recognize as her own, but she lacked the English language skills and the confidence to correct her teacher. Although "Pat" is a perfectly normal way of shortening "Patricia" in U.S. personal address, for Covarrubias, who lives in the United States to this day, being addressed as "Pat" became a constant reminder of her relative cultural outsider status.

KINSHIP TERMS

Much like proper names, the use of **kinship terms** in personal address accomplishes far more than identifying individuals to whom someone is biologically related. Communication scholar Kristine Muñoz identified four functions of kinship terms in personal address (Fitch, 1991). She illustrated each of these types with rich and varied uses of the Spanish term "*madre*" ("mother") she witnessed in Colombia.

1. *Biological relationship.* Kinship terms can signal a strictly biological relationship between speaker and addressee. In Colombia, calling a woman "*madre*" (or "*mamá*") can signal the relationship of biological child to the female biological parent.

2. *Vicarious or potential biological relationship.* Kinship terms can signal an addressee's future kinship status or a kinship status they are likely to have with another, nonpresent person. Kinship terms are often used in this way to signal a close personal relationship with someone or to perform **positive politeness**. In Colombia, a husband might refer to his wife as "*mami*" as a term of endearment that implies they will have children in the future. In one of Muñoz's examples, a male service person warns a female stranger in her 50s that she is not allowed to park in a certain spot by saying "No, *madre*, sorry, but you can't park here. You have to move your car somewhere else" (p. 267). Although calling the woman "*señora*" ("madam" or "ma'am") would have been appropriate, the woman reported that she thought "*madre*" was a much more deferential option. Implying that, due to her age and gender, the woman could be someone's mother indicated the man's respect for her in a culture where (potential) motherhood is highly valued and respected.

3. *Real or desired interpersonal relationship.* The use of kinship terms can indicate that the speaker has or is seeking a particular type of interpersonal relationship with the addressee with whom they don't have a biological (mother-child) relationship. Intimate forms of *"madre"* can be used in Colombia to signal metaphorical solidarity between equals (e.g., one sister calling another *"mamita"*) or between non-equals. An expression of this latter option can be seen in cases when a speaker tries to ingratiate themself with a woman who has relatively more power (e.g., a male shopkeeper calling a female shopper *"madrecita"*).

4. *Symbolic value attached to the person.* Speakers can use kinship terms in a metaphorical sense to extend some characteristics and values associated with the kinship category to addressees, regardless of their gender. Colombians, for example, apply *"madre"* and its various forms in this sense to men to signal a close, appreciative relationship with them by invoking their positive personal qualities, which are culturally associated with motherhood. As an example, Muñoz describes a farewell party for the male chair of an academic department where one of the male faculty members said about the honoree, *"Ha sido todo una mamá para nosotros"* ("He's been a real *mamá* for us"; p. 268). What he meant was that the departing chair had taken good care of his colleagues and the department as a whole.

You may have noticed that these four functions of kinship terms are arranged along a spectrum ranging from biological/universal to the cultural/local. The biological relationship kinship terms (mother, father, aunt, cousin, etc.) indicate elements of universal experience in spite of the fact that different cultural groups often have different kinship systems. By contrast, understanding the symbolic meanings of kinship terms requires accessing **local knowledge.**

The Misuse of Kinship Terms

Lack of familiarity with the various local meanings of kinship terms can lead to uncoordinated interactions in intercultural communication. In the excerpt below, Jennifer, whose first language is Polish but who speaks English as well, experiments with using a kinship term with a Korean speaker, Young, with whom she has a close interpersonal relationship. Jennifer is 22 years old, and Young is 25. Jennifer possesses some degree of local knowledge: she understands the use of Korean kinship terms (such as *"enni"* ["older sister"]) is considered "girly" and "cute." As they chat on Facebook, the conversation doesn't go quite as she had planned.

EXCERPT 6.2. (from Kim & Brown, 2014, p. 272, simplified)

1	Young [in Korean, uses an intimate form of Jennifer's name]	Work hard on your essay, Jennifer-nun!
2	Jennifer [in Korean]	OK thanks enni ha ha ha
3	Young [in Korean]	ha ha ha don't call me that!!! Don't call me enni ha ha ha I dislike being older ha ha ha
4	Jennifer [in English]	I have NEVER called you enni so far, weird … ha ha ha ha ha ha
5	Young [in English]	you don't need to say that!!!! Please ha ha ha ha ha ha
6	Jennifer [in English/Korean]	[English:] really? [Korean:] why? [English:] You dont like?
7	Young [in English]	I feel rly getting old when im called enni. Just call me 'Young' as YOUNG!!

Fortunately, Jennifer doesn't do irreparable damage to her friendship with Young: they quickly make light of her use of "*enni*" and move on. Kim & Brown (2014) explain that Young's rejection of "*enni*" on the basis that being addressed in this way makes her feel old is only a part of the story here. The use of "*enni*" ('older sister') as an address term also establishes a close but hierarchical relationship between the speaker and the addressee. Young rejects the term in order to affirm the close, egalitarian relationship she enjoys with Jennifer. Although Jennifer made an honest attempt to use the term to signal an existing close relationship, she didn't take into account the full range of (possible) meanings implied in the term's use.

CULTURAL PRAGMATICS SAYS

Yes, Jennifer made a mistake here, but by making it, she also took her first step toward rebuilding culture that can help her achieve coordinated interaction in the future with Young and other Korean speakers.

The Effect of Migration on the Use of Kinship Terms

Cultural norms and expectations regarding the use of kinship terms in personal address change over time and across generations of speakers, often as a result of migration. One frequent result of migration is the formation of **diasporas**, groups of people from the same home country relocating to and maintaining social ties in a different country. Speakers in diasporas often have to reconcile ways of speaking they brought with them from home and the ways of speaking their young borrow from the host country. Young members of diasporas sometimes become experts at playing one set of norms and expectations regarding the use of personal address terms against another in order to get their way, communicatively. The applied linguist Zhu Hua (2010), for example, reports an interaction among a mother and her two young sons, all members of the Chinese diaspora in the United Kingdom. The older brother, Chris (aged 10), born in China, wants to persuade his younger brother, David (aged 5), born in the UK, to let him (Chris) build a model car for his younger brother. David doesn't like this idea and wants to build the car himself. In the transcript below, the use of kinship terms is highlighted in bold letters.

EXCERPT 6.3. (from Hua, 2010, p. 203, simplified)

1	David [in English]	Mum, Chris doesn't let me.
2	Chris [to David, in Mandarin]	Elder brother [**gege**] will let you look.
3	David [in English]	I can do it myself.
4	Chris [in English]	No.
5	Mum [to Chris, in Mandarin]	Xinxin [Chris's Chinese name], let younger brother [**didi**] play.
6	Chris [in English]	He can't do it.
7	David [in English]	I can.
8	Chris [in Mandarin]	Elder brother [**gege**] will do it and show you.
9	Mum [to Chris, in English]	Let him try. He can do it.
10	David [in English]	Chris.
11	Chris [in English]	What?
12	David [in English]	Give it to me. [Tries to grab.]
13	Chris [in English]	Mum, David's snatching it. Don't be rude.
14	Mum [in English]	David. Don't snatch. Can you let him have a go, Xinxin?
15	Chris [to David, in Mandarin]	Elder brother [**gege**] will do it for you. He's doing it for you.
16	David [in English]	No.

Chris refers to himself as "*gege*" (Mandarin for "older brother") in lines 3, 8, and 15 in order to assert his authority over David. In doing so, he follows a Chinese convention for the purpose of persuasion: the older brother can be expected to tell his younger brother what to do! His mother affirms the difference in hierarchy and authority by addressing David as "*didi*" ("younger brother") in line 5 while appealing to Chris to allow David to play in spite of his status as *gege*. David, however, who wants to put the car together himself, resists his brother's attempts by using the English system of personal address and repeatedly addressing his older brother by his English first name (lines 1, 10).

BARRIERS TO COORDINATED INTERACTION

1. **Missing the pragmatic meaning of address terms.** In any social group, persons can be addressed in a variety of ways. When speakers apply an address term to another speaker, they are choosing a term from a set of appropriate terms their expressive system makes available to them. Think about an American mother who, in the course of their relational history, has addressed her daughter as "Joanne" (first name), "Jo" (diminutive form of first name), "Jitterbug" (nickname), "love" (term of endearment), "Joanne Abigail Hendricks" (official premarital name), "Mrs. Peck" (married name), "Judge" (official title), and "Your Honor" (honorific). In any particular encounter she may have with her daughter, her *choice* of address term will be meaningful. Choosing the term of endearment can indicate intimacy; selecting the official premarital name can signal anger; opting for the honorific can invoke pride. In intercultural encounters, you may be hindered not only by lacking local knowledge of the full range of locally available address terms but also by the lack of being aware of how the choices speakers make among options is locally meaningful.

2. **Damage to identity.** When you violate someone's cultural expectations or preferences by addressing them with an inappropriate address term, you run the risk of not only upsetting them but also causing temporary or lasting damage to that person's sense of self or who they are relative to you and others. This risk is higher when you are addressing others who have relatively lower power or prestige or who lack the linguistic ability to push back and demand that you use a different address term. Try not to underestimate the power of address terms to put people into social categories or identities they don't wish to claim as their own.

3. **Damage to relationship.** Beyond undermining others' identities, you also run the risk of undermining your relationship with others by not applying (or misapplying) local address terms. Fortunately, many speakers exercise a degree of leniency when it comes to the use of address terms in intercultural encounters. Such leniency can give you a chance to notice that you have violated cultural expectations or meanings and quickly select another, more appropriate term. But don't take such leniency for granted, especially in situations where you are in a relatively powerless position relative to a cultural other. Instead, for the sake of building and maintaining relationships with speakers who rely on expressive systems other than yours, do your best to map local systems of address terms as quickly and thoroughly as possible.

REFLECTION QUESTIONS

1. List address terms other speakers regularly apply to you. Who applies particular address terms to you? What identities do those terms signal? What types of relationships do they index?

2. Can you think of terms of person reference that apply to you but others would not use to address you?

3. Think of a person in your life for whom you use a range of different address terms. What types of address terms do you use? Is the selection among those terms meaningful in your speech community or in your relational history?

4. Can you think of address terms that are unique to your speech community?

5. Are you able to recall a time when someone addressed you in a way that threatened your sense of self or the relationship you had with that person?

7

"Were They Trying to Be Rude?"

Doing Things With Speech

DANA: I have always identified with the south of Vietnam, where my family is from. I grew up speaking Vietnamese, as my grandparents weren't fluent in English, and I assumed my dialect was "the norm." It was only during the spring of 2015 that I encountered the different cultures of the northern and middle regions of Vietnam. Starting in Hanoi and ending in Saigon, I was exposed to the hustle-and-bustle culture of the north, and I was shocked by the behaviors exhibited. With a population of about 7.5 million people, the preferred mode of transportation was mopeds. However, if you were traveling down a long stretch of the city road, there would only be about three stoplights. It seemed as if this system of transportation wouldn't work without accidents or aggressive drivers, and indeed, I encountered plenty of the latter during my trip. In many cases, if a driver was offended in some way, s/he would hop off their moped and begin verbally assaulting the person they found responsible. Never before had I heard such long strings of Vietnamese profanity used in such a normal situation. After both drivers were satisfied with their verbal assaults, they would hop back onto their mopeds and speed off like nothing ever happened. During my stay, I never

In this chapter, you will learn:

- how speech becomes action and attends to face concerns

- about the contexts of speech acts

- how speech acts combine into act sequences and genres

understood why this was such a common occurrence. Why couldn't the drivers just curse at each other to themselves and avoid confrontations? From my experience and my parents' knowledge, I understood that there were many different subcultures within Vietnam. You have the aggressive go-getters of the North, the laid-back and relaxed Hue, and the relaxed but efficient South. Of course, I'm partial to Hue and South Vietnam, but in general, this simple outline of the differences in cultures holds true. That being said, the typical North Vietnamese citizen is all about getting things done in a quick manner, but stopping to confront other drivers clearly impedes on that goal. Are these confrontations a result of pent-up frustrations or just something to distract them from their daily duties?

BILLIE: I have been a Christian my entire life. From birth until I left for college, I attended my parents' nondenominational church and only attended a few Catholic ceremonies like confirmation for my cousins. I was never captivated by my parents' church, which is why I was so excited to visit other churches once I left for college. One of these instances occurred two summers ago when I attended Orchard Road Christian Center. I attended one Sunday sermon and followed that up with several visits to their college youth group gatherings on Thursdays. I had already declared Flatirons Community Church as "my church," but I felt the Holy Spirit stirring in this place, especially after that first Sunday sermon. It was during one of the Thursday night gatherings that a worship leader, Chris, asked us all to gather around our main worship leader, Jennifer, and pray for her. We were told to place a hand on her and begin praying. While Chris was praying out loud, I heard whispers around me that started from one voice and grew to everyone around me. All of these college-age Christians started to speak in tongues. They were producing sounds and nonidentifiable words while surrounding our worship leader. I was shocked and began to panic, wondering if I should join in or leave; I had no idea what to do. Never had I ever heard anyone speak in tongues or talk about people speaking in tongues in my 21 years of attending church. I spoke with Chris a few weeks later about this event, and he explained how people have been blessed with spiritual gifts and pointed me to 1 Corinthians 12. This section of the Bible talks about how certain people are blessed with special talents that are directly linked to God, such as prophecy, distinguishing spirits, and the ability to speak in tongues and/or translate a speech of tongues. I had heard passingly of the act of speaking in tongues but never knew that there is a culture that has continued this speech act into the modern day.

M ore often than not, the words we say to others in interaction mean more than their immediate surface-level content. The meaning of words you find in a dictionary constitute their **referential meaning**. In the context of interaction, our words and their combinations with one another and with other features of communication (such as turn taking, intonation, pauses, etc.) become **communicative**

actions. Actions, in turn, take on **pragmatic meaning**—meaning that derives from context-bound language use.

To clarify this distinction, let me borrow an analogy from the anthropologist Clifford Geertz (1973). Concentrate on your right eye. Now quickly contract your eyelids one time. You have just used a certain set of muscles in your face to cover your right eyeball with your eyelids for a split second. Now, imagine being in the company of your friends and doing the same thing while making eye contact with only one of your friends, unnoticed by other friends. You haven't just contracted your eyelids: you *winked*. As a winker, Geertz explains, you are

> communicating, and indeed communicating in a quite precise and special way: (1) deliberately, (2) to someone in particular, (3) to impart a particular message, (4) according to a socially established code, and (5) without cognizance of the rest of the company. ... Contracting your eyelids on purpose when there exists a public code in which so doing counts as a conspiratorial signal *is* winking. (p. 6)

When you place this simple facial movement into the context of social interaction, you get nonverbal communication with a widely recognized name (wink) and pragmatic meaning (signaling or confirming your intent to collude with a person unbeknownst to others). In other words, you *acted* socially toward someone else. We can perform actions with verbal or oral communication resources as well, often much more complicated ones than a wink.

Actions can be a source of confusion, misunderstanding, and miscommunication in the context of intercultural communication, particularly when you lack awareness of the shared "socially established code" that allows members of an unfamiliar speech community to make sense of the pragmatic meaning of actions. Dana's account of her rich point is a vivid description of how someone might struggle with making sense of confusing communicative conduct. Why do North Vietnamese moped drivers feel compelled to stop, get off their mopeds, and take the time to shout profanities directly at one another in the middle of traffic instead of doing so while driving away? To Dana, this makes very little sense, especially given her stereotype about Northerners as the kind of people who don't waste time and like to get things done quickly.

In this chapter, we will first look at how actions are constituted in various contexts. Then we look at cases in which speech as action becomes an issue in intercultural communication due to mismatched interpretations of its meaning. Next, we look at how different cultural expectations about sequences of acts can also result in uncoordinated interaction. Finally, we focus on generic speech and its role in social interaction.

The philosopher J. L. Austin (1962/2014) was the first scholar to recognize that, in some cases, when people use language, they aren't simply making "statements"—that is, they are not saying things about facts in the world that are true or false—but rather they are performing "actions" that either constitute (or fail to constitute) socially shared reality. Many of our utterances are performative: they don't simply describe an action: they *are* the action. When I say "I name this boat *Seas The Day,*" the boat will actually bear that name, given the right set of conditions (i.e., there is in fact an unnamed boat that I have the right to name at this time). Acts can fail, Austin stated, when, despite the speaker's personal *intentions*, the *conditions* that make them "work" aren't there. If I am not the boat's owner, for example, and if the owner didn't give me the right to name it, my speech act is likely to be unsuccessful no matter how hard I try to name that boat.

CULTURAL PRAGMATICS SAYS

The intention to communicate meaningfully doesn't guarantee that you will communicate meaningfully. You can intend to apologize, but if you don't have the right ingredients in place, your apology is not likely to be accepted. (Think about it this way: no matter how much you intend to bake Hawaiian pizza, you will not be able to pull it off without pineapples.)

Speech Acts

The linguistic anthropologist Dell Hymes (1972) expanded the meaning of **speech acts** by claiming that they represent the level of linguistic phenomena where language understood as formal grammar and vocabulary was transformed into a locally recognized form of language in use in the context of actual social situations. More simply put, Hymes thought speech acts captured language use that *counted as action* for members of a speech community. For example, a speech act can transform what is formally a question into a request ("Can you pass the ketchup?") or a greeting ("How are you doing?") as long as there are local communication norms in place that guide the transformation and there is a situation in which a question can legitimately take on these meanings.

Speech Acts in Context

Hymes added that there are three kinds of context in which speech acts take on meaning. The first one of these is the **act sequence**, a progression of speech acts that are culturally meaningful. For example, in a Q&A following a lecture, audience questions and lecturer answers are expected to alternate and make sense relative to one another. Participants' decisions to depart from the usual progression of an act sequence doesn't automatically result in uncoordinated interaction, but the departure itself can be meaningful. During a Q&A, when two or more audience members ask questions without allowing the lecturer to answer them, they may be communicating that the lecture left them with strong feelings of enthusiasm or skepticism. The second type of context is the **speech event**, a social event with a locally recognized beginning and end governed by the norms inherent in the speech acts that constitute it. For example, a lecture is a speech event that begins with introducing the speaker and ends with thanking the speaker and the audience for their participation. The Q&A is an act sequence that constitutes one element of this speech event. Third, a **speech situation** is a type of social situation in which speech is appropriate and to be expected. Note that speech is not expected in all social situations in which we participate. Speech communities have different ideas about which social situations in what places count as speech situations for what types of participants. In his study of a White working-class neighborhood in Chicago, the communication scholar Gerry Philipsen (1976) observed that a gathering of adult males on a street corner was locally considered a typical speech situation, as was the gathering of adult females on a porch. Speech events and speech acts can vary within the context of speech situations.

From Speech Acts to Speech Genres

Hymes (1972) adds that some speech acts or act sequences can solidify into relatively stable **speech genres**, locally recognized and named generic forms of language use "such as poem, myth, tale, proverb, riddle, curse, prayer, oration, lecture, commercial, form letter, editorial, etc." (p. 65). In the second rich point narrative at the beginning of this chapter, Billie names a speech genre: *speaking in tongues*. What makes speaking in tongues a genre is that it contains a locally recognized, rule-governed sequence of acts for which participants have a local name, or label, that helps them identify and enact this type of speech and interpret it as meaningful. Billie's narrative illustrates how awareness of local speech genres can facilitate coordinated intercultural interaction between speech community insiders and outsiders.

There are important differences between speech genres and speech events. Speech events can contain multiple speech genres, whereas the reverse is not true. The meanings of speech genres can change

A Practical Question

"I am not religious. Do I have to consider speaking in tongues, or any kind of prayer, as actual communication?"

As an individual with private beliefs, you don't; as an intercultural practitioner, you do. From a cultural perspective, what matters is what members of a speech community see themselves doing, on their own terms. Understanding communication from their point of view is what will allow you to work toward coordinated interaction with them.

depending on the event in which they are performed—think about African American preaching as an element of religious liturgy or as a source of entertainment when it is imitated by comedian Steve Harvey in a stand-up routine about the difference between a White "service" and what some Black speakers affectionately call "*chuuch*" (The Official Steve Harvey, 2018). Finally, speech communities often treat speech genres as sites of creative performance and innovation, whereas the same cannot be said of speech events.

SPEECH ACTS

In intercultural encounters, the nature of speech as action can derail coordinated interaction in two ways. First, you and your conversational partner may have a different understanding of what performing a particular type of speech act takes. Second, you and your partner may simply have a different interpretation of the same act. I will use West African promises to illustrate the first of these problems and the Western speech act of *lying* to illustrate the second.

What Does It Take to Make a Promise?

"I'll be at the party Friday night!" When you say this to a friend, you are not simply describing your location at a certain point in time that will occur in the future. Rather, you are making a promise. When we make a promise, we are following a set of implicit rules that allow this speech act to constitute a genuine promise. Among other things, you have to be in the presence of someone to whom you are making the promise, you have to speak the same language, you should not be under duress, you should not be pretending or telling a joke, you should be referring to a future act, the person to whom you are making the promise should prefer that you do what you are promising to do, and you should sincerely intend to do what you are promising to do (Searle, 1965). However, you may run into problems when you try to apply these rules to promises made to you by non-Western speakers. The linguist Inge Egner tells the following story of a promise a speaker from the West African country of Côte d'Ivoire (Ivory Coast) made to her:

> A few weeks before an important ceremony at the Abidjan base of the NGO I work with, I went to an Ivorian friend's house to hand him an invitation to the ceremony and the reception afterwards. When I did so, he said, "I shall be there." However, in the course of the following conversation, he mentioned that on the day of the ceremony, he would be 600 kilometers away from the capital on an important government mission. When I pointed this out to him by saying something like "So then you won't be able to be there for the ceremony," his answer was "I shall be there. I'll do everything to be there." He never came. (Egner, 2006, p. 444).

From a Western perspective, it is easy to interpret what Egner's friend said as a relatively careless lie. Not only did he state a falsehood (i.e., that he intended to be at the ceremony), he also did very little to conceal that falsehood (i.e., he revealed that he was going to be far from the location of the ceremony). What the speaker should have done, from the Western perspective, was apologize, politely refuse the invitation, and explain the reason why he would not be able to attend the ceremony. This would have been the polite thing to do: the speaker would have communicated that he appreciated the invitation and that they respected Egner enough not to make a promise to her that he could not keep. Doing so would have serviced both the friend's and Egner's **positive face**: the friend would have come across to Egner as a responsible person, and Egner would have been cast as a respectful person worthy of honesty.

However, Egner later learned that the Western perspective on promising did not capture her friend's interpretation of what he was doing. For speakers in Côte d'Ivoire and in other West African countries, to openly say to someone they couldn't do something the other person expected or preferred them to do constitutes a serious **face threat**. Refusing an invitation, even on the grounds that the invitee physically can't be at the event to which they are being invited, tells the person extending the invitation that the invitee doesn't care about the relationship. Egner's friend was following a cultural rule: when it is clear to all parties involved that you will not be able to make it to the event, *say* that you will be there. No one will *actually* expect you to show up. For him, the polite thing to do was to appear interactionally cooperative. The divergent rules Western and West African speakers apply to promising are grounded in a divergent hierarchy of **cultural premises** relevant to this type of situation. For Western speakers, in situations where a promise is made, the most important premises are "Tell the truth!" and "Be sincere!" By contrast, West African speakers place other premises at the top of the hierarchy: "Do what is socially required!" and "Be compliant!" Does this mean that West African speakers will *always* prize compliance over rejection and that Western speakers *never* tell white lies? Of course not. Egner's observations apply to promises—whether they apply to other speech acts is an open question.

Also, does this mean that in West Africa, you can never make another speaker give you a promise that they will keep? Egner eventually figured out that what she should have done was ask a follow-up question after what she thought was a promise: "Is that a promise?" If the friend had intended to actually be at the ceremony, he would have said "yes," and that "yes" would have constituted a commitment. Answering "no" would have confirmed that he was being polite.

Was That a Lie?

As it turns out, then, Egner's friend wasn't lying. Or was he? How do we decide whether what he said *counted as* a lie? At the surface level, a sentence constitutes the speech of "lying" if it meets three conditions: it is a false statement; the speaker knows that it is a false statement; and the speaker intends to deceive an addressee (Agar, 1994). But these conditions, as they are formulated here, reflect a Western cultural perspective that foregrounds speakers' individual intent and abstract, absolute truth according to which what someone says either accurately reflects facts in the world or not. From this perspective, "I shall be there" meets two of the three conditions of lying: it was a false statement, and the speaker knew that it was false. (He didn't intend to deceive Egner—he simply assumed she would understand local conventions of promise making and would not interpret the statement as an expression of commitment.)

But what happens when you encounter a speech community in which members use different criteria to determine what *counts as* a lie? While doing ethnographic fieldwork in Mexico City, the linguistic anthropologist Mike Agar (1994) had to realize that even when Mexican speakers seemed to say things that were factually untrue, they did not intend to deceive—they were doing a range of other things. In some cases, they followed the cultural preference for having a pleasant moment (*pasar un buen momento*), for keeping the conversation pleasant by creating a positive, slightly rosy image of world. This preference trumped a concern for expressing factually true statements. For example, a Mexican speaker named Luis told Agar that a business transaction they were planning to conduct with a third party (one that Luis had arranged) was going to go smoothly. As it turned out, the transaction did not go smoothly at all; in fact, everything that could go wrong did. Luis told Agar that all of this was "normal" and explained how the transaction fell apart. Luis's explanation made Agar realize that Luis had, in fact, anticipated problems that were common in Mexico, but because there was a slim chance that the problems wouldn't occur, he had left out the negatives and emphasized the positive in order not to ruin a pleasant moment. There is no reason to obsess over worst-case scenarios, Luis implied; we can deal with the negatives as they happen.

Agar also reported feeling frustrated by Mexicans' tendency to make plans and not stick to them.

> Lots of things get planned. We'll do this at 11, that on Thursday, and this week-end, we'll take a trip to Cuernavaca. Instead, it turns out we do this at 5, that on Monday, and the trip to Cuernavaca is canceled. Multiple events are scheduled with certainty and then shift around or disappear. ... What I eventually learned was that no one expects things to work out all the time. Problems come up and other activities become possible. ... The important thing ... is to have a pleasant moment, not to follow a schedule you set up a week ago. The rule I currently use is that you don't have to do anything you said you'd do, but you should call the host or hostess or organizer and let them know you're not doing it. If you just don't show after you've promised to appear, that's a bit rude, but if you don't show and let them know you're not going to, even a couple of hours after the event started, nobody bats an eye. (p. 157)

Is this lying? The easy answer is it depends on who you ask. The more complicated, and more pragmatic, answer is that in order to coordinate your interactions with members of the Mexican speech community in intercultural encounters, you need to build culture from your observations of how Mexican speakers prefer to participate in conversations, approach tasks, and make plans for the future. Like Agar, you might find that, from the Mexican cultural perspective, individual intention and knowledge of and adherence to facts matter less than maintaining harmonious social ties through social interaction under conditions of uncertainty.

ACT SEQUENCES

Individual speech acts can become the source of intercultural miscommunication, but so can act *sequences*. Speech communities often have clear expectations about the order in which speech acts ought to follow one another. If these expectations are violated, uncoordinated interaction may ensue. Let's take a look at two examples from the personal experience of American communication scholar Donal Carbaugh (2005) of intercultural interactions in which cultural expectations regarding sequences of acts were violated.

The Sequence of Personal Introductions

In the early 1990s, Carbaugh was visiting Linacre College at the University of Oxford in the United Kingdom as a researcher. One day, a local man chatted him up in a pub during lunch. Carbaugh recalled their increasingly awkward conversation in this way:

EXCERPT 7.1. (from Carbaugh, 2005, p. 15)

He said	Hello.
I replied	Hello.
He said	What brings you here?
I	I'm visiting Linacre College.
He said	Oh, yes, are you a student?
I	In a broad sense, yes [*laughing*], but I've come to join two research teams.

He	Oh, what are you studying?
I	One group is studying communication and identity. The other is studying environmental discourses.
He	Oh, yes, mighty interesting. Are you a member of the college?
I	[Pause] I'm here at the invitation of Professor Harré.
	[Pause]
He	What is it that you study?
I	Cultural patterns of communication and intercultural encounters.
He	Oh, you're an anthropologist?
I	No, not really, although my undergraduate degrees were in anthropology and communication, but what I study mostly are communication process-es. In the United States, we have academic departments whose primary purpose is to study communication.
He	[Surprised] Oh, yes, uh-huh.

The miscommunication here, Carbaugh explains, results from different cultural expectations about what type of information you should share about yourself first when you are introducing yourself to a stranger. The Oxford man was seeking information Carbaugh wasn't providing. The introduction was going "well" by local standards until Carbaugh said he was visiting Linacre College. Once he was asked if he was a student, Carbaugh began to highlight his personal academic background and his affiliations with local researchers. What the Oxford man needed to know before everything else, as Carbaugh learned later, was his position in the local hierarchy of colleges and academic ranks. If he responded to the question "Are you a student?" with "I was elected by college members to be a visiting senior member of Linacre College," the man would have been perfectly satisfied. However, giving this answer would have run up against Carbaugh's U. S. American preference for minimizing social hierarchy in initial conversations and instead highlighting personal experience, interests, and connections. This is not to say that Americans aren't interested in social hierarchy and the British don't care about the unique experiences of individuals, but this is not the type of information they prefer to hear *first* in the context of a friendly, semiprofessional introduction.

The Sequence of the Academic Lecture

The *order* in which communicative actions are culturally expected to appear is not the only source of misunderstanding: expectations about *the number and types of acts* included in the sequence can also cause interaction problems. Carbaugh's second example reflects a common complaint Hamé Finns (Finnish speakers from the cen-tral region of Finland) make, in the context of friendly conversation, about American academics and their expectations about what lectures should look like.

An American academic visited here just last year from [insert any American] University. He gave an hour-long lecture about social science [insert your topic], then paused for discussion. He must have waited a whole 5 seconds! [said sarcastically]. After no discussion was produced by us (the audience), he began chiding the audience, and after that didn't produce any discussion, he got angry and started calling us names! He embarrassed himself and all of us, and they quickly adjourned the meeting. [Laughter]. (p. 20)

As Carbaugh explains, Finns and Americans have different expectations about what needs to happen between two sections of the academic lecture—namely, the lecture itself when the presenter speaks and the follow-up question-and-answer (Q&A) session. These expectations are grounded in culturally specific rationales. After a lengthy (hour-long) information-rich lecture, Finns expect to engage in some quiet reflection and come up with meaningful questions before they engage in the Q&A with the lecturer. This expectation rests on an image of the ideal Finn as reserved, thoughtful, careful with words, and someone who will not take up anyone's time with half-baked thoughts. Americans, by contrast, don't tend to see the need for reflection and prefer to go straight to questions and answers. There is less cultural demand placed on audience members to evaluate the social worthiness of their comments and questions. They can more or less take it for granted that what they have to say will be respected as an expression of their selves. Carbaugh argues that this latter orientation to speaking up in public is the preference of a diverse society where people expect to be different from one another and therefore wish to learn as much about their differences as possible through talk "so that some common life can be woven out of these threads of difference" (p. 22). Finns, who live in a relatively more socially homogenous society, expect more commonality and less talk.

These instances of miscommunication are difficult to clear up for at least two reasons. First, we tend to be unaware of our own cultural norms, rationales, expectations, and preferences regarding performing and interpreting speech acts and act sequences. To put it more precisely, we aren't aware of them until a cultural "other" violates them. Second, in moments when our expectations are violated, we tend to quickly reach for our national, cultural, and racial stereotypes to explain the **rich point** we have just experienced. Speakers who believe entire groups of people can't be trusted or are pompous or too shy to speak are much more likely to jump to conclusions about the *people* who violated their expectations than to patiently observe their *practices* and draw insights from those observations about local **expressive systems**.

SPEECH GENRES

Much of our speech is generic in the sense that it unfolds in predictable ways, but it is generic to varying degrees. Compare, for example, a family conversation at the dinner table with a religious liturgy. It is possible to identify generic features of the American dinner table conversation: participants talk about a restricted range of topics—talk about recent events in the family is usually acceptable, while talk about family members' sex lives is not—while allowing each family member to have their say, to change the topic of conversation, and to have side conversations. Religious liturgy can be much more tightly orchestrated. The structure of the Catholic mass, which I attended regularly as a child, makes room for very little variation in the sequence and the content of acts it comprises.

If we open up "speech" to include all forms of language use, we can distinguish **primary genres** (genres of everyday communication, such as rejoinders and personal letters) from **secondary genres** (genres derived from everyday communication, such as novels and speeches; Bakhtin, 1986). It is also worth distinguishing **local genres** (genres that are unique to particular speech communities) from **translocal genres** (genres that "travel" across cultural boundaries).

A Practical Question

"How do you know you are dealing with a speech genre?"

If a speech act or act sequence has a relatively stable content, style, and structure it maintains across contexts (e.g., speech events and speech situations) and has a locally intelligible label attached to it that members of the speech community use as a shorthand reference, you are likely looking at a speech genre. For example, when you are invited to a *job interview*, you have a pretty good idea of what type of communication is likely to occur, in what type of setting, and with what types of participants.

A Local Genre

To give you an example of a local genre, think about complaining. In the U.S. context, when you complain, you are likely either expressing dissatisfaction, pain, or annoyance (e.g., you are complaining about a broken arm), or you are making a formal accusation against someone (e.g., you are complaining to your elected political representative about your local police department's excessive use of force). In some cultures, you can witness more elaborate forms of social complaining that take on a ritual, communal function. Growing up in Hungary, I spent many hours sitting around the table after a meal with friends and relatives complaining about anything and everything going on in the world. Hungarians like to think of themselves as a depressed, bitter people, so I concluded group complaint sessions were expressions of a national psychology—that is, until I learned about Israeli *kiturim* ("griping") and Bulgarian *oplakvane* ("mourning," "crying"). Israeli griping sessions (Katriel, 1985) involve informal Friday-night conversations among members of the middle class who complain about the "situation" in Israel. Participants complain about the dismal state of the country and mournfully recall the golden age of the "realization" of the State of Israel, when people still knew how to act like members of a community with a shared purpose and future. When Bulgarians gather to *se oplakva* ("complain"; Sotirova, 2018), they also complain about the "(Bulgarian) situation" (corruption, potholes, drunk drivers, etc.), but they go about it in a slightly different way: they compare the "situation" to other countries in Europe where things are going better. Both *oplakvane* and *kiturim* have a spiral structure: someone raises a complaint, others acknowledge the complaint is legitimate and is somehow linked to the national "situation," everyone agrees that the "situation" is terrible and express remorse—no solutions are offered!—and around they go again. Although Israelis and Bulgarians are equally unhappy with the practical potential of these complaining practices ("Complaining won't change anything!" "Complaining kills all hope!"), they are also deeply invested in its ritual function. **Communication rituals** are act sequences that, when correctly performed, pay homage to a sacred object (Philipsen, 1987). The *kiturim* and *oplakvane* rituals are bittersweet celebrations of the community, the shared sense of "being in the same boat," constituted through acts of airing one's frustrations with the national "situation."

A Translocal Genre

Although these complaint sessions resemble one another, they are homegrown genres of speaking. Other genres are carried from one speech community to another by the rising tide of globalization. One example of such a genre is the Anglo-American *presentation*, the kind you would expect to hear in a corporate meeting. Dale Carnegie's 1937 book *How to Win Friends and Influence People* popularized the "American friendly" style of interpersonal behavior in business and organizational communication. This style gradually spread to the corporate *presentation* as well and demanded that speakers maintain eye contact with their audiences, project warmth and sincerity, organize their presentations according to a linear logic, and use sophisticated presentation technologies. Transnational corporations then held up the *presentation* genre as a model of corporate communication to be emulated by employees all over the world. A study of corporate employees in China, Hong Kong, and Finland (Pan, Scollon, & Scollon, 2002) showed that non-English speakers did very little to resist the spread of this translocal genre. Although they struggled with tensions between their own cultural preferences and expectations regarding communication and the demands of the *presentation*, study participants "expressed a Cargo Cult-like belief in the Anglo-American style of presentation, saying that because Americans were successful, they themselves would also be successful if they adopted the same style" (p. 101). In addition, once the *presentation* became the default genre of global corporate communication, it was difficult to argue for the value of local expressive forms it replaced.

Anglo-American speech genres such as *presentation* or *public speaking* are packaged and marketed globally as **for-anyone-anywhere genres**—that is, as genres of expression that ought to be available to, and preferably spoken by, everyone around the world (Boromisza-Habashi & Reinig, 2018). Enthusiastic campaigns to make such genres available to all speakers as valuable communication resources tend to overlook the difficulty of integrating such genres into local expressive systems.

BARRIERS TO COORDINATED INTERACTION

1. **Misconstruing the action speech is designed to perform.** If speech is action, then misunderstanding speech means misunderstanding what speakers are attempting to accomplish with speech—that is, an utterance's pragmatic meaning. One useful rule of thumb for intercultural communication is that whenever you encounter a rich point, assume (1) members of the speech community are trying to *do* something with words or other locally available symbolic resources, and (2) the nature of the action they are performing may not be obvious to you. This rule is not asking you to be naïve—sometimes what looks like an insult is actually an insult—but it is suggesting you defer interpretation and judgment, if possible, until you understand an action on cultural members' terms. Such understanding derives from making observations and asking questions.

2. **Resorting to stereotypes to explain unfamiliar speech acts.** When the actions words perform become a rich point for you, try to hold your stereotypes that apply to a target community at bay. Stereotypes are convenient interpretive shortcuts that help you make sense of confusing situations quickly. But the speed and convenience stereotypes offer are rarely paths to coordinating interaction across cultural boundaries. As Agar (1994) says, if you become preoccupied with the harmful stereotype that "Mexicans lie," you develop a blind spot for the possibility that they may simply be telling different types of truth. American stereotypes about the "silent Finn" distract from the variety of actions Finns perform with silence (Carbaugh, 2005). More often than not, stereotypes give you a false sense of certainty and plunge you deeper into miscommunication in actual intercultural encounters.

3. **Disregarding institutional and global pressures on speakers.** Globalization sometimes forces speakers around the world to perform speech acts, act sequences, and genres that feel unfamiliar or strange to them or perhaps are at odds with their expressive systems. When you see a speaker struggle with performing translocal speech acts and managing the pragmatic meanings of those acts, remain open

to the possibility that what you are witnessing is a speaker trying to do things with familiar words in unfamiliar ways. The successful performance of such acts is not just a matter of one's ability to speak a language: it is a matter of working with that language in ways that feel foreign. (If you want to get a better feel for what I'm arguing here, try to drive a nail into a plank of wood with pliers instead of a hammer.)

REFLECTION QUESTIONS

1. Can you think of a social situation that doesn't count as a speech situation (that is, a type of social situation in which no participants are expected to speak) in your speech community?

2. Recall a time when you were arguing with someone about the pragmatic meaning of something you said. What did you say, and what were the competing interpretations of that action?

3. What is a routine act sequence in which you regularly participate? Think about what cultural premises about human relationships this act sequence affirms.

4. Name a local and a translocal speech genre you regularly perform.

5. Do you think the speech genre of *speaking in tongues,* as described in Billie's rich point narrative at the beginning of this chapter, may have a ritual function? Why or why not?

8

"Is That Appropriate to Talk/Joke About?"

The Topic of Talk

CASEY: I experienced a rich point while I was studying abroad in Shanghai, China this past summer. I was in my Chinese language class at East China Normal University in Shanghai. We were learning about marriage and Chinese culture surrounding men and women's rights and lives. As this was an intensive summer language program, the exchange happened in Mandarin. We were discussing this topic when my teacher suddenly asks if I am married. This alone was not surprising; I said, "No, not yet." She then looked worried and asked me, "Why not?" and announced, "You're 20 already, aren't you afraid that if you don't get married soon you'll be alone forever?" Her concerned response was what gave me pause. Was she implying that I should be worried that I am somehow going to have a less fulfilling life because I was not yet married? I felt uncomfortable in this situation, as it is not typical in American culture for people to ask why someone isn't married yet or to insinuate that they should get married as soon as possible.

WYATT: The first time I heard a "yo mama" joke was in 7th grade on the school bus. I had never heard one before, so it came as

In this chapter, you will learn:

- the distinction between, and the importance of, topic selection and topic management

- how the topic of humor makes a difference in intercultural interactions

- that ethnic humor as a type of intercultural communication is a complex and creative "balancing act."

quite a shock at the time. The bus had just started leaving school, and I hear, "Hey Wyatt!" I turned around and a kid named Chris, a friend of a friend, was looking at me. Chris called out, "Yo mama so fat she has her own area code!" I was dumbfounded. This guy I barely knew had just insulted my mother to my face. At that point I was more surprised than offended, so I responded, "Excuse me?" He smiled and said, "Yo mama so fat her blood type is Nutella." Looking back, that second one was actually hilarious, but I remember it so vividly because I could not believe he would just say that to me out of the blue. I never did anything to Chris, so why would he say that? I had never heard of someone insulting a close family member so casually. At the time, it was like he just called my girlfriend ugly. But then he explained "you mama jokes" to me, and within a week, I was saying the jokes to my friends, and it became a trend throughout middle school.

O ften, though not always, social interaction is "about" something. This "about-ness" of communication is what I will refer to as the **topic** of communication in this chapter. A fundamental challenge in intercultural communication is figuring out what range of **conversational topics** (subject matters introduced into conversation) count as "fair game" in what kinds of conversations. You can expect most cultural groups you encounter to have some informal rules for topics you ought to avoid. Think about the U.S. American **cultural rule** according to which you shouldn't discuss sex, religion, and politics at parties or with strangers. In a stunningly diverse society such as the United States, this rule makes perfect sense: strangers are quite likely not to share your view of sexuality, your religious beliefs, or your political orientation, and therefore bringing up topics related to these areas of human experience can lead to awkward conversations. Also, sex, religion, and politics are often controversial, "heavy" topics in contemporary U.S. society, and you can't expect strangers to be invested in entering into deep conversations with you about these topics, no matter how enthusiastic you may be about them. In fact, in the U.S. context, broaching the subjects of sex, religion, and politics is often a signal that someone wants to enter into a deep conversation with you, which implies they are *assuming* you are interested in building a (closer) relationship with them.

During my international student days, these unspoken rules and meanings were not at all obvious to me nor to German students I had met in the States. I quickly discovered these students and I had something in common: we all enjoyed bringing up politics in casual conversations. I learned that, in the context of talking to Germans whom I had barely met, the choice of politics as the topic of conversation signaled to the other person that—by displaying a willingness to talk about a sensitive subject matter—I was invested in the conversation and that I was available for moving beyond a stranger-to-stranger relationship. Of course, I didn't become friends with every German with whom I talked about politics, but the selection of that topic at least planted the seed of that possibility in the moment. I discovered equally quickly that this strategy did not work with U.S. students, who were quickly turned off by the topic of politics. They saw politics as a divisive and "heavy" subject that was incompatible with initial friendly conversations. Politics was also incompatible with the activity known locally as "hanging out," the context in which my U.S. friends tended to form closer relationships. "Keep it casual" was a key conversational rule that applied to "hanging out," and the topic of politics was considered far from casual. Needless to say, my lack of familiarity with this rule didn't keep me from making friends with U.S. students, but politics as a conversational topic was not what helped me get there.

Casey's rich point account at the beginning of this chapter also illustrates the intercultural challenge of **topic selection**—that is, identifying particular subject matter as an appropriate conversational topic and introducing it into an ongoing conversation. One's marital status counts as a relatively harmless conversational topic in the United States. However, as far as U.S. speakers are concerned, the *reason* for one's marital status is no stranger's business, and implying a woman ought to be married in order to avoid a lonely existence is a very effective way to nip a conversation in the bud. So is, by the way, insulting someone's mother, although, as Wyatt's rich point story illustrates, there are **speech genres** that radically change the social meaning of insults. The "yo mama" joke is one such speech genre. Conceived in the African American **speech community**, such jokes were designed to insult and entertain at the same time (Morgan, 2014). "Yo mama" jokes were elements of a **speech event** called "the dozens," in which typically male participants playfully but competitively insulted one another in front of an audience of friends and acquaintances in order to make their fellow "contestant" lose their cool. Like so many other African American speech practices, "yo mama" later spilled over into U.S. pop culture (see, for example, Adult Swim, 2010).

Forms of humor other than jokes can also be the source of problems in intercultural interactions. One day in graduate school, while "hanging out" in the grad students' office between classes, my friend Mario began asking me about what life was like in Hungary. Mario was a big, friendly guy and a proud New Yorker who liked to tease others in a harmless, good-natured way. I was glad to be asked about my home country, and I began to tell him about how life in Hungary was pretty good in the early 2000s. State socialism and Soviet occupation were things of the past, the economy was doing well, people were still excited about Western-style democracy and open borders, and my home town, Budapest, was becoming a busy, prosperous international city. "Well," Mario responded with a familiar sly smile, "that's totally not how I imagine where you grew up. When I think of that part of Europe, I imagine housing projects with gray apartment blocks and chickens running across the road." As is often the case in rich points, my mind immediately went in a number of different directions at the same time. *I get it, this is a harmless tease. Wow, I guess grad school doesn't protect you from the influence of Hollywood movies' stereotypical representation of Eastern Europe. That comment kind of stung.* I remember his comment to this day because of that sting: like many Eastern Europeans, I too harbor a certain inferiority complex toward the global West. In the wake of his comment, all my insecurities as an international student from a relatively less affluent and powerful part of the world bubbled to the surface and kept me from coming up with a clever comeback.

Don't worry, this chapter is not trying to persuade you never to crack a joke around people from other speech communities or to feel like you have to walk on eggshells in order not to offend someone with your topic selection. We will, however, address three aspects of conversational topics you should be aware of as you build culture and try to achieve coordinated interaction with cultural others: **topic selection**, **topic management** (the conversational actions speakers perform with topics), and **humor**, including **ethnic humor** (humor centered on interethnic and interracial relations) as a particularly complex case of topic selection.

TOPIC SELECTION

As you interact with cultural others, you will sometimes find yourself having to answer the question "Is this an inappropriate topic to discuss?" **Intercultural practitioners** tend to face this question when they notice the interaction in which they are involved is becoming uncoordinated: your conversational partner seems to be avoiding the topic you are raising or they have fallen silent altogether and you find yourself giving a monologue.

Speech communities have different ideas and preferences about topic selection. Consider, for example, the example I used at the beginning of this chapter: initial conversations with others in informal encounters among speakers from the U.S. and Germany. The applied linguist Catherine Evans Davies (2004) writes that *typically,* these two groups of speakers bring not only a different set of topics to initial conversations but also a different set of cultural orientations to such encounters. U.S. speakers developed the **speech genre** of "small talk" for this particular type of communication encounter. Small talk fits into an **indirect** style that seeks to minimize imposition on one's conversational partner in order to give them a variety of response options and to avoid topics that force participants to take **stances** on social issues. This style assigns more importance to respect and relationship building than to truth about issues and works very well in a diverse culture where people are likely to hold quite different views on any topic, especially a controversial one. The result is a conversation that's relatively low on information about participants and their views and relatively high on affirming that everyone involved are competent, likeable people. By contrast, in the context of first conversations with strangers, German speakers tend to place more emphasis on information than on social bonding. Germans, who traditionally value directness and honesty, tend to use more **direct** speech that leaves less room for interpretation and response options and creates more opportunities for the discussion of controversial issues. This style is arguably rooted in Germans' experience of a more homogenous society in which speakers need to worry less about causing offense or awkwardness by introducing potentially sensitive topics into conversations.

This example highlights that topic selection in intercultural interaction is not a simple matter of "Don't talk about *X* with cultural group *Y*." As you reflect on what topics you should select and what topics you should avoid with a particular group of cultural others, use what you know about that group to answer these questions:

- In what type of conversation are you participating, and with whom? (An initial conversation with a stranger? A deep conversation with a friend? A friendly conversation with a member of another gender? A professional conversation with a coworker?) Is the discussion of certain topics restricted to certain categories of people in this group?

- Based on your observations and/or readings, what kinds of topics tend to be raised in such conversations/with such conversational partners in this cultural group? Does raising those topics tell you something about the group's preferred communication style?

- What does the selection of those topics tell you about the group's view of itself as a social unit? (Do they see themselves as a group of equals? A group of non-equals? A group of unique individuals or representatives of a social category, such as family members, friends, citizens, employees, and so on?)

TOPIC MANAGEMENT

Like other elements of communication, conversational topics do much more than convey information. "There are vitally important issues in the study of topic besides the question of what (the) topic is. We must also ask such questions as how communicators 'do' topic and what topic itself does in the interaction" (Nofsinger, 1990, p. 46). Once you recognize that topics "do" things in interaction, you should expect to encounter cultural variation in how speakers manage topics.

Who Has the "Right" to Introduce Topics?

The anthropologist Charles Briggs (1986) had a firsthand experience with this type of cultural variation while he was studying the woodcarving industry in a small village not too far from Santa Fe, New Mexico. Like all anthropologists doing fieldwork, Briggs was eager to learn about the daily life of the Mexicano ethnic community in the village, including local methods and meanings of woodcarving. To that end, he tried to interview his most knowledgeable elderly local informants about their daily lives. To his great frustration, the elders responded to his questions with vague allusions to the Bible. No angle, no line of questioning seemed to work. Briggs later learned that his preferred method of information gathering—that is, interviewing—violated a range of cultural norms and expectations in the Mexicano speech community, including norms of topic selection. Young Mexicanos were primarily expected to learn from their elders through observation and imitation, not direct questioning. But in the rare instances when elders used conversation to teach young adults, elders were expected to select topics, and adult learners were only expected to ask questions within the topic areas introduced previously by the elders. In addition, young adults were expected to ask questions only by directly referring to what an elder had just said ("What did you mean when you said X?"). When Briggs asked the elders questions with the intent of learning, he introduced new topics and thus inadvertently encroached on elders' conversational privileges.

Organizing Topics

Intercultural miscommunication related to topic management can happen even in encounters where participants are in agreement regarding who can introduce new topics. Let's look at the example of business communication between U.S. American and Asian speakers (Scollon & Scollon, 2001). Speakers from these two parts of the world tend to agree that a person who initiates a conversation also has the right to introduce the topic of conversation. This makes intuitive sense, right? In a business environment, why would you start a conversation if you didn't have something to discuss? But, as usual, the devil is in the details when it comes to social interaction. When, for instance, American business professionals want to argue a point, they typically introduce the topic (the argument) first and then provide the evidence supporting the argument. This is called a **deductive argument pattern.** Chinese professionals, by contrast, tend to prefer an **inductive argument pattern:** evidence first, argument last. This pattern confuses U.S. listeners who find themselves wondering, *What are we talking about? What is the topic of this conversation?*

Before you generalize the preference for the **topic-delayed organization** of talk to all Asian speakers in all contexts, it is important to remember that these patterns are typically observed in business-related contexts. In other contexts, U.S. speakers may use topic-delayed organization, and Asian speakers may use a **topic-first organization.** For example, Asian speakers of relatively higher social status (e.g., teachers) are often expected to introduce the topic of conversation because speakers of relatively lower status (e.g., students) try to avoid introducing a topic as a sign of respect. (In fact, as a surprising sign of the survival of Confucian cultural norms in a post-Confucian society, lower-status Chinese speakers often avoid starting a conversation with a higher status speaker and instead only signal that they are ready to be addressed.) Also, in cases where the topic of conversation is predetermined by the context—for example, in service encounters—Asian speakers have no trouble beginning conversations by stating the topic first (e.g., "I'd like a bag of chips, please").

Beyond the introduction of topics, topic management also includes building and maintaining relationships among topics. To stay with the example of American vs. Asian business meetings, U.S. business meetings often feature an **autonomous organization of topics**, whereas Japanese business professionals tend to opt for an **interdependent organization** (Yamada, 1990). Individual U.S. speakers tend to introduce a topic first and then use a relatively higher number (compared to other meeting participants) of **turns at talk** to elaborate on the topic. This style results in fewer topics raised and a monological meeting style. Japanese speakers, by contrast, raise more topics and take fewer turns discussing each topic. As a result, these meetings feel more dialogical. Unfortunately, both groups tend to stick to their own patterns even in meetings where members of both speech communities are present, which results in the mutual reinforcement of cultural stereotypes: Americans see the Japanese as patronizing ("They try to keep us talking!"), and the Japanese see the Americans as overly aggressive ("They keep steamrolling us with their views; we can't get a word in edgewise!").

As it is often the case, there are also cultural and institutional reasons for these different patterns and styles. In the business context, U.S. speakers tend to foreground individual initiative and autonomy, while Japanese speakers value group strength. In addition, while U.S. business professionals tend to make important decisions in business meetings, their Japanese counterparts often make key decisions in informal conversations between formal meetings and use formal meetings to celebrate the consensus they have accomplished (Miller, 1994).

The Influence of Globalization

Globalization exerts subtle but noticeable influence on topic management in various types of communication and erases some cultural differences that seemed much starker just a decade or two ago than they do today. This influence can happen in two ways: through addition or hybridization. New globally recognized communication styles can be added to local ways of speaking when topic management in global styles is seen as more optimal from a global perspective. Sometimes existing styles of expression are **hybridized**—that is, combined with nonlocal styles, to meet global expectations. Let me give you an example of each of these. The first example comes from Kenya (Miller, 2002), where a number of universities have recognized that traditional forms of Kenyan public speaking will not help students give Western-style presentations in the global business environment. Kenyan public speaking links together anecdotes into a circular structure, where each anecdote subtly hints at the point (or topic) of the speech. The topic itself often remains entirely unstated, and the audience enjoy figuring out the speaker's point. As you can imagine, this presentation pattern would not go over well in a corporate boardroom, a point not lost on Kenyan universities and students. A result

The culture you build for a speech community is always *partial*. Like the Kenyan students in this example, cultural others you interact with often stand at a crossroads between multiple communication systems—here, a local Kenyan system and a global system you are most likely aware of. Focusing on the Kenyan side of these students' cultural story would miss the global side.

of this incompatibility is that Kenyan universities today offer courses in Western-style public speaking to undergraduate students who seek to "make it" in the business world. There, they learn a linear presentation style that begins with an introduction (which includes clearly stating the topic of the presentation), continues with the body (evidence), and ends with a conclusion that restates the topic in light of the evidence.

An example of hybridization resulting from globalization comes from China. As a professor working at a U.S. university, I regularly receive emails from Chinese graduate students or early-career faculty wishing to work as visiting scholars in my department. They email me because they see their research interests overlap with mine, and they need a faculty member to act as their sponsor in order to be eligible for a visa. Over the years, I noticed that the style of the first email in which they introduced themselves to me and stated their purpose changed: applicants included fewer respectful pleasantries and compliments on the value of my work and more information about their own achievements and credentials. The shift in topics marks a cultural shift (Xiao & Gao, 2016). This type of email is known in China as the *Taoci* email. Prospective Chinese students or academic visitors target U.S. academic supervisors with *Taoci* emails for the purpose of increasing admissions or scholarship opportunities. The emails are carefully designed to build a relationship and rapport (*guanxi*) between the applicant and the supervisor: their language is intended to draw the two together like a magnet (*ci*). Traditionally, Chinese speakers attempted to achieve *guanxi Taoci* by showing respect (including flattery) toward higher-status individuals, identifying shared personal contacts, and assuming the liberty to stay in contact. However, more recent academic *Taoci* emails combine traditional Chinese *guanxi*-seeking strategies with Western/global self-promotion. Today, applicants recognize that U.S. academics expect and appreciate the right amount of self-promotion and therefore incorporate it as a topic in their *Taoci* emails. A number of websites and discussion boards are available to Chinese speakers where successful applicants share best practices for deciding how much self-promotion is appropriate in *Taoci* emails and how it can be mixed in with more traditional topics related to "pulling *guanxi*."

As an intercultural practitioner, if you want to test your level of mastery of a previously unfamiliar expressive system, try to be funny. If members of the cultural group laugh—not at you, but at what you've said—you can be sure you are no longer a novice speaker. The next section gives you insight into why topic selection is a key element of humorous speech.

HUMOR AND TOPIC

What should you joke about with cultural others? What topics should you steer clear of in order to avoid causing offence? The answer to these questions will vary across speech communities. This section will give you some points to consider as you decide how to use humor in intercultural encounters. After an introduction to cultural universals and variation in humor and a review of all of the different ways in which humor can fail, we will look at a type of humor with a particularly sensitive topic: ethnic humor.

Humor Around the World

Humor can look a little different from culture to culture: its form varies, and so does the range of social tasks speakers try to accomplish with humor. Nevertheless, you will find humor anywhere you go in the world (Guidi, 2017). Some topics of humor—such as sex, obscenity, and the figure of the "fool"—are also present in every speech community. The functions of humor, though culturally variable, fall into three broad categories:

1. social control (calling out violations of local norms and rules, holding violators accountable, and thereby affirming the local system of norms and rules);

2. social play (fun, entertainment); and

3. building **joking relationships** (the types of social relationships where tension and conflict are common, as in relationships between in-laws or competing groups, and where participants use ritualized forms of humor to maintain social harmony).

Failed Humor

Does the fact that humor has so many universal features mean that telling jokes in intercultural encounters shouldn't cause problems? I'm afraid it doesn't. Humor can go wrong in plenty of different ways. In a study of failed humor in interactions between native and non-native (Chinese, Japanese, Korean) speakers of English in the United States, two linguists, Nancy Bell and Salvatore Attardo (2010), who specialize in the study of humor identified seven ways in which humor can cause uncoordinated interaction:

1. failure to process humor (e.g., not hearing it properly because the speaker mumbles or speaks too fast)

2. failure to understand the meanings of words and/or their connotations (e.g., a U.S. speaker referring to a Japanese speaker as a "guru," not realizing that, in Japan, the word is associated with dangerous cults such as Aum Shinrikyo)

3. failure to recognize irony, sarcasm

4. failure to recognize the humorous **interactional frame** (misunderstanding or missing the cues in someone else's talk that signal that what is being said is [not] to be interpreted as humor, and missing a joke or hearing a joke where none was intended as a result)

5. failure to understand wordplay (e.g., knock-knock jokes)

6. failure to appreciate the joke ("I get that this was humor, but I don't get why it's funny")

7. failure to join in the joking (being unable to keep up with native speakers' pace of joking conversation and/or inability to perform "being funny")

The selection (2, 3, 5, 6) and management (1, 4, 7) of humorous topics—or humor as a topic—can lead to uncoordinated interaction in which participants relying on different cultural systems of communication are unable to pursue the conversation or their social goals in a way that feels satisfactory.

A classic example of category #4 on Bell and Attardo's list comes from European history. Have you heard the expression "Let them eat cake"? Legend has it that when Marie Antoinette, the Austrian wife of 18th-century French king Louis XVI, was informed that the poor of France lacked access to basic necessities, including bread, she responded: "If they don't have bread, let them eat brioche!" (*"S'ils n'ont pas de pain, qu'ils mangent de la brioche!"*) Her statement was widely interpreted later as either evidence of her and the rest of the monarchy's utter cluelessness about the state of the country ("If they ran out of bread, they should just switch to brioche!") or as flippant disregard for the poor, who obviously did not have access to luxury baked goods. I should mention that historians today dispute the attribution of the expression to Marie Antoinette. Nevertheless, what's interesting about the expression is that it was meant to be ... humor! In Austria, there is a type of dark humor known as *Schmäh* (pronounced roughly as "shmay"). *Schmäh* humor consists of slightly insulting, sarcastic statements or acts that seemingly target particular individuals or groups of people but are really meant as commentary on the terrible state of the world shared by the speaker and the butt(s) of their joke. The world is so awful, a well-told *Schmäh* implies, that all we can do is laugh about it. According to an Austrian interpretation (Agar, 1994), if Marie Antoinette had indeed uttered her famous statement, she was not revealing her ignorance about, or disregard for, the plight of the people of France: just the opposite. What she meant was: "I know about the devastating suffering of the poor, and there is nothing any of us can do to make it go away. All we can do is laugh it off." From her Austrian perspective, telling a *Schmäh* was more genuine and powerful commentary on the tragic state of affairs in her adopted country than a simple description. To French revolutionaries, her statement was an excellent justification for her eventual execution.

The "moral" of this story is that intercultural practitioners face a double risk as they try their hand at humor in a cultural environment with a relatively unfamiliar expressive system. First, they may apply (dark) humor to a topic that is much too sensitive for members of the cultural group and face social backlash. Second, when a speaker uses subtle forms of humor, their audience may miss the irony or sarcasm and the implied (sympathetic) social commentary, interpret the topic of the statement differently from the speaker, and sanction the speaker for the violation of local norms. ("Is she actually talking about telling the poor to eat brioche? What on earth is she thinking?")

Social media greatly exacerbate these risks by fracturing and multiplying the audiences of our expression. According to Agar, Marie Antoinette failed at humor because she failed to anticipate her audience's reaction to *Schmäh*, not because she couldn't anticipate who her audience would be. Today, an intercultural practitioner's attempt at humor on social media can easily find its way to unfamiliar audiences with unfamiliar expectations, even within the same cultural group. The backlash is also likely to be swifter—although perhaps less bloody—than in 18th-century France.

A Practical Question

"Should I attempt subtle forms of humor like sarcasm, irony, or dark humor in intercultural encounters?"

I would recommend that you don't overuse these types of humor. What makes subtle (indirect) humor subtle is that it requires a lot of **inferencing**. Inferencing draws heavily on cultural background knowledge, which your interactional partner will likely not have.

Ethnic Humor

Both types of risks—choosing the wrong topic and prompting different interpretations of a topic—are very much present in the brand of humor commonly referred to in the U.S. as "ethnic humor." If done well, this type of humor is exhilarating because it not only exposes the daily experience of interracial and interethnic relations in a society and holds those who commit social wrongs accountable but also entertains. Watching a skillful performer of ethnic humor in any speech community is like watching an acrobat perform a particularly dangerous routine with ease: the risks and the benefits are equally high.

Topic choice in ethnic humor is tricky because one or more ethnic or racial groups targeted by such humor may object to some topics relevant to race and ethnic relations. The documentary *You Laugh but It's True* (Meyer, 2011), a film about the early career of Trevor Noah, the South African comedian and current *The Daily Show* host, offers insight into this feature of ethnic humor. The film features White South African stand-up comedians taking issue with their Black colleagues' choice of apartheid as the topic of their comedy.

David Newton	Maybe it's a therapeutic thing for them [Black comedians]. Maybe it's good to talk about the apartheid thing. But when do you say enough is enough?
Mel Miller	The Black and White experience, it's enough now. It's gone. It's finished. We must get past that.
David Newton	A Black guy will get up, and one of the first things [he would say is], "So, you know what it was like when we were in the townships [apartheid-era urban ghettoes]?" And I'm like, you've got to be kidding me.

In the following scene, Noah and another Black comedian, Loyiso Gola, are seen discussing these objections.

Loyiso Gola	This shit only was fifteen years ago.
Trevor Noah	Yeah, it ended fifteen years ago, but then you must remember it's not like it's [instantly over]. Do you know what I mean? It's not instant.
Loyiso Gola	I don't understand. People always say, hey you Black people must get over this apartheid shit. No one in the world will go, yeah, you know, you know, you Jews must forget [the] Holocaust ...

Of course, no amount of criticism from fellow White comedians could keep Noah and Gola from using their experiences with apartheid as a topic of their comedy, but they were also aware that their humor antagonized peers and turned away some White members of their audiences.

From time to time during Noah's career, some members of his audience also misinterpreted, or produced competing interpretations of, the topic of his ethnic jokes. After France had won the FIFA World Cup in the summer of 2018 with a team consisting mainly of players of African descent, Noah celebrated the national team's victory on *The Daily Show* in this way:

> Yes! Yes, I'm so excited! [*Chanting*] Africa won the World Cup! Africa won the World Cup! Africa won the World Cup! Africa won the World Cup! [*Does Wakanda salute from the movie Black Panther.*] I mean look, I get it, I get it, they have to say it's the French team, but look at those guys, huh? [*Image of French national team appears.*] Look at those guys. You don't get that tan by hanging out in the south of France, my friends. Basically, if you don't understand, France is Africa's backup team. Once Senegal and Nigeria got knocked out, that's who we root for, you know? (*The Daily Show*, 2018)

Noah's words touched a nerve in France, a country where public discourse about national belonging, multiculturalism, and race had been intensifying for decades and reached fever pitch around the time of the World Cup. Followers of the French liberal assimilationist tradition (including the government) were leaning into the argument that French citizenship unites all members of French society and supersedes differences based on race, ethnicity, or national origin. These speakers spoke out against racist nationalists who pointed at the national soccer team and bemoaned the loss of French identity. In a public letter to Noah, the French ambassador to the United States at the time, Gérard Araud, claimed:

> France is indeed a cosmopolitan country, but every citizen is part of the French identity and together they belong to the nation of France. Unlike in the United States of America, France does not refer to its citizens based on their race, religion, or origin. To us, there is no hyphenated identity, roots are an individual reality. By calling them an African team, it seems you are denying their Frenchness. This, even in jest, legitimizes the ideology which claims Whiteness as the only definition of being French. (French Embassy U.S., 2018)

In response to the ambassador and to his many French critics, Noah later explained (*The Daily Show With Trevor Noah*, 2018) that his jokes were meant to be a celebration of his own and the players' shared African heritage and of Africans' accomplishments in the world. He also forcefully pushed back against what he saw as the ambassador's denial of the players' African origin: "This is what I find weird in these arguments, is that these people go, 'They are not African, they are French.' And I'm like, why can't they be both?" In essence, he dug in his heels and reasserted a U.S. liberal view of multicultural societies that honors hyphenated identities and doesn't force individuals to treat their "roots" as a private matter.

In this high-profile conflict between two culturally rooted liberal positions on diversity, the conflict itself is expressed as disagreement over the topic of Noah's humor. Was the topic of his humor pride in African identity or the denial of African French players' national identity? The conflict was never resolved.

At this point, you may be wondering: Given that ethnic humor can produce so much disagreement and feed all kinds of social anxieties, should intercultural practitioners avoid it? I, for one, don't think so. Notice that in both of the cases involving Trevor Noah, he was not only doing ethnic humor—he was also doing politics, as was the young Arab man who once introduced himself to me, a White stranger, by saying, with a big grin on his face, "Hi, I'm Osama, but I'm not a terrorist." Ethnic humor has considerable potential as a

CULTURAL PRAGMATICS SAYS

This exchange between Noah and Araud is an excellent example of the *opposite* of what intercultural practitioners do. Instead of building intercultural frames, both sides stuck to their own cultural frames. Notice, though, that neither side was interested in coordinated interaction—they were more invested in communicating their political positions.

A Practical Question

Would you like to try your hand at ethnic humor in situations in front of a multiethnic audience? Whether you are talking to an audience of one or thousands, the use of ethnic humor in intercultural encounters is a complex balancing act that presents speakers with a combination of challenges. The linguistic anthropologist Marcyliena Morgan (2014) offers novice users of ethnic humor some pointers:

1. Develop deep knowledge of local cultural forces at play, including racial/ethnic stereotyping and the history of interracial and interethnic relations, to be able to speak about difference in a credible way.

2. Take into account that your conversational partners or larger audience may not be ethnically or racially homogenous.

3. Find ways to stay in control of the interpretation of your humor while remaining funny.

4. Use communication resources such as indirectness creatively in order to maintain **positive social face**.

5. Be mindful of local cultural norms that shape what topics you have the "right" to joke about and in what ways as well as who has the authority to enforce those norms, and how.

6. Find ways to offer hope, not only criticism.

communication resource speakers can use for the purpose of challenging the ways of thinking and practices of dominant social groups in the name of equality and social justice. Intercultural practitioners should explore the creative possibilities of ethnic humor in interactions with cultural others while also being mindful of the possibility of uncoordinated interaction and negative social consequences that can result from the use of such humor.

Ethnic humor reminds us about two important features of coordinated interaction. First, coordinated interaction doesn't necessarily take the shape of harmonious, smooth interaction that all parties involved find pleasant. Ethnic humor can produce interactions that are coordinated in the sense that both (or all) sides share an understanding of what the speaker is *doing*, even if they don't agree with, or have mixed feelings about, the sentiments the speaker is expressing. Second, as you can see from the Trevor Noah examples, coordinated interaction is sometimes a less desirable outcome for participants of intercultural interactions than taking a stand about issues that matter.

BARRIERS TO COORDINATED INTERACTION

1. **Making uninformed choices about topic selection and topic management.** You introduce a new topic in conversation with cultural others and get blank stares or evasive responses. You begin the discussion of an item on the agenda in a business meeting with cultural others, and you find yourself giving a long monologue to which no one is responding. After you have recovered from feeling confused or disappointed, doubting yourself, or tapping into your stereotypes about the other group, ask yourself whether you have any relevant information in response to these questions: From your cultural others' point of view, who has the authority to introduce new topics? At what point in the conversation are they expected to introduce topics? What topics are "fair game" in this context? How is this group likely to sanction you for raising inappropriate topics or raising topics inappropriately? What do you have to win (or lose) by conforming to their expectations about topic selection and management (for example, by switching from a topic-first to a topic-delayed organization)? If you don't have relevant information, start observing, reading, and asking questions.

2. **Using ethnic humor inappropriately or ineffectively.** When you see your use of ethnic humor going wrong in intercultural (including interethnic or interracial) encounters, you should ask yourself questions similar to the ones listed above. Do you have the conversational "right" to perform ethnic humor in this context (in this setting, with these participants, engaged in this type of activity, etc.)? If you are a strong believer in the universal right to free speech, keep in mind that free speech doesn't free you from the social consequences of your speech. In addition, even if in a given intercultural encounter you do find yourself at liberty to use ethnic humor, think carefully about what you want to accomplish with its use. Do you want to entertain, critique, self-deprecate, or something else? Then, once you know what you want to accomplish, think about using humor as a communication resource in ways that allow you to accomplish those goals. The lists of possible reasons for failed humor and tips for performing ethnic humor above should offer some useful pointers.

REFLECTION QUESTIONS

1. Find two examples of social interaction that don't have an obvious topic.

2. This chapter points out that U.S. speakers tend to use a topic-first organization in business meetings. Can you think of contexts in which U.S. speakers tend to use a topic-delayed organization?

3. Think about the last time you argued that someone should do something for you. Did you use an inductive or deductive argumentation pattern? In what types of social situations would you be more likely to use a deductive argumentation pattern (stating your point first, then providing evidence)? How about an inductive argumentation pattern (evidence first, argument last)?

4. Write down the first two jokes that come to mind. Is their primary function social control or social play?

5. Do you have a hyphenated identity? Are both (or all) elements of that identity sources of pride for you? Why? How do you celebrate those identities that you are proud of?

9

"Wait, Was That Sexist/Biased/ Racist?"

Moral Issues in Everyday Life

VAL: Just over a month and a half ago, I got back from studying abroad in Florence, Italy, for 4 months. On an average day in Florence, one can smell fresh bread being baked, hear a beautiful language being spoken, and see happy people walk down the street with smiles on their faces. Not once did it cross my mind that I would get constantly catcalled by men of all ages as I walked down those ancient cobblestone streets. On my first day in this foreign country, I was traumatized after being whistled at by a man who had to be the same age as my grandfather. This degrading form of communication was not something I was expecting in Italy after living and witnessing it in the United States for the past 20 years. Many of my professors in Florence told us to look at it as a compliment and to not pay much attention to it. We were advised that if a group of girls walking down the street got catcalled by a man or men, they were supposed to look it as a compliment instead of harassment. This notion differs greatly from what we are taught and what we believe in the United States.

SUNNY: A few years ago, I spent a weekend in Oregon with the family of my boyfriend at the time. This was my first time meeting

In this chapter, you will learn:

- what it means to be a pluralist

- about the benefits of treating your encounters with sexist, racist, or politically biased speech as intercultural encounters

- about case studies of taking a cultural approach to morally objectionable speech

them. I was nervous, of course, as we sat down for dinner and started to get to know one another. His brother-in-law was quick to start the conversation off, talking about illegal immigrants, specifically Mexicans. He started talking about how Mexicans come to the U.S. and use all of our resources, take American jobs, and bring in drugs. He talked about how they are all criminals, mooching off our system, and talked about how much money they cost American taxpayers. He rambled on about how Mexicans would use the emergency room at the local hospital and U.S. citizens would have to foot the bill. The language he used to describe Mexicans was very derogatory and extremely alarming to me. He talked about how he, and other members of the community, were taking things into their own hands and how he was now an active member of the Oregon Militia. He went on to explain how they regularly went down to the Mexican border with guns and would shoot at Mexicans trying to cross the border. Needless to say, I was shocked beyond belief. I am a liberal, a progressive, and my values and world ideology does not align with this type of thought. I sat there and wondered, "How could he say these things?!?" I will be the first to say I knew nothing about the Oregon Militia. It was only during this weekend visit that I got a peek into the anti-government, racist, and hostile world of what I would call extremists. I never expressed my liberal views to the family members, as I was a guest, but I left in awe of the differences in our lives, values, and worldviews.

W hen someone says something to you that strikes you as sexist, racist, or politically biased, the experience can be disorienting, to say the least. You may feel a combination of anger, surprise, confusion, frustration, vengefulness, and self-doubt. How can they say that?!? Who do they think they are?!? I had no idea they were racist, sexist, biased. … How am I going to put them in their place? And was that really racist? Was that sexist? Was that their personal opinion, or are they expressing the views of a political party or movement?

Such statements can be parts of a large-scale society-wide pattern, as in Val's rich point account above, or they can come out of nowhere, as in Sunny's. They can occur in public spaces or in private conversations. They may be verbal or nonverbal. They may come from familiar or brand-new peer groups. No matter the context, no matter the communication resource the offender chooses, responding to the offender in the moment is one of the most difficult challenges we face in our communicative lives.

There are, of course, many more ways to cause others offense in socioculturally diverse societies where people have many ways to categorize one another as "different." I chose to focus on sexism, racism, and political bias in this chapter because these are the ones my students at the University of Colorado Boulder tend to experience as **rich points** in their daily lives.

CULTURAL PRAGMATICS AS A STARTING POINT

This book is organized around the idea of **cultural pragmatics**. As an approach to intercultural communication, cultural pragmatics holds that the fundamental challenge of communicating with cultural others is figuring out how (and if) we can go on interacting with one another and pursuing our shared or separate goals despite our differences. Cultural pragmatics will not teach you everything you need to know about sexism, racism, and political bias. You will find other sources to learn more about race as a relatively new way of describing difference among people (Jackson & Weidman, 2004) that emerged during the modern slave trade under the conditions of capitalism (Wade, 2005) and has shaped social and institutional relations in Western societies ever since. You can turn to yet other sources to learn about how male-dominated societies around the world find ways to sustain gender hierarchies (Eltahawy, 2015; hooks, 2015). Excellent explanations of how political movements and campaigns are shaped not only by personal moral conviction but also by the technologies they use (Kreiss, 2016; Tufekci, 2017) abound. Finally, you can explore scholarship on **intersectionality**—that is, how sorting people into intersecting and interacting social categories of race, class, gender, sexuality, ability, and so on can reinforce social hierarchies and relationships of **discrimination** (Krølokke, 2009; Scott, 2017).

Cultural pragmatics prompts you to understand rich points that involve language use that strikes you as sexist, racist, or politically biased *as* intercultural encounters. Treating statements that go against some of your deepest moral convictions for the purpose of assessing the possibility of coordinated interaction with the offender seems counterintuitive at best and morally wrong at worst. Why not simply interpret biased statements as evidence of the person's inherent bias, condemn both the speaker and what they said, and disengage? You might quite reasonably refuse to waste your time on morally corrupt individuals.

But what if you have to deal with sexists, racists, or politically biased individuals in your daily life? Unfortunately, catcalling in Florence isn't likely to cease just because the young woman in the first rich point above found it objectionable. Neither is a member of the Oregon Militia likely to give up his views of Mexicans to make his brother-in-law's new girlfriend comfortable. Clearly, these two students were eventually able to disengage from the discomfort they experienced, but this option is not always available, or desirable, to someone with a racist coworker, a political activist who is committed to eradicating sexism in U.S. society, or someone whose spouse is of an opposing political persuasion. This chapter focuses on cases when *disengagement is not an option or is not (immediately) desirable.*

The option of disengagement was not immediately available to me, either, as a teenager who had just returned to Hungary from his year-long visit to the United States. Like many other international students (Bardhan & Zhang, 2017), I was first exposed to public and private discourse about race and racism for the first time in the

United States. I learned that I was "White" and had certain privileges that my "Black" peers didn't have. Although even at the age of 12 I was well aware that some fellow Hungarian citizens fell into the category of "ethnic groups" (such as the Jewish, Roma, and Swabian minorities), prior to my first extended visit to the United States in 1988, I had never heard any talk about my family having a race or belonging to an ethnicity. I only found out how deeply I was influenced by American race talk when, a few days after my return to Hungary, I found myself panicking at a family gathering: *"Whoa, my family is racist!"* The way they talked about ethnic minorities checked every box on the list of racist ways of speaking. When I pointed out to my parents how some of the things my aunts, uncles, and cousins said at that gathering definitely sounded like racism, they smiled at me dismissively and said, "You've become Americanized." As a teen whose budding political views were swiftly invalidated with that one infuriating statement, I had to figure out communication strategies for dealing with racist talk and attitudes in my family without burning all bridges to my social support system. In the end, I was able to convince some of my closest family members to respect my values and to refrain from racist statements around me. (I've also learned to accept that they will always see my view of racism as an element of my "American" identity.)

PLURALISM

We live in a world marked by a plurality of beliefs grounded in often incompatible views of the world. Your views on race, gender, and politics may be different from mine, your peers', or your instructor's. You can approach this condition as an unfortunate state of affairs or you can accept it as inevitable. If you choose to do the latter, you have taken the first step toward becoming a pluralist.

Pluralism, the philosophical foundation of cultural pragmatics, is based on the following basic principles:

- **Difference matters.** We live in a diverse world where it is virtually impossible to live a life where social contact is limited to those who share one's own convictions. In U. S. American society, some cultural and political forces suggest achieving ideologically homogenous communities is not only possible but desirable. This isn't the case. Difference matters, and will continue to matter, because of changing demographics, the desire to lead better lives in organizations and markets, sustained commitment to achieve "liberty and justice for all," and heightened popular interest in diversity (Allen, 2011).

- **Every "faith" matters.** Our lives are organized around "faiths." I am using the term "faith" here in the broadest possible sense to include all deeply felt convictions (Connolly, 2005), some of which are tied to **cultural norms** and **premises**. People of all stripes—religious people and secular scientists, liberals and conservatives—have "faiths," or sets of basic assumptions about what the world is, how it works, and how we should live in it. When someone does something that goes against the grain of our faith, we feel like the bottom has just fallen out of our world. The pluralist acknowledges the coexistence of a plurality of "faiths" and fights to uphold conditions that allow them to coexist. Exercising modesty, the pluralist also acknowledges that their own "faith" can seem contestable, or downright ludicrous, from the perspective of another.

- **Personal convictions matter.** Pluralists are not relativists. While relativists follow the "When in Rome, do as the Romans do" principle, pluralists refuse to give up the personal convictions that derive from their "faith," and they equally refuse to give up their commitment to societies that accommodate diversity. You can be a conservative and a pluralist or a Marxist and a pluralist. Pluralists are not secularists, either. No pluralist would demand that people give up their religion or spirituality and participate in society following abstract norms of rationality.

- **Interdependence matters.** Beyond coexistence, people in diverse societies depend on one another for goods and services and for accomplishing peace, justice, and prosperity. We rely on people of different "faiths" every day to work toward goals that matter to us and to others of our "faith."

- **Communication matters.** Interacting with others creates opportunities to make the most of our interdependent lives in diverse societies. Communication is the playing field where we attempt to coordinate our interactions, our goals, and our lives. We negotiate, we persuade, we share our stories, we praise, and we hold each other accountable in social interaction.

Cultural pragmatics, as it applies to intercultural communication, helps you translate these principles into practice. Suppose you witness some form of expression that strikes you as sexist, racist, or politically biased. What can you do? One option available to you is condemning and sanctioning the speaker. You can shun speakers whose speech you find objectionable on moral grounds, or you can build a coalition of friends or like-minded strangers willing to condemn their speech with you. In the workplace, you can investigate your organization's policies regarding offensive speech and harassment and pursue sanctions against speakers on the grounds of those policies. Sanctioning offensive speakers in these ways is particularly warranted if their speech directly threatens individual targets' well-being and livelihood or if it contributes to **discrimination**, the intentional or unintentional disadvantaging of members of a minority group by a majority group (Billig, 2006).

But what if you are not interested in shunning or sanctioning particular speakers? What if, for example, you are committed to persuading a parent that their speech is morally wrong? Or what do you do if someone you love says something racist? What if you want to talk an elected official who doesn't share your political views into changing a policy that directly affects your life? In other words, what if there is *some degree of interdependence between you and the speaker*? The cultural pragmatic approach suggests you can try a few things before you condemn your conversational partners' speech, condemn them as racists, sexists, or political "sheep," and sever social contact with them or seek to punish them in other ways. You can do all of the following without either compromising your "faith" or assuming your "faith" speaks for itself and anyone in their right mind should be able to see the world as you do.

1. Stop and think about who this person is to you and whether maintaining a relationship with them is worth your while.

2. If it is, think about what you would like to accomplish by discussing their offensive speech with them. (Do you want to make sure they never say such things again? Do you want to persuade them they are wrong? Are you genuinely curious to find out what brought them to say those things?)

3. Treat sexist, racist, or politically biased speech as a rich point. This involves positing, for the moment, that the speaker is not a morally corrupt person who is a danger to society but that what they are saying is informed by a worldview different from your own.

4. Approach them about the rich point as you would someone from a different culture. Talk to them to learn something. Exercise due diligence. Ask questions about what they meant when they said what they said. Try to reconstruct their point of view. At the same time, think about whether, and to what extent, their point of view is compatible with yours.

5. Based on what you have learned, consider whether you can go on communicating and sharing your life with a person who holds those views, what communication with them ought to look like, and if persuasion is an option. (Does their racism, sexism, or political bias run deep, or is it posturing or a passing phase? Should you try to avoid topics like race, gender, and politics around them? Can you convince them to think differently? Do you have to alter or sever your existing relationship with them?)

I can't emphasize this enough: treating sexist, racist, and politically biased speech as rich points and as windows on cultural difference does *not* mean endorsing, or even tolerating, such speech. A cultural approach to such speech means giving the other a chance before disengaging with them, treating them as part of a problem, or giving up on conversing with them about race, gender, or politics.

I suspect that by now you have picked up on an important benefit of following the lead of cultural pragmatics: as you make a (significant!) effort to understand someone else's politics, you end up clarifying your own. In particular, you will walk away with a better understanding of your own view of life in a diverse society. Such understanding can take the form of answers to the following questions:

- What are your views about diversity in society?

- What do you think counts as sexist, racist, or biased speech?

- How does such speech shape social relations in your community, city, region, or country?

- What other interpretations of these types of speech are possible? How do you think those who hold those interpretations damage society?

- How do you think those who endorse those interpretations might disagree with you? How might they see you damaging society?

- (How) do you think those who disagree with you about these interpretations could be convinced to think like you? What would you need to hear to be persuaded to think otherwise?

In this chapter, we will review three case studies to illustrate what treating sexist, racist, and politically biased speech as rich points might look like. These case studies model the type of cultural inquiry that generates information you can rely on when you feel you have to respond to sexist, racist, or politically biased speech with persuasion. First, we will look at a particular type of expression in the Spanish-speaking world (Bailey, 2017) that has a sexist overtone because it discriminates against women in public. Then I will introduce you to a classic study of a type of expression in the U.S. designed at once to avoid charges of racial prejudice and to preserve the racial status quo (Bonilla-Silva & Forman, 2000). Finally, we will look at a study that seeks to make sense of political differences between conservatives and liberals in the U.S. as cultural differences (Hochschild, 2016). After a description of each form of talk, I will outline the interpretation of each from the perspective of one "faith" (which I *personally* share) and then summarize cultural information that can aid someone of that "faith" in their persuasive efforts.

Before we get to the case studies, I would like to temper your expectations. Remember: cultural pragmatics will not tell you what to do. It will not tell you how to convince others to see the world—including bias and discrimination—from your

A Practical Question

"This sounds good in theory, but does it work in real life?"

It does. Rhetoric (Burke, 1945), linguistics (Lakoff, 2004), and social psychology (Feinberg & Willer, 2015) have shown that persuasion works better if one acknowledges the moral values of the person they are trying to persuade and uses those values to frame persuasive arguments.

point of view. Human interaction is too complex and too deeply rooted in context for generic advice to be genuinely useful. Also, some prejudiced or biased individuals will be resistant to persuasion because their identities are too tightly wrapped up in their positions. For folks like that, opposing or contesting your views becomes a resource for performing their identities (Boromisza-Habashi, 2010). However, in cases where there is even a slim chance of persuasion, careful description of sexist communication practices and the context in which they occur can offer you resources you can factor into your communication strategies.

CASE STUDY #1: THE *PIROPO*

The practice of *piropos* is widespread in the Spanish-speaking world, including Spain, Cuba, Mexico, Venezuela, Peru, Costa Rica, and Argentina, and similar practices have been documented around the Mediterranean, particularly Italy (Bailey, 2017). The original meaning of the word *piropo* is "red garment" or "ruby." Today, *piropos* encompass a wide range of unsolicited flirtatious or sexual comments men direct toward passing females in public. The relationship between the term's original and contemporary meaning is unclear. Some expressions resemble American *pickup lines*, others sound more like *catcalls*, and others sound like *street harassment*, pure and simple.

- *¡Qué ojos!* ("What eyes!")

- *¡Tus ojos me encandilan!* ("Your eyes dazzle [blind] me!")

- *Por vos cruzaría la Antártida en alpargatas.* ("For you, I would walk across Antarctica in espadrilles.")

- *¿De qué estrella te caiste?* ("What star did you fall from?")

- *¡Qué curvas y yo sin frenos!* ("What curves, and me without breaks!")

- *¡Si fueras mango, te chuparia hasta la pepa!* ("If you were a mango, I would suck you all the way to the pit!")

The Interpretation of *Piropos* as Sexist Speech

From an American feminist perspective (which also happens to be my perspective), all of these forms of *piropos* appear as socially and morally unacceptable harassment. After all, women's near universal reaction to this and other types of unsolicited public comments by men is fear (Kissling, 1991). The effects of *piropos* radiate beyond particular situations, sustain women's fear for their own safety in public places, and feed the patriarchal expectation that the woman's primary place is in the private sphere of the home and that she is therefore a legitimate target for engagement, pursuit, and harassment for men in public regardless of her personal preferences and desires. Unfortunately, free speech laws inadvertently give men the license to harass women in public (Nielsen, 2004).

Cultural Insights About a Competing "Faith"

Suppose that you, as someone who shares the above interpretation of *piropos,* find yourself in a situation where you decide you have to explain your position on *piropos* in a persuasive manner. Say you want to hold an uncle accountable for his tendency for giving *piropos*, you want to explain to a male coworker from a Spanish-speaking country why *piropos* are morally wrong, or you want to explain to a friend why you think *piropos* are a means of oppressing women. Consider some important cultural "leads" in Bailey's study:

> ### A Practical Question
>
> "Do you want me to start persuading men who harass me in the street to stop?"
>
> No. For one thing, I want you to be safe. Also, *piropos* are chance encounters with men you are not likely to see again. This chapter focuses on the possibility of persuading people with whom you have a sustained (professional, personal, family, etc.) relationship—people with whom you are interdependent.

1. **Men's beliefs about *piropos*.** There are three important insights we gain from Bailey's study about men's typical beliefs about *piropos*. First, "[m]en and women regularly disagree on whether *piropos* are a verbal gift to women or a form of harassment, with men tending to see a wide range of them as flattery that they claim women enjoy, and women tending to see some of them as flattering and desirable and many as offensive and harassing" (p. 199). Men tend to believe that *piropos* are not only harmless but flattering to women. Second, men are unaware that women tend to interpret *piropos* as a reminder of their subordinate social position in their respective societies. Third, *piropos* are an important resource for men to display their heterosexual masculinity in public. The audience for such displays includes women who are targets of *piropos* and other men who overhear them. As a result, you can't accept a *piropeador* ("someone who gives *piropos*") or someone who finds the practice acceptable to easily accept arguments that *piropos* are morally wrong.

2. **Cultural norms of conduct in public places.** In Western countries such as the U.S., we tend to follow the norm the sociologist Erving Goffman (1966) called **civil inattention.** This norms prompts us to respect strangers' **negative face** wants in public—that is, their desire for autonomy. In plain English, we want others to leave us alone in public places, unless of course they have a legitimate reason to bother us (e.g., asking for directions, warning us that we've dropped something,

etc.). This cultural norm is not as widely observed in Spanish-speaking countries. Rather, there is an expectation that strangers will respect one's **positive face** wants and try to engage. As a result, don't accept people who support *piropos* to respond positively to the "everyone wants to be left alone in the street" argument.

3. **Changing cultural gender norms.** In a number of countries where *piropos* are used, they are becoming less and less acceptable. Younger generations of women openly challenge the gender hierarchy that allows men to claim that *piropos* are a form of flattery. In recent years, there have been efforts in Peru, Chile, Panama, and Mexico to create legal sanctions against sexual harassment in the street. This is important for two reasons. First, as you express concern for women who are targets of *piropos,* keep in mind that women are fighting back. Second, don't accept the argument that *piropos* are morally acceptable because they are "cultural." Not only are they morally objectionable from a Western perspective, an increasing number of women from the same "culture" are finding it unacceptable.

CASE STUDY #2: CONTRADICTORY TALK ABOUT RACE RELATIONS

For their classic study of racial attitudes among White undergraduate students in the United States, sociologists Eduardo Bonilla-Silva and Tyrone A. Forman (2000) conducted in-depth interviews with 41 students at a Southern university, a Western university, and a Midwestern university. To avoid interviewer bias, the authors hired five White students to conduct the interviews and tried to match the genders of the interviewers and interviewees. They then conducted a detailed discourse analysis of students' talk to find out how they made sense of race relations between Blacks and Whites.

Bonilla-Silva and Forman noticed two interesting patterns in students' responses. First, all students carefully avoided the type of language we think of as classic (or Jim Crow) racism—namely, direct statements about, or descriptions of, Black racial inferiority or White supremacy. Second, the vast majority of students struggled to express consistent views on such issues as interracial marriage or affirmative action. When asked about interracial dating, one of the students said this:

> I mean ... I would say that I really don't have much of a problem with it but when you, 'ya know, if I were to ask if I had a daughter or something like that, or even one of my sisters, um ... were to going to get married to a minority or a Black, I ... I would probably ... it would probably bother me a little bit just because of what you said. ... Like the children and how it would ... might do to our family as it is. Um ... so I mean, just being honest, I guess that's the way I feel about that. ... I just don't think it would be a healthy thing for my family. I really can't talk about other people. (p. 61)

There seems to be a contradiction here between "not having much of a problem" with interracial marriage in general but having a problem with a family member bringing "a minority or a Black" into the student's family. Another student spoke about affirmative action in this way:

> ... I don't know what I think about this. I mean, yeah, I think affirmative action programs are ... needed. But ... I don't know. Because, I mean, I'm gonna be going out for a job next year, and I'll be honest, I'd be upset if I'm just as qualified as someone else. And individually, I'd be upset if a company takes, you know, like an African American over me just because he is an African American. I think that would—'ya know? I wouldn't.

Again, the speaker contradicts the general statement that "affirmative action programs are ... needed" and his description of how he would feel if an African American candidate with the same qualifications were to be hired instead of him as a result of an affirmative action program.

The Interpretation of Contradictory Race Talk as Colorblind Racism

From a politically progressive perspective, which Bonilla-Silva, Forman, and I personally share, this type of contradictory talk appears as color-blind racism. This talk is racist in the sense that it seeks to preserve the racial status quo in the United States—namely, the social and economic dominance of the already dominant racial group (Whites). It is also color-blind in the sense that it seeks to avoid overt racist statements about racial inferiority or superiority. The collective effect of color-blind racist talk is that it challenges or undermines efforts to achieve racial equity by calling into question the legitimacy of concrete practical measures designed to achieve inclusion.

Cultural Insights About a Competing "Faith"

If you share this interpretation of contradictory talk about race relations in the United States (which I'm not taking for granted!), you will most likely run up against what Bonilla-Silva and Forman call a *color-blind ideology* as you try to convince White coworkers, friends, and family of the value of concrete measures to achieve inclusion (such as providing additional training, funding, and employment opportunities for persons of color). Speakers express color-blind ideology in the form of six broad types of argument:

1. Promote abstract notions of liberalism (such as "race should not be a factor when judging people") instead of concrete, context-bound notions of liberalism or the distribution of social goods ("We should do X to address racial inequality").

2. Provide a cultural explanation for inequality ("Blacks weren't raised with the right work ethic") instead of systemic explanations ("Blacks have been left behind by the system").

3. Avoid racial references in talk about racial matters, as opposed to naming racial matters (such as affirmative action, school busing, or interracial dating).

4. Explain racial issues (such as segregation or limited interracial marriages) as the "natural" outcome of "natural" processes, as opposed to discrimination.

5. Describe racial discrimination as limited, rare, and declining in significance, as opposed to a feature of society.

6. Invoke a "live and let live" attitude toward racial inequality ("Kids should be exposed to all kinds of cultures, but it cannot be imposed on them through busing") instead of supporting particular special programs to address racial inequality.

If and when you try to persuade speakers who talk like this about the value of equality, racial integration, and affirmative action, you will have to contend with some basic, deeply felt tenets of their "faith": "Overt racism is immoral, but so is interference with people's personal choices and merit-based personal success. In personal relationships, freedom of personal choice takes precedence over a concern with social integration. If someone personally chooses harmonious (and racially homogenous) family life over welcoming a Black person into the family, that's their choice. In the job market and the workplace, 'equality' and 'equal opportunity' mean that no one gets unfair advantage over others. You accept the hand you were dealt, and you do your best to succeed. Affirmative action is unfair because it interferes with the existing system of rewards for merit and personal effort."

A Practical Question

"What exactly am I supposed to do with this information?"

The simple gesture of acknowledging your conversational partner may hold these beliefs goes a long way toward showing them you aren't trying to "get them" or prove them wrong but that you are trying to persuade them to accept your position.

CASE STUDY #3: CRITICIZING ENVIRONMENTALISM AS LIBERAL BIAS

The cultural sociologist Arlie Hochschild (2016) traveled to Louisiana to unravel a mystery: local working- and middle-class folks were well aware of the direct detrimental effects of the chemical and oil industries on their health and environment, yet they supported these industries and the financial incentives their state extended to them. She was particularly interested in how the Tea Party's—and, later, presidential candidate Donald Trump's—pro-industry message resonated emotionally with voters. She organized focus groups, conducted in-depth interviews with supporters of the Tea Party, environmental activists, scientists, and bureaucrats, and directly observed the lives of some Tea Party supporters who were gracious enough to invite her to their homes, churches, and events. She witnessed them battle cancer, mourn the loss of the bayous where they spent their childhood years, and enthusiastically support the governor of Louisiana's decision to support private companies over public services.

Many Tea Party supporters Hochschild talked to were deeply concerned about what they saw as unfair environmental regulation championed by liberals, bureaucrats, and Obama-era Washington. For them, the Clean Air Act, the Clean Water Act, and the Endangered Species Act became symbols of liberal attempts to undermine investment in the state and take away their livelihoods. How can endangered species such as the brown pelican, the Louisiana state bird, have more rights than hardworking people? A key reason why Tea Party politicians succeeded in Louisiana, Hochschild argues, is because they understood these frustrations.

The Interpretation of Criticism of Environmentalism as Right-Wing Bias

Hochschild and I share a common political perspective on the natural environment: we regard it as a public good. A clean environment is a critical condition of public health, and health is best regarded as a human right. From this perspective, the knowing and willful pollution of the environment appears as a direct attack on the interests and rights of the public. While it is clear that petrochemical companies generate jobs (although, as Hochschild documents, few of those jobs go to the people who suffer the long-term effects of industrial pollution), their environmentally harmful activities endanger the environment as a public good, encroach on low- and middle-income individuals' right to healthy lives, and destroy the prospect of a healthy, thriving society. This view is part of what Hochschild calls "the liberal deep story" (p. 236), a narrative version of liberal "faith."

Cultural Insights About a Competing "Faith"

In American political life, as we learn from Hochschild, the liberal deep story is in competition with a right-wing deep story in which the environment plays a different role. While the central metaphor of the liberal deep story is the "public square," the right-wing story is organized around the metaphor of "waiting in line." In this cultural story, White, Christian, predominantly male folks with various degrees of education are standing in line for the American Dream, which is just over the top of a hill. One moves forward in line by being patient, working hard, supporting one's family, and suffering life's hardships without complaint. Life is hard, but capitalism leads those who wait and do their best to live by Christian values to prosperity. However, there are also those who cut the line. These include (some) women, minorities, immigrants, refugees, and public sector workers—and yes, the brown pelican—who are getting preferential treatment from the federal government over those standing in line. This feels deeply unfair and morally wrong to those in line who see themselves as having made innumerable sacrifices to get where they are. ("Pollution is the sacrifice we make for capitalism," said one of Hochschild's interviewees.) In this story, the environment is a resource to be used to advance human prosperity, and environmental protection rules rob enterprising individuals and businesses of this precious resource. This is a powerful American story, some versions of which have gone global. Any persuasive efforts directed at those who live by this story will have to take it seriously.

A Practical Question

"Will persuasion based on acknowledging the other's cultural and/or moral beliefs always work?"

No, it won't always work. But sometimes it will. See the "Barriers to Coordinated Interaction" section to think about the limits on the potential of persuasion.

To summarize, by thinking through competing "faiths," including yours, you achieve greater political self-awareness, which can put you on a path toward learning about the deep social, cultural, and historical roots of different attitudes toward diversity. Even further, you may discover that you—yes, you!—have a role to play in the creation of social conditions among which members of your diverse society can live safe, fulfilling lives.

BARRIERS TO COORDINATED INTERACTION

1. **Lacking a clear practical goal.** In this chapter, I am encouraging you to explore the possibility of treating expression you interpret as sexist, racist, or politically biased as cultural expression. The goal of such an exercise is to engage speakers who produce such expression for practical purposes—that is, for the purpose of getting something from them (their agreement, compliance, support, vote, silence, etc.). Such practical purposes can vary considerably, from convincing your coworkers who refuse to recycle to do so to persuading a family member to treat your significant other, who is of a different race, with kindness. Before you make such attempts, however, you have to be very clear on what that "something" is; otherwise, you will run the risk of getting bogged down in endless debate instead of moving toward your goal.

2. **Lacking a clear understanding of relevant positions on a social issue.** Another area where you need clarity is where you stand and where your conversational partner stands. What is your view of a diverse society? What are your principles and convictions? What are theirs? Do your "faiths" overlap in some ways? (If

they do, you may have found a foothold for persuasion!) Don't underestimate the complexity of your own position or theirs, and also don't underestimate the emotional investment you and they have in your views. Also, as you try to reconstruct their worldview, make sure your disagreement is about deeply felt, highly politicized issues and not something else (e.g., competition for a promotion, a disagreement over finances, personal conflict, etc.).

3. **Pursuing coordinated interaction beyond reasonable limits.** As you attempt to engage with speakers of a different "faith," always remain open to two possibilities: (1) the engagement might force you to morally compromise your "faith," and (2) your conversational partner may not be genuinely invested in aligning their speech and/or actions with yours—in other words, they may not be interested in coordinated interaction. In both of these cases, disengagement remains an option.

REFLECTION QUESTIONS

1. Pluralists are often charged with being relativists in disguise. On what grounds might someone argue this? What are some counterarguments?

2. Review my explication of the "faiths" from the perspective through which *piropos* seem sexist, color-blind speech seems racist, and right-wing views on the environment seem politically biased. Do you agree with my position? If not, what's your position?

3. To what extent do you think Bailey's cultural insight about *piropos* applies to pick-up lines, catcalls, and street harassment in the United States?

4. Do you think student attitudes toward race have changed since the late 1990s, when Bonilla-Silva and Forman conducted their interviews? If so, how? If not, why not?

5. Can you think of a public figure in the United States or elsewhere who has successfully appealed to members of an opposing political "faith" on environmental issues? What did they say?

"Why Aren't They Saying Anything?"

The Amount of Talk and Silence

RAY: This summer, I worked as a project engineer intern at a worksite that I helped manage. Our company had four laborers that were consistently on-site: two Mexican immigrants, a high school graduate from Colorado Springs, and a White carpenter in his mid-40s. During our lunch breaks, I noticed that the two Mexican workers, Alan and Carlos, talked and joked around a lot. Meanwhile, Kevin, the carpenter, and I rarely spoke much. This was not merely the norm on the site that I worked this summer. Following my sophomore year, I worked construction at the airport and often noticed the Latino workers joking around together and creating a lively atmosphere. Once again, the American, and predominantly White, workers on-site typically kept to themselves. It seemed that the Latino workers thrived on their exhaustion, embracing the "misery loves company" mentality, whereas the White workers seemed to deal with the doldrums of the workday in their own introverted manner.

PARIS: I was working as a snowboard instructor at my local mountain, Campgaw, in New Jersey. Once a week, I instructed a group of kids from the local Hasidic synagogue. The parents never

In this chapter, you will learn:

- about various ways in which choices regarding how much one speaks can become meaningful

- that silence is more than "not saying anything"

- to distinguish cultural and noncultural meanings of silence

acknowledged me when they dropped off or picked up their kids from the lesson, even when I tried to tell them about their child's progress. It was almost as if I was invisible. The kids did not listen to me either. Having babysat since I was 13, this was different than the typical kid not listening to you, just because they are kids. I was blatantly ignored. It got to a point where their safety was at risk. They did not listen to the rules of the mountain and would take off when my back was turned. Kids and adults would cut to the front of the lift lines and cut people off while going down the mountain. I saw many accidents where they would run into someone from behind because they completely disrespected mountain etiquette: the person downslope always has the right of way. As an instructor at Campgaw, when I would see them cut in line, I would tell them they had to go to the back. I was often ignored. When I was able to stop them, I had to report it, and if they had caused problems before, they usually got their pass taken away. Sometimes they wouldn't say much to me, especially the women and children, but the men would usually raise their voice at me, claiming that they did not do anything wrong and that I was being ridiculous. These experiences made me feel confused because I had never felt so disrespected. I also felt confused when the men would tell me that I was wrong, when I knew what they were doing was wrong and frankly rude and inconsiderate.

These accounts of rich points illustrate the importance of the amount of talk and silence in encounters with cultural difference. Ray highlights cultural groups' preferences regarding the amount of talk in a particular context (here, men taking breaks from physically demanding work). As Paris expresses her frustration with a group she approaches as culturally different, she calls our attention to how social groups may regard silence as the preferred mode of communicative contact between members of particular social categories (here, contact in public places between women and children on the one hand, and female strangers on the other).

How much talk is too much, or too little, from a cultural perspective? What are the various types of silence, and do they have cultural meanings? The answer to these questions is, as always: it depends on the social group you are approaching as culturally different from you and your group. This chapter will help you learn to recognize some of the ways in which the amount, or lack, of talk matters in intercultural encounters.

THE AMOUNT OF TALK

Cultural preferences regarding the amount of talk speakers produce can vary across **speech communities**. Let's take a look at such variation at two different scales: the scale of particular social situations and the scale of entire speech communities.

Scale 1: Particular Social Situations

While doing ethnographic fieldwork among the Western Apache in Arizona, the anthropologist Keith Basso (1979) noticed they had a particular brand of humor dedicated to making fun of "the Whiteman." They particularly enjoyed roasting Whites for the way they talked. Basso wrote down an Apache cowboy's spontaneous impersonation of a White man using letters of the alphabet to identify participants. On a hot, clear evening, the cowboy (J), his wife (K), and their kids have just finished dinner when there is a knock on the door. The couple stop their conversation in Apache. J opens the door and finds his clan brother (L) standing outside. He **code-switches** to English to address the guest:

EXCERPT 10.1. (from Basso, 1979, pp.46–47)

J   Hello, my friend! How you doing? How you feeling, L? You feeling good?

[J now turns in the direction of K and addresses her.]

J   Look who's here, everybody! Look who just come in. Sure, it's my Indian friend, L. Pretty good, all right!

[J slaps L on the shoulder and, looking him directly in the eyes, seizes his hand and pumps it wildly up and down.]

J   Come right in, my friend! Don't stay outside in the rain. Better you come in right now.

[J now drapes his arm around L's shoulder and moves him in the direction of a chair.]

J   Sit down! Sit right down! Take you loads off your ass. You hungry? You want some beer? Maybe you want some wine? You want crackers? Bread? You want some sandwich? How 'bout it? You hungry? I don't know. Maybe you get sick. Maybe you don't eat again long time.

[K has stopped washing dishes and is looking on with amusement. L has seated himself and has a look of bemused resignation on his face.]

J   You sure looking good to me, L. You looking pretty fat! Pretty good all right! You got new boots? Where you buy them? Sure pretty good boots! I glad ...

[At this point, J breaks into laughter. K joins in. L shakes his head and smiles. The joke is over.]

J purposely violates Apache cultural expectations that apply to this type of situation—an unannounced visit by a member of one's clan—in every possible way (e.g., calling L a "friend," not waiting for him to state the purpose of his visit, talking loudly, making direct eye contact and comments about his appearance, etc.), including talking way too much. To an Apache who finds this type of excessive talk annoying or downright inappropriate, J's parody is hilarious.

Other social groups have particular expectations regarding the appropriate amount of talk in particular contexts. When I moved to the United States as an adult, one of the first things I noticed is how much White suburban parents talked to their kids when they were acting out. Mothers and fathers used rich and varied combinations of reasoning, cajoling, words of wisdom, and threats, changed the tone of their speech from pleading to serious to agitated and back again, and avoided physical contact (e.g., picking up their kids throwing a tantrum) to the very end. Naively, I assumed this was how all American parents talked to their kids until I read the communication scholar Gerry Philipsen's (1975) work on a working-class neighborhood in Chicago in the 1970s. In that social environment, only mothers used the strategy of talking to misbehaving kids. Expectations toward fathers were quite different. In this community, the appropriate amount of speech varied across social contexts. In all-male relationships participants saw as symmetrical—that is, where they saw one another as equals—men were expected to talk a lot; in asymmetrical relationships, they were expected to talk a little; and in relationships where they asserted power, they were not expected to talk at all. "To speak 'like a man' in Teamsterville," Philipsen explains, "required knowing when and under what circumstances to speak at all" (p. 20). From the Teamsterville perspective, a child is not an adult male's equal. A child talking back to an adult male is laying claim to a symmetrical relationship, which is unacceptable and merits physical instead of verbal disciplining. Men who did not conform to this expectation risked having their "male" identity questioned.

This case is a useful reminder that, across different speech communities, the **functional load** of speech—that is, the social meaning of the very *choice* to speak instead of staying silent—can vary. A direct result of such patterned variation is that the same social situation may be considered a **speech situation** in some speech communities, whereas in others it will be regarded as a social situation that doesn't require any, or only minimal, verbal expression.

Of course, in socioculturally diverse places like cities, you will notice that there can be a fair amount of disagreement about how much speech needs to occur in specific social contexts. Just think about all the discussion and controversy surrounding how much, if at all, drivers working for rideshare companies like Uber and Lyft should talk to their passengers and Uber's 2019 decision to offer "Quiet Rides" to their customers willing to pay a premium. (Recently, a fellow Uber rider demonstrated to me a more cost-effective way of avoiding talking to the driver: immediately after getting into the car and giving the driver and me a friendly greeting, she put on a pair of large over-ear headphones.)

Scale 2: Speech Communities

Let's "zoom out," so to speak, to a scale of observation where we can compare entire speech communities' cultural expectations regarding the appropriate amount of talk.

Back in the 1960s, the British sociologist Basil Bernstein (1964) noticed that working-class and middle-class students used different principles for planning, organizing, and regulating their communication. He called these principles codes, attributing a meaning to the term that slightly differs from the way "**code**" is defined in concepts such as **code-switching** and **code-mixing**. Working-class students seemed to make use of a **restricted code** that shifted emphasis from verbal expression toward nonverbal communication and the **indexing** of shared, taken-for-granted knowledge. The restricted code allowed these students to interact meaningfully using relatively few words across a wide variety of situations. Middle-class students also made use of the restricted code, but they also had another code at their disposal, which Bernstein called the **elaborated code**. This code prompted students to use relatively more words (more complex vocabulary and grammar) to produce speech that could be understood without sharing relevant background information with the speaker or witnessing their nonverbal cues. The elaborated code directed students to talk to others as persons with experiences and backgrounds different from their own; the restricted code motivated students to speak as if their conversation partners shared their experiences and backgrounds. Working-class students, Bernstein noted, only had access to the restricted code.

The anthropologist E. T. Hall, who is widely credited as the founder of the intercultural communication discipline, was intrigued by Bernstein's distinction between these two types of codes because it helped him make sense of the fact that some speech communities tended to use relatively fewer words to communicate, while others seemed more talkative. Perhaps, Hall reasoned in his influential book *Beyond Culture* (1976), speakers in more wordy cultures talk more not because they have more to say or because they are better speakers with more elaborate linguistic resources but because they can take less for granted about their conversational partners. Conversely, cultures that tend toward the silent end of the spectrum have to say less because they have more shared knowledge, history, and understanding of the situation they are in. This line of thought led Hall to distinguish **high-context cultures,** where speakers could lean heavily on shared frames of reference and say a lot with very few words, from **low-context cultures,** in which speakers had less shared knowledge to draw on and therefore needed to rely more on spoken words.

A Practical Question

"How does the distinction between restricted and elaborated codes apply to my life?"

To better understand the distinction between restricted and elaborated codes, think about chatting with a close friend or significant other with whom you can communicate almost without words, as opposed to explaining your credentials to an HR representative in the course of a formal job interview. Matching these codes to particular contexts is an important element of cultural competence.

Hall's distinction inspired Claire B. Halverson, a scholar who specializes in organizational behavior and training, to ask the question: Can differences between high- and low-context cultures cause communication problems in multicultural teams in organizations such as corporations, schools, and factories? Her answer, as I'm sure you have guessed, was "yes." Team members from high- and low-context cultures, for example, had different—and sometimes conflicting—expectations about appropriate forms of communication. These different expectations, in turn, could give rise to misunderstanding, **miscommunication**, prolonged conflict, and diminished team effectiveness. She identified five differences that pertained directly to social interaction:

TABLE 10.1. Cross-cultural expectations about social interaction

Characteristics of high-context cultures	Characteristics of low-context cultures
High use of nonverbal elements; voice tone, facial expression, gestures, eye movement carry significant parts of the conversation.	Low use of nonverbal elements. Message is carried more by words than by nonverbal means.
Verbal message is implicit; context (situation, people, nonverbal elements) is more important than words.	Verbal message is explicit. Context is less important than words.
Verbal message is indirect; one talks around the point and embellishes it.	Verbal message is direct; one spells things out exactly.
Communication is seen as art form—a way of engaging someone.	Communication is seen as a way of exchanging information, ideas, and opinions.
Disagreement is personalized. One is sensitive to conflict expressed in another's nonverbal communication. Conflict either must be solved before work can progress or must be avoided because it is personally threatening.	Disagreement is depersonalized. One withdraws from conflict with another and gets on with the task. Focus is on rational solutions, not personal ones. One can be explicit about another's bothersome behavior.

Halverson & Tirmizi, 2008, p. 32

Halverson developed a 20-item questionnaire called the Cultural-Context Inventory for determining whether one's cultural preferences are closer to the high- or low-context end of the spectrum. Respondents are invited to agree or disagree with statements such as "When communicating, I tend to use a lot of facial expressions, hand gestures, and body movements rather than relying mostly on words," "When communicating, I tend to spell things out quickly and directly rather than talk around and add to the point," and "In an interpersonal disagreement, I tend to be more emotional than logical and rational." The trouble with these questions is that the impressions we have about our own communication habits are usually quite different from how we actually interact with others. This type of information can, however, be a useful conversation starter between members of social groups who recognize their expectations about the appropriate amount of talk are not culturally universal.

Communication research can also provide us with potentially useful information about cultural groups' relative positions along the spectrum between high- and low-context cultures. This research has shown, for example, that recent immigrants to the United States from Latin American countries are located further from the low-context end of the spectrum than typical Anglo-American speakers (Albert & Ha, 2004).

From the perspective of the approach this book represents (cultural pragmatics), distinctions between elaborated and restricted codes and high- and low-context cultures are useful because they point you, the **intercultural practitioner**, to a set of communication patterns and practices you can observe and a set of topics you can explore with cultural others. Following a **rich point**, as you try to make sense of why your conversational partner talked more or less than you had expected, you can begin seeking answers to questions like these:

A Practical Question

"Why are you assuming that I'm not aware of my own communication habits?"

Let me invite you to do an experiment. Try recording a conversation with a friend, and then transcribe your conversation verbatim, noting down every little pause, "uh," "um," and "like." I am sure you will learn new things about your communication habits.

- In what types of situations does this person talk less/more than I expected?

- If they talk less than expected, what other types of communication resources do they rely on? Do they use nonverbal means? Do they invoke your shared interpersonal history or other elements of the context in which you are interacting?

- If they talk more than expected, do they seem to want to discuss topics or information that you see as taken for granted? Why may they not be taking that information for granted? What does this say about their view of you (as an individual or as a member of a particular social category such as "female" or "coworker") and your relationship?

- Does the amount of talk they use with you differ from the amount of talk they engage in with others? What does this say about their view of your relationship?

THE MEANINGS OF SILENCE

In intercultural encounters, silence can be the source of interactional trouble. For example, speakers from the United States are often confused by their Japanese conversational partners' silent pauses. In the context of business meetings, such silences make U.S. speakers frustrated and irritated and prompt them to fill the silence with rephrased versions of their questions (Fujio, 2004). From Japanese participants' perspective, such incessant talk robs them of the opportunity to think before they answer. In a study of telecollaboration between Japanese and American students, when a Japanese speaker tried to use silence to signal they were having trouble formulating a response and they needed their U.S. counterpart to engage in some helpful guesswork, the U.S. speaker became anxious and started overexplaining their previous point (Akiyama, 2017). In the university classroom, U.S. teachers consistently misinterpreted the silence of Chinese students in four ways:

> [c]ross-cultural misunderstandings occur when Chinese students' silent behaviors in class as a way to show respect to the teacher or as a concern over wasting other students' time is thought of as a lack of respect or lack of engagement in the class; when Chinese students' sense of politeness in class by avoiding expressing conflicting ideas and opinions in order to maintain group cohesion and harmony is interpreted as a lack of independent thinking; when Chinese students' face-saving strategies in keeping silent to avoid making mistakes in speaking or to be modest are thought of as indications of the lack of communicative competence; and when Chinese students' willingness to speak up in class is not directly transferred to action because of their anxiety in speaking in a second language in front of L1 [native] speakers" (Liu, 2002, p. 52).

As you can tell from these examples, silence in conversation is not simply a lack of speech. If you look at silences—ranging from split-second pauses to minutes-long periods of quiet—in actual social interaction, you will soon realize that, from the perspective of how much communication gets done, the distinction between speech and its absence seems somewhat arbitrary (Boromisza-Habashi & Martínez-Guillem, 2012). Because it is so laden with communicative meaning, silence can be a challenge for those participants in intercultural encounters who don't have a shared sense of what kind of communication gets done when talk ceases. In order to accomplish coordinated interaction, speakers from different speech communities need to discover not only the various meanings of silence but also their own deeply ingrained expectations about silence in particular contexts. "[S]ilence can be seen as positive or negative by members of any culture, as it is measured against what is expected in that context" (Tannen, 1985, p. 98).

Sometimes the meaning of silence is cultural in the sense that silence is used differently in different groups of speakers. Speakers do things with silence: they enact politeness, they manage identities and social relations, they ask for help, and so on, and they do so in ways they believe are appropriate and effective, perhaps even creative. In other cases, speakers' silences are not (purely) cultural: they struggle to put together a sentence in a second, third, or fourth language, they are taking their time to figure out exactly what they want to say, they are out of breath, and so on. In what follows, we will look at these two categories of silence.

A Practical Question

"Is there a quick way to tell if a cultural other's confusing silences are culturally meaningful?"

Unfortunately, there isn't. Following the tenets of cultural pragmatics, you can assume that they are and use that assumption as a hypothesis to be tested through further observation, interviewing, or reading.

Culturally Meaningful Silence

In this section, I will use scholarship on silence in two cultural groups, Native Americans and Finns, to give you an idea of the wide range of cultural meanings silence can have and to encourage you to investigate the ways in which silence can matter to cultural others in your own life. In an early study of culturally meaningful Native American (Apache) silences, Keith Basso (1972) observed that the Apache prefer to remain silent in six types of situations:

1. *Meeting strangers.* Meeting people who aren't one's kin for the first time is regarded as a situation marked by social distance. In that context, there is no need for formal introductions, and the stranger will speak as they see fit. Strangers who talk immediately and much are regarded with suspicion.

2. *Courting.* At the beginning of their relationship, romantic partners are considered strangers to one another. The longer a couple is together, the more they will talk.

3. *Children coming home from White boarding schools.* Parents first refrain from talking to their kids, sometimes for days. Rather, they watch them for some time to see how they have changed and whether they have adopted Whites' habits.

4. *Getting cussed out.* People who cuss out someone who insulted them are considered dangerously irrational. Talking can lead to getting hurt.

5. *Being with people who are in mourning.* There can be three reasons for not talking to those in mourning: (1) talking requires too much physical effort from them; (2) talk is unnecessary, we all know what happened, and there is no need to

elaborate it and cause more pain; and (3) mourning changes people, so it's best to wait and see who they turn into.

6. *Being with someone for whom they sing (during curing ceremonies).* Only the presiding medicine man and his aides will speak during the ceremony because the "power" of the medicine man entering the patient renders the patient "holy" and thus strange.

Although at first these situations seem quite different, there is an important thread that connects all six: ambiguity and unpredictability. The Western Apache preferred to stay silent in contexts where they weren't sure what to expect from another person.

The Western Apache preference for silence when communicating with strangers became the source of cultural miscommunication when the University of Arizona and a group of European research institutes proposed building an observatory on top of Mount Graham (Carbaugh & Wolf, 1999). Located 20 miles south of the border of the San Carlos Apache Indian Reservation, Mount Graham and the surrounding area were considered a sacred site by many in the local Apache tribe. However, when tribal members were asked at public meetings to make a case for why the mountain was sacred, they gave responses that predominantly White scientists described as "maddeningly vague." From the Apache perspective, silence was the appropriate response to the question, for two reasons. Many outsiders attended the public meetings, which meant speech counted as inappropriate conduct in that context. In addition, the Apache believed silence about sacred places expressed respect for those places and helped preserve their traditional forms of life. Unfortunately, the Apache's silence (or "vagueness") about Mount Graham prevented them from arguing against the observatory in public forums in a way the scientific community at the University of Arizona found persuasive. In the end, three telescope observatories were built 2 miles down the road from Mount Graham.

The cultural preference for silence across social contexts extends to other Native American tribes beyond the Western Apache. For example, the functional load of speech among the Blackfeet, who live in Northern Montana, is rather low as well. One particular context in which young members of the tribe tend to discover—or rediscover—this cultural preference is in the public speaking classroom (Carbaugh, 2005).

If you have ever taken a public speaking course in high school or college, I probably don't have to explain to you in great detail how stressful the experience can be. Students of any cultural background tend to fight personal battles with a combination of stage fright, anxiety, sleepless nights, and imposter syndrome in this course. (As someone who has taught the course at my university, I am familiar with these battles.) Taking a public speaking course is hard enough; now imagine taking it as someone who grew up with these ideas about public speaking:

- Public speaking is called for when one's community, or some of its members, need to be spoken for.

- Typically, the best person to speak for the community is a male elder of the tribe who has accumulated the expertise and wisdom of a lifetime and whom other elders have tutored to speak in public.

- Speaking in public is a risky activity: a speaker can mistakenly cultivate disagreement in the community and disrupt individuals' connectedness to the tribe. Such connectedness—which is best experienced in silence—is an important source of personal well-being.

Young Blackfeet students who learned to regard public speaking in this way in the process of primary **language socialization** have a devastating experience in the public speaking classroom, where, from their perspective, they are being called upon to step into a socially consequential role and speak like their community's fate depends on it. Some students, Carbaugh reported, freeze up entirely and refuse to speak in front of the class; others find creative workarounds. One Blackfeet student, for example, got up in front of the class, took out a pair of nunchucks, performed a 7-minute routine, and concluded his "speech" by pronouncing: "Like an eagle." In this way, he gave a public performance while keeping speaking to an absolute minimum, he displayed eloquence by using a figure of speech (a simile), and he claimed the right to do so by displaying unique expertise.

On the other side of the Atlantic, you will find another social group that prizes silence over speech, particularly in encounters with strangers. As a people who consider silence as their "natural way of being" and who prize terse, matter-of-fact talk (Carbaugh, Berry, & Nurmikari-Berry, 2006), Finns are not much for U.S.-style small talk. In the words of a Finnish speaker:

> Communication in Finland can be described in one sentence: if you've got nothing to say, shut up. If you, on the other hand, have something to say, say it straight, brutal but truthful, whatever it is. Don't try any slick small talk. Again, the Finnish culture shows not only its elegance but also its efficiency: wordless communication is, in fact, always the most truthful. (p. 215)

Small talk, from a Finnish perspective, requires one to say things when one has "nothing to say" and should therefore stay silent. How could you have something to say to a stranger you have just met and with whom you are quite unlikely to develop a long-term relationship? The invitation to engage in small talk, for many Finns, is not simply an annoying imposition on one's tranquility and personal space but also a violation of their sense of Finnishness ("We Finns don't do small talk"). It also goes against the grain of local **cultural rules** of conversation:

1. One should not state what is obvious.

2. If speaking, one should say something worthy of everyone's attention.

3. One should not invoke topics or themes that are contentious or conflictual (or more positively, one should keep present relations on harmonious ground).

4. One should be personally committed to or invested in what one says.

5. What you say properly—the unobvious, socially worthwhile, noncontentious, personally involving statements—forms a basis for subsequent interactions and social relations. (Carbaugh, 2005, p. 42)

U.S.-style small talk violates every rule above, with the exception of Rule 3. Small talk involves stating the obvious ("Man, it's hot today …"), saying things of little informational value ("I'm good, thanks!"), not having a lot of personal commitment to what one says ("We should have coffee sometime!"), and not expecting that an episode of small talk will lead to future exchanges or social relations. Nonetheless, as Finnish society is becoming more culturally diverse and Finns interact with speakers from the rest of the world, they are learning to relinquish the silence they would otherwise prefer. As the *Wall Street Journal* reported, some Finns have gone to the extent of taking lessons in small talk (MacDonald, 2019).

There are two important caveats you should keep in mind as you try to make sense of cultural others' unexpected silences. First, it is unlikely that you will encounter a cultural group whose cultural rationale for silence is entirely unique. For example, the communication scholar Charles Braithwaite (1990) showed that Western Apache silences in encounters with strangers can be found in other speech communities. He identified five speech communities in which "[s]ilence as a communicative action [was] associated with social situations in which the relationship of the focal participants is uncertain, unpredictable, or ambiguous" (p. 323). He also found that in 13 other speech communities, silence had a different communicative function: it was "associated with social situations in which there is a known and unequal distribution of power among focal participants" (p. 324). Second, even communities that value silence over speech demand speech in some situations. For example, when Whites make discriminatory statements against American Indians, they perceive the silence of other Whites not as an appropriate response to the situation but as complicity (Covarrubias, 2008).

Noncultural Meanings of Silence

Once you start building culture for another speaker whose silences led you to experience a rich point, it may be tempting to interpret all of their patterned silences as carrying some sort of cultural meaning. I would encourage you to remain open to the possibility that some of their silences are not rooted in a particular worldview.

Let's return to the example of Finns. Although the Finnish preference for silence is well known, some Finnish silences have noncultural explanations (Carbaugh, 2005). Some Finns may avoid engaging in small talk with U.S. speakers because they have stereotypical notions about how much U.S. speakers like to talk. Others may respond to an unfamiliar situation with silence. In workplace settings, Finns don't expect to talk to visitors or colleagues they see for the first time. Their expectation is that the visitor is there to explore the workplace first and will make themselves available for conversation on another occasion. Yet other Finnish speakers may not be entirely fluent in English and may need a few seconds to compose an intelligible response. Language fluency can be a challenge for other speakers as well. Speakers from Hong Kong whose native language is Cantonese but speak English at a relatively high level of proficiency struggle to participate in English-language business meetings where they are required to engage in spontaneous interaction or analysis, as opposed to giving preprepared reports (Du-Babcock, 1999). Unfortunately, English speakers often interpret the silence of these bilingual speakers as a lack of ideas or analytic ability.

> **CULTURAL PRAGMATICS SAYS**
>
> Our speech community membership shapes the way we speak, but it doesn't determine our speech. Noncultural factors (fatigue, nervousness, speech impediments, linguistic proficiency, etc.) may also have a role to play in how individuals communicate.

Sometimes speakers' silences in particular types of situations result from a combination of cultural and noncultural considerations. During class discussions, Japanese students in Australian classrooms (Nakane, 2008) and Turkish students in American classrooms (Tatar, 2005) were often silent in order to maintain their own **positive face**. Sometimes they found the use of this strategy necessary because they were not confident about their English language proficiency and were concerned about appearing incompetent. At other times, however, they chose to remain silent because of a cultural imperative not to openly disagree with their instructors, whom they considered authority figures, and to only speak when they had a thoughtful and carefully considered contribution to the discussion. Neither the Australian nor the U.S. students were following the same cultural imperatives, which ended up benefitting them in the context of the classroom. Instructors tended to consider them more engaged and having a greater ability to think critically than their Japanese and Turkish counterparts.

Finally, don't discount the possibility that the explanation for silences between you and a cultural other—especially those silences that stretch over days, months, or even years—is to be found neither in culture nor in practical matters like different levels of linguistic proficiency but in your interpersonal history: prolonged conflict, different interests, unrequited love, and so on (Muñoz, 2014).

BARRIERS TO COORDINATED INTERACTION

1. **Missing the meanings of variations in the amount of talk.** Most of us humans are quite sensitive to speakers who talk more or less than we expect. This means you can count on others to signal when you violate their expectations regarding the appropriate amount of talk. Stay alert to such signals in intercultural encounters, and when you see or hear them, try to determine whether they are clues to cultural actions or preferences. Do they think you talk too much or too little for someone in your social (gender, racial, age, class, national, etc.) category? Are you failing to perform membership in that category according to their expectations? Or if they talk more or less than you expected or talk to you more or less than they used to in the past, are they indirectly saying something about who they think you are or should be? The amount of talk and variations in its amount across speakers, contexts, and occasions can be important communication resources whose meaning may vary across speech communities.

2. **Missing the meanings of meaningful silences.** From a U.S. cultural perspective, it is easy to read silence in social interaction as a lack of coordinated interaction. Just as the number zero is not the equivalent of "nothing," silence is not a vacuum that should have been filled with words. Remember: speakers do things with silence; silence can count as meaningful communication in culturally specific ways. As a result, silence can be a functional element of coordinated interaction. If you try to fill it with talk at all costs you might miss something your conversational partner is trying to tell you. They may be asking you for help, **altercasting** you into a social identity (friend, stranger, authority figure, etc.), reprimanding you, telling you they don't have anything important to say at the moment and they don't want to waste your time by saying it, or that what they have to tell you is too important for words. Keep in mind, though, that not all meanings of silence are cultural—they may also be practical or interpersonal.

REFLECTION QUESTIONS

1. Find Halverson's Cultural-Context Inventory online (http://www.resilitator. com/images/pdf/CulturalContextInventory_ASRC.pdf), and fill it out. Are you learning useful information about your cultural background? If so, useful in what sense?

2. When was the last time you used silence to communicate something to a particular person? Were you able to get your message across? Try to recall, in as much detail as possible, what you did and what you were trying to accomplish.

3. Can you think of people around whom you are more likely to be silent than around others? Who are those people? Why do you feel compelled to be silent in their company?

4. How would you describe the value of public speaking? Who do you think should develop public speaking skills? Why?

5. Many people dislike the idea of small talk but keep engaging in it regardless. Why do you think this is? What do people accomplish socially with small talk?

11

"But Why Wouldn't They Smile at Me?"

Embodied Interaction

EMAN: This summer I had the opportunity to travel abroad to Europe. During my short visit to Warsaw, I experienced a rich point that made me feel discomfort as well as curiosity. In American culture, it is normal and almost expected to smile to people you don't know out in public. However, in Poland, they do not follow that American norm of smiling at someone they don't know. Instead of smiling, people from Poland stare at you. This is their way of smiling at a stranger. I first experienced this the first day I arrived in Warsaw and was walking around exploring the city. I was walking in the main square of the city and walked past a young woman around my age. We ended up making eye contact and instead of her smiling at me like an American would, she stared at me with a blank face.

KYLE: My rich point took place in Chiang Mai, Thailand. Chiang Mai is a northern region of Thailand, home to vast jungle forests filled with breathtaking ancient temples and a speech community and culture so different from my own that it nearly felt alien. I was hiking up an ancient temple, exploring one of the many holy sites located in the region. Upon reaching the summit of the

In this chapter, you will learn:

- various categories of embodied interaction

- about the relationship between speech and embodied interaction

- how embodied communication can facilitate or hinder intercultural interactions

temple, I met an employee of the temple, a boy, no older than me, dressed nearly identical to myself. I greeted him with the polite and traditional verbal greeting that I had practiced in preparation for the trip and offered a handshake, but he responded by silently smiling and gently bowing his head instead. Not knowing how to react, I quickly withdrew my hand and smiled and bowed instead, to which he nodded. While only one word was exchanged, it later became apparent to me that gestures played a much larger role in introductions, goodbyes, and thank-yous than I had known as various bows, smiles, and other motions became a common part of my travels.

EMBODIMENT vs. NONVERBAL COMMUNICATION

It is not difficult at all to find popular advice online about what sorts of familiar body movements one should avoid in particular countries of the world in order not to cause offense. Don't give people the thumbs up in the Middle East. Avoid the peace sign in the United Kingdom. The okay sign (making a circle with your thumb and index finger while extending your remaining three fingers) is a rude gesture in Venezuela, Turkey, and Brazil. The "come here" gesture performed with the index finger in the United States offends the Japanese.

All of these examples fall into the category of gestures called **emblems** or **quotable gestures** (Streeck & Knapp, 1992): members of **speech communities** in which they are used can easily replace them with words. In the U.S. context, for example, "Peace out!" "Great job!" "Okay!" and "Come here!" do more or less the same interactional work as these gestures themselves.

However, the range of embodied actions—communicative "doings" we perform with combinations of our various body parts, sometimes in the company of words, sometimes not—extends far beyond emblems. If you thought doing things with words was complicated, add to the mix the face with all of its moving parts, nonverbal sounds, body posture and orientation, distance from others, and so on and so forth, and you get amazingly complex, culturally variable **expressive systems** communication scholars and other disciplines are only beginning to map out. Some embodied actions, such as smiling at strangers as we pass them in public (as in Eman's rich point above) are expected in some speech communities and seem uncalled for in others. In some speech communities, as Kyle's rich point narrative illustrates, greetings are verbal genres; in others, they are not. The meanings of individual movements tend to vary quite a bit depending on the (interactional, social, spatial, cultural, etc.) contexts in which they appear.

You may have already noticed I prefer to use the term "embodied communication" instead of the more common term "nonverbal communication." Before I explain my preference, let me tell you a story that got me thinking about embodiment in intercultural communication encounters. In my teenage years, I loved reading the novels of the Hungarian poet and novelist Dezső Kosztolányi. (In case you are wondering how to pronounce his name, it's roughly *De-zhu Kos-to-luh-ny*.) Like many responsible adults, Kosztolányi struggled with the unfortunate fact that he was living a rather boring life. So he did the logical thing—well, logical for an artist—and invented an alter ego for himself whom he called Kornél Esti. Esti was a reckless, self-assured, and somewhat cynical gentleman with a heart of gold who went gallivanting around Europe in the 1930s and found himself in a series of weird and wonderful encounters with people he met along the way. In one such adventure (Kosztolányi, 2011), he meets a train guard on a long and boring train ride across the country of Bulgaria. Esti, who speaks 5–6 words in Bulgarian, including "yes," "no," and "Do you smoke?" decides to entertain himself by convincing the equally bored Bulgarian guard that he is a native speaker of Bulgarian. Esti pretends to be a pompous Bulgarian intellectual and dazzles the guard with his gold-tipped cigarettes in order to appear like someone who can reasonably patronize the guard and remain silent when he feels like it. After smoking in silence for a while, Esti makes his move:

> I yawned and sighed, and then put a hand on his [the guard's] shoulder and raised my eyebrows so that they formed huge question marks, tilted my head back and murmured "Well?" The guard smiled; he must have discovered in this amicable form of interest some memory of childhood, or the behavior of a friend who inquired of him in this way, "How are things?" He began to speak. He uttered four or five sentences. Then he fell silent and waited.

> I too waited. I had good reason to. I was wondering what answer I should make. After a brief uncertainty I decided. I said "Yes."

> Experience has taught me that much. Whenever I'm not paying attention to the conversation or don't understand something I always say "Yes." This has never yet brought me any trouble. [...]

> That my reasoning was not unfounded was demonstrated brilliantly by the consequences. The guard became much more communicative. Unfortunately, he then fell silent once more and waited. This time I showed interest with a "Yes?" in an interrogative tone, somewhat redolent of incomprehension and uncertainty. That—if I may so express myself—opened the floodgates. [...] From the way words poured from his mouth, the way he chattered and jabbered on, it became clear that even in his dreams he would never imagine I was a foreigner. This belief, firm though it seemed, I had to support. [...]

> How did I manage that? Not with words. I put on an act, like an actor—a first-class actor—with all my might. My face, my hands, my ears, even my toes moved

as required. But I had to beware of exaggeration. I mimed attentiveness, not that forced attentiveness which is suspect in advance, but that sort which is now lax and abstracted, now catches fire and flares up. I thought of something else as well. Sometimes I indicated by a gesture that I hadn't understood what he'd said. You will naturally think that would be the easiest of things. Well, you're wrong. That, my friends, was the hardest part. Just as I had not understood a single word of his ceaseless flow, I had to take care not to let my admission be too sincere and convincing. Nor did I miss my mark. The guard simply repeated his last sentence, and I nodded as if to say 'Ah yes, that's quite different.' (pp. 126–127)

Esti and the guard's conversation, which includes some interpersonal drama and Esti trying to figure out why the guard is showing him the photo of a dog, continues for hours. In the end, Esti gets off and says goodbye to the guard with a final "yes."

Even though I knew Esti's adventures were fictional, as a teen I found the possibility of pulling off this type of stunt exciting. Today, I'm less excited about the prospect of deceiving well-meaning Bulgarians and more interested in what Esti's story tells us about embodied communication.

First, nonverbal communication research often assumes that a one-to-one relationship exists between individual body movements and their meanings. The notion of embodiment *doesn't treat meaningful movements we perform with our bodies as discrete units with discrete meanings*. Instead, it draws our attention to combinations of movements—the movements of the face, the hands, the ears, and even the toes, as Esti put it—and the actions those combinations accomplish.

Second, *research on embodiment doesn't separate the meanings of movements from the meanings of words in social interaction;* rather it opens up the possibility that they may form a single action together, at the same time. Typically, nonverbal communication research suggests a strict separation between verbal and nonverbal activities and tries to understand their meanings separately. The beginning of the excerpt illustrates these first two points nicely. Esti sighs to indicate he is about to initiate a conversation and then puts a hand on the guard's shoulder, arches his eyebrows, tilts his head back, and murmurs "Well" to inquire "How are things?" without speaking those words in Bulgarian.

Third, *embodiment research recognizes that the status of communicative actions as verbal or nonverbal communication isn't always clear-cut.* Nonverbal communication research typically makes this distinction quite readily. The excerpt above doesn't offer a clear example of the point I'm making here, but consider whistled speech (Meyer, 2015). Whistled languages are often found in places where speakers separated by geographic features such as valleys or rivers have to find a way to communicate across long distances. So speakers in some speech communities of France, Greece, Turkey, Thailand, Laos, French Guyana, Mexico, the Canary Islands, Spain, Ghana, Alaska, Brazil, and Morocco developed whistled versions of the local languages in dialects. On clear days, speakers of whistled Spanish, known locally as *Silbo*, on the island of

La Gomera in the Spanish Canary Islands could communicate with one another at a distance of 5 miles! Now, are these whistles verbal or nonverbal communication? In a sense they are: there is a one-to-one relationship between words and phrases and whistles in whistled languages. In another sense, they aren't: strictly speaking, whistles are combinations of nonverbal or nonlinguistic sounds. Or, to choose an example that's perhaps a bit closer to home, why do "ew" and "huh" count as playable words in Scrabble (according to the online Merriam-Webster Scrabble Word Finder in 2019) but not "mhm"? Examples such as these suggest that if we want to understand how speakers communicate in meaningful ways, making the distinction between verbal and nonverbal communication is more or less unnecessary.

Nonetheless, we sometimes do experience **rich points** in intercultural interaction related to body movements that do not contain verbal or linguistic elements. Both students' accounts at the beginning of this chapter illustrate such rich points. These rich points call our attention to the fact that different speech communities may have different **cultural norms of interaction** and **norms of interpretation** attached to such movements. As a result, from the perspective of cultural pragmatics, it makes sense to isolate these movements and to use them as the first step toward cultural investigation. For simplicity's sake, in the rest of this chapter, I will refer to such movements as examples of nonverbal communication.

In the rest of this chapter, we will look at three types of nonverbal communication that have attracted the attention of intercultural communication scholars: proximity, facial expressions, and gesture. We will also explore how elements of nonverbal communication found their way into online discourse in the form of emoticons, emojis, and memes and brought with them cultural expectations about their use.

TYPES OF NONVERBAL COMMUNICATION

In the broadest possible interpretation of the term, nonverbal communication includes all nonlinguistic resources we humans can mobilize for the purpose of communication. Consider this definition (Patterson, 2012):

> Any communications medium that carries visual and vocal information is a vehicle for nonverbal communication. Thus, the images on television, films, the internet, and even in photographs are examples of nonverbal communication. In addition, the audio channels of mediated communication provide vocal cues,

CULTURAL PRAGMATICS SAYS

In popular discourse, nonverbal or embodied actions are often called "body language." This is incorrect. Embodied actions are not languages (Patterson, 2012), nor are their online representations in the form of emojis (McCulloch, 2019). Nevertheless, they are as important elements of a speech community's expressive system as language-based actions.

including pitch, volume, intonation, and pauses that are elements of the non-verbal system of communication. (p. 731)

Patterson narrows down this vast range of communication resources to those we use in face-to-face encounters. We still end up with a large set of resources, all of which speakers can combine at will in the process of context-bound social interaction. Static features of nonverbal communication tend to be less embodied; dynamic behaviors are more embodied.

- *Static features*

  - Design and arrangement of the physical setting of social interaction (e.g., the arrangement of furniture, decorations, the choice of indoor vs. outdoor, public vs. private settings)

  - Allocation of time (e.g., arriving early, on time, or late to a meeting)

  - Personal appearance characteristics (e.g., clothing styles, accessories)

- *Dynamic behaviors*

  - Distance between, and relative orientation, of the bodies of participants

  - Gaze (e.g., meeting or avoiding someone's gaze, length of meeting someone else's gaze)

  - Facial expression

  - Posture and movement (arranging and moving one's body in space)

  - Gestures (the strategic use of mobile body parts in interaction, particularly movements of the head, shoulders, hands, and arms)

  - Touch (physical contact between participants' bodies)

  - Vocal behavior (e.g., features of speech such as pitch, loudness, emphasis, and tempo, pauses, silence; identifying objects by imitating the sounds they make, etc.)

  - Olfactory cues (the communicative properties of smell [e.g., the use of perfume or deodorant, controlling the strength of body odor])

In nonverbal communication scholarship, interaction by touch is often called **haptics**, interaction by the allocation of time **chronemics**, interaction by physical distance or proximity **proxemics,** interaction by body movement **kinesics**, and interaction by nonlinguistic vocal behavior **paralanguage**. All of these communication resources and their combinations with one another and with linguistic or verbal communication can be potential sources of rich points.

Although all of these forms of embodied communication are equally useful and meaningful, in the rest of this chapter, I will focus on three categories my students tend to find the most intriguing: proxemics, facial expression, and gesture.

PROXEMICS

E. T. Hall, the "godfather" of the field of intercultural communication, developed an interest in nonverbal communication when he noticed that cultural groups seemed to follow unexpressed rules for interpersonal communication. This unexpressed or "hidden" dimension of culture was inaccessible to outsiders. Hall, who thought of the "hiddenness" of culture as the main obstacle to successful intercultural interaction, built his research agenda around identifying and expressing "hidden" expectations regarding nonverbal communication. He was particularly interested in how members of cultural groups seemed to be saying something about the nature of their interpersonal relationships to others with the distance they put between their bodies.

Types of Social Distance

In his book *The Hidden Dimension,* Hall (1966) describes the cultural expectations about proxemics in his own social group, White middle-class Americans. He identified four types of distance between two persons and some of the kinesics associated with each type in the following way:

- *Intimate distance*

  - Close (0–0.5 ft.): pelvis, thighs, head can touch; skin and muscles communicate; one person can put their arm around the other

  - Far (0.5–1.5 ft.): one can easily hold or grasp the other person's extremities (hand, arm, knees, shoulder, etc.)

- *Personal distance*

  - Close (1.5–2.5 ft.): one person barely has elbow room

  - Far (2.5–4 ft.): one person has elbow room; one person can reach out and touch or grasp one of the other's extremities

- *Social distance*

    - Close (4–7 ft.): both persons have elbow room; one person needs to stretch to touch the other

    - Far (7–12 ft.): both persons needs to stretch to touch the other or to pass an object

- *Public distance*

    - Close (12–25 ft.): it's possible for one person to run from another

    - Far (25+ ft.): the distance around important public figures

As you can see, all four categories of distance between bodies imply a particular type of social relation (intimate, personal, social, public). All cultural groups, Hall argued, and even animals distinguish these four categories of social relations, but measurable physical distances associated with each type of relation are likely to vary.

Hall acknowledged that circumstances may cast people into physical situations where their cultural expectations are violated. One of those situations is in public transportation. During rush hour, you quickly find yourself at a close/intimate distance from random strangers. Luckily, subway riders have defensive devices which take the real intimacy out of intimate space in public conveyances. The basic tactic is to be as immobile as possible and, when part of the trunk or extremities touches another person, withdraw if possible. If this is not possible, the muscles in the affected areas are kept tense. [...] In crowded elevators the hands are kept at the side or used to steady the body by grasping a railing. The eyes are fixed on infinity and are not brought to bear on anyone for more than a passing glance. (p. 118)

A Practical Question

"Once I figure out how a cultural group translates physical distance into social relations, can I just go ahead and use a typical physical distance to initiate the corresponding type of relationship I want to have with them?"

It's not that simple. *Expressing* an existing relationship with your body is easier than using your body to *claim* a type of relationship that doesn't yet exist. Treat proxemics like any other form of communication. Imagine saying to someone you barely know, "We are now intimate." That would go over about as well as suddenly standing only a few inches away from them.

Cultural Variation in Proxemics

In his book titled *The Hidden Dimension,* Hall compared cultural preferences in national groups such as Germans, French, the English, the Japanese, and Arabs regarding proxemics. These groups, he argued, had different conceptions of personal space, different levels of comfort regarding crowds, and different ways of using, or avoiding, physical contact. In terms of proxemics, Hall observed that South Americans, Southern and Eastern Europeans, and Arabs maintain relatively smaller personal space, while Asians, Northern Europeans, and North Americans tend to maintain relatively larger personal space between themselves and other members of their cultures. Later research could only partially support these observations, particularly because generalizing to the cultures of entire geographic regions is a crude way of describing cultural uniqueness and differences. Further, Little (1968) cautions that the type of interpersonal relationship between people may have as much, if not more, effect on proxemics as culture.

Nonetheless, such research continues for a very good reason: imagine a dyad where one participant has a cultural preference for closer and the other for greater interpersonal distance. As the latter moves their body further from the former's, the former might try to decrease the distance between their bodies. In an extreme case, these adjustments might result in a slow-motion chase around the room, which is fertile ground for intercultural misunderstanding and miscommunication (Beaulieu, 2004).

Another key question for intercultural practitioners is how tolerant cultural others are toward others who violate their sense of personal space. Instead of simply asking members of various cultural groups about their preferences, Hasler & Friedman (2012) recruited East Asian and European university students to perform virtual tasks in small teams using avatars. The tasks required students from the two groups to interact with one another one-on-one, using their avatars, in same-culture and mixed-culture dyads. The researchers then measured the distance between the virtual bodies of participants. They found the distance between the avatars of Asian participants was much greater than the distance between the avatars of European participants. However, the

A Practical Question

"If there is so much cultural variation in proxemics, how can I find out about another cultural group's space preferences?"

Beaulieu (2004) devised an ingenious experiment for gauging different cultural groups' preferences related to interpersonal distance. She invited students at her university from various cultural groups for interviews about campus life. She set up an interviewer in a room against the wall opposite from the door and placed chairs next to the door. When interviewees walked in, the interviewer simply asked them to pull up a chair. Beaulieu then measured how interviewees positioned their chairs relative to the interviewer. You can also find ways to track how closely cultural others you don't know very well position themselves relative to you in spaces where you are stationary (e.g., sitting down or doing something that requires you to stay put).

distance between the virtual bodies of mixed-culture dyads was only a bit greater than the distance between same-culture European dyads. The researchers interpreted this to mean East Asian participants were more willing to adapt to European proxemic preferences than European participants and therefore were more tolerant toward violations of their personal space. However, the researchers concede that communication between avatars in virtual worlds may be quite different from communication in the physical world between people who control those avatars.

The study of proxemics is naturally connected to the study of other types of embodied conduct. It is possible to classify cultural groups as **contact cultures** (groups where members engaged in, and facilitated, physical touch) and **noncontact cultures** (groups where physical touch is neither sought out nor facilitated; Watson, 1970). Members of contact cultures tend to not only touch others more frequently but also tend to use more sustained gaze, more direct physical orientation, and closer personal distance than noncontact cultures.

As I write this chapter, the COVID-19 pandemic has been raging all over the world for 5 months. It is much too early to study how the practice of physical distancing will transform the use and social meanings of proxemics in intra- and intercultural interactions, but I am fairly confident the pandemic will shape embodied interactions globally for years to come.

FACIAL EXPRESSIONS

Humans perform a range of communicative actions with their faces. Streeck and Knapp (1992) distinguish three categories of facial actions:

1. *facial actions with pragmatic functions*: signaling what type of action is being performed (e.g., raised eyebrow = question);

2. *facial actions as metacommunicative comments*: usually full-fledged facial expressions (e.g., sad face) that specify the meaning of what someone is saying (serious talk vs. joking); and

3. *facial actions as narrative components*: enacting a narrated event (e.g., imitating how a participant of the narrated event acted).

Universal Facial Expressions of Emotion

In the early days of research on embodied communication, researchers debated whether the nonverbal cues humans use were a product of nature or nurture. In the 19th century, Darwin argued that humans everywhere (and even nonhuman primates) use the same facial muscles to express emotion and therefore, facial expressions can be thought of as universal. Anthropologists pushed back on his claims in the 1970s and claimed facial expressions of emotion cannot be universal, given the considerable cultural variation in how humans use their faces to express emotion. Today, we have good cross-cultural evidence that humans, both in industrial and nonindustrial societies, use universal facial cues to convey seven basic emotions (Matsumoto & Hwang, 2013):

- anger

- disgust

- fear

- happiness

- sadness

- surprise

- contempt

We also have reason to believe these cues or expressions are not only universally recognized but also innate. Researchers have found that congenital blind people use similar facial expressions as sighted people; blind people's facial expressions are more like their kin's than strangers'; monozygotic twins' facial expressions are more alike than those of dizygotic twins; newborn babies share some emotion expressions (crying, smiling, distaste), and by preschool, children display all universal emotions; universal human facial expressions can be observed in nonhuman primates (chimpanzees), and they can recognize these expressions as well as humans. "Universality, however, means something quite specific in the context of emotion expression research: Universality did not mean that *all* people of *all* cultures recognized the emotions in the face; rather universality meant that, in general, people of all cultures studied are better than chance in recognizing emotional expressions" (p. 703).

What this implies is that cultural groups may have different interpretations of the same universal facial expression. Americans and Japanese, for example, tend to attribute different types of social personalities to smiling people (Matsumoto & Kudoh, 1993). While Americans rate smiling faces as more intelligent and more sociable than neutral faces, Japanese attribute less social significance to smiling. Consequently, Americans often attribute lower sociability and intelligence to Japanese speakers, while the Japanese distrust Americans who strike them as all smiles. In a different context, Spanish public service interpreters and intercultural mediators in Catalonia routinely have to "translate" the smiles of Chinese immigrants to government employees (Vargas-Urpi, 2013). Chinese immigrants would often smile a compensatory smile (*peixiao*) or a bitter smile (*kuxiao*) in situations in which they felt uncomfortable—for example during courtroom proceedings. While Chinese speakers used these smiles to avoid appearing angry or frustrated (and thereby saving **face**), Catalonian government employees interpreted them as signals that immigrants were not taking the ongoing situation seriously.

Facial Expressions Go Online

Universal expectations about the relationship between smiles and happiness can be the source of humor that spans cultural boundaries. If you grew up in an industrialized nation like the United States, you are probably used to stock photos of smiling people in advertising. Typically, actors featured in stock imagery tend to flash so-called **Duchenne smiles,** or "genuine smiles." Such smiles are expected to include these elements: exposed teeth, raised corners of the mouth, raised cheeks, crow's feet in the corners of the eyes, slightly lowered eyelids, and arched eyebrows. As it turns out, violating these expectations can result in more than a fake smile. As my compatriot, András Arató, an electrical engineer from a small town in Western Hungary, found out, it can turn you into a meme. You may know Arató by his meme name, Hide the Pain Harold. Arató achieved meme status after a stock photographer took shots of him in various professional settings—posing as a doctor in a hospital, answering the phone in an office, and so on. In 2011, internet users became fascinated with his unusual smile, which had all the right ingredients for a Duchenne smile, with the exception of lowered eyebrows and a pinched muscle over the bridge of the nose. These features are commonly associated with the facial expression of pain and suffering.

FIGURE 11.1. Hide the Pain Harold

As a result of this discrepancy, Hide the Pain Harold became an overnight internet sensation in the United States. As he recounted in a TEDx talk, Arató's—or rather, Harold's—fame then spread to Europe, Russia, and, later, to Asia (Arató, 2018).

Beyond serving as meme fodder, the universality of emotion expression also facilitated the movement of nonverbal communication to interaction online. Emoticons ("emotion icons" consisting of punctuation marks) and emojis ("picture words" or graphic icons) facilitate intercultural interactions on a daily basis. Over the years, these nonlinguistic cues helped speakers reduce message ambiguity, communicate not only particular types of emotions but also their intensity (Hwang & Matsumoto, 2013), **frame** episodes of social interaction, and nuance message meaning (Danesi, 2017). Just think about how many different smiley emojis are available to us to communicate all degrees of happiness, from moderate (e.g., the classic smiley) to extreme (e.g., the emoji with half-moon eyes, arched eyebrows, a smile, and flushed cheeks). Emojis and emoticons representing the facial expression of emotions tend to be less culturally specific than kinesic (movement-based) emojis.

Emojis, however, are unlikely to become a global **lingua franca** (Danesi, 2017) with the potential to replace language-based communication. In practice, their meaning-making function is restricted to illustrating or nuancing linguistic communication along with infusing communication with visual humor and informality. Also, different cultural groups may have different expectations about emoji use, expectations that typically depend on whether they interpret an exchange as formal or informal. For example, in a study of U.S. students' communication with Malaysian and Chinese students in communication courses, U.S. students felt peeved by non-U.S. students' use of emojis during an initial exchange of electronic messages (Sandel, Buttny, & Varghese, 2019). U.S. students felt that emojis—which signal some degree of relational closeness and emotions across cultural groups—were inappropriate in a type of encounter they saw as formal and institutional. Chinese and Malaysian students, by contrast, enjoyed using emojis from the outset with each other and U.S. students, as they saw their exchanges as

A Practical Question

"Many companies today use collaboration software that facilitates the use of emojis. Are you saying that, in a way, such software endangers the success of international collaborations?"

Not necessarily. Like other communication technologies, collaboration software is also changing intercultural communication. Because such technology is relatively new, it is difficult to say exactly what types of challenges it poses to coordinated interaction across cultural boundaries. In the spirit of cultural pragmatics, according to which indeterminate situations call for inquiry, instead of trying to develop a wholesale understanding of how such software changes intercultural interaction, try to observe whether and how, for example, the use of emojis helps you manage intercultural collaborations.

friendly rather than formal and task oriented. In another study, Japanese business-people highlighted avoiding the use of emojis and emoticons in intercultural business negotiations as a key communication skill (Yoshida, Yashiro, & Suzuki, 2013).

GESTURES

Perhaps more than any other type of nonverbal communication, gestures are tightly coordinated with ongoing speech. Streeck and Knapp (1992) distinguish two main categories of gestures: **emblems** (or quotable gestures) with conventional meanings that don't depend on interactional context, and **iconic gestures, which** have a natural resemblance to what they denote (e.g., a gesture might accompany the phrase "to rush out of" indicating the path the "rusher" followed). Speakers perform six types of actions with gestures (Streeck, 2015):

1. tracing the outlines of objects and manipulating them

2. orienting other participants to visible objects at a distance (e.g., pointing)

3. depicting nonpresent phenomena or modeling imaginary and abstract worlds (e.g., indicating "time" by signaling a line or progression with one's hands)

4. elaborating or highlighting the topic of conversation with postures and actions of the hands (e.g., crossing one's arms or rubbing the upper arm with the opposite hand to indicate "being cold")

5. embodying and displaying aspects of **speech acts** that are being performed (e.g., praying gesture to embody prayer)

6. regulating the communicative actions of others (e.g., holding up a finger to indicate one wishes to continue talking)

In the context of social interaction, one gesture can perform more than one of these actions at the same time.

Cultural Variation in Gestures

Both the meanings and appropriate amounts of gestures can vary across cultures. For example, indicating time and its progression as a straight line is not a cultural universal (Rodríguez, 2019). Among the speakers of Chol, a Maya language spoken in Chiapas, Mexico, time is indicated with combinations of upward and downward hand movements, arched hand movements, and others, but not hand movements depicting a straight line. Cultural variation in the amount of gesturing speakers do can be the result of environmental factors. For example, Kendon (2004) speculates the reason why the amount and frequency of gesticulation in Naples strikes people from the northern parts of Europe as peculiar may be found in city life. Traditionally, people in in the densely populated and noisy city of Naples spent a lot of time in the noisy outdoors, and they needed to gesture more to attract and hold the attention of others and to make themselves understood—hence, rich Neapolitan gesture culture.

Globalization, especially the global flow of visual representations of nonverbal communication through movies, television, and the internet, is producing a set of emblems recognizable across cultural boundaries. These emblems include gestures for come, go, hello, goodbye, yes, and no. Communication technologies, Matsumoto and Hwang (2013) argue, "may be helping to homogenize gestures into a worldwide emblem dictionary, and if so, it may be only a matter of time that a homogenized, universal set of emblematic gestures replaces culture-specific ones" (p. 714).

Gestures in Social Interaction

I am not sure if such a worldwide dictionary is indeed in humanity's future, but we have evidence that gestures play a significant role in intercultural interaction, particularly when speakers have limited or no proficiency in each other's languages. A typical social setting in which such encounters often occur is markets in major cities. Two researchers spent 4 months observing and recording interactions at a Chinese butcher's stall at the Bull Ring market in Birmingham, England (Blackledge & Creese, 2017). The participants of these interactions were shoppers, the two Chinese proprietors, Kang Chen and Meiyen Chew, and their English assistant, Bradley. They reported three typical interactions in which gestures had a role to play but did not always result in coordinated interaction.

- **Example 1:** A customer with limited English proficiency approached Bradley and wanted to buy pig intestine. Both Bradley and the customer used gestures to represent large and small intestine, using their arms to show large and small, and Bradley pointed to his stomach to refer to intestine. Bradley then shrugged and said "no more" to indicate they no longer sold the product. In this interaction, Bradley was able to communicate that they no longer sold small intestine to a customer who did not share the same first language as him.

- **Example 2:** Three men of southeastern European descent approached the stall. One wanted to buy a chicken from Bradley. Bradley made a motion as if to cut off the feet and head of the chicken. The man said "yes" at first, then said "no only" and motioned to his throat. Bradley cut off both the feet and head, demonstrating that shared gesture does not always result in the desired result.
  Another man, after leaving the stall and then returning, asked Kang Chen how much for the rest of the chicken. He said, "35." The man handed him a 20.

Kang Chen then tried various ways of communicating "35," saying it slowly, using his fingers to show three and five, and drawing a three and five in the air. He finally said, "no, 35," and the customers left with big grins on their faces. The researchers concluded that the smiles indicated social play. Along with the continued presentation of the 20-pound note, the customers wanted to deliberately cultivate misunderstanding for the sake of making a joke.

- **Example 3:** A Chinese woman approached the stall and pulled her three middle fingers to her palm, a Chinese gesture for "six." To clarify, she said the Mandarin word for six. Bradley, either understanding the gesture, the word for six, or both, selected six pig intestines and handed them to her, saying, "one ninety-nine." The interaction was successful, even though there is little clarity about what Bradley understood verbally and what gestures he understood.

These examples demonstrate not only humans' creativity in combining bits and pieces of shared language and gesture for the purpose of coordinated (or uncoordinated) interaction across cultural boundaries but also the fact that it is difficult, if not impossible, to separate the functions of gestures from the functions of linguistic communication resources. It is often similarly difficult to say with certainty whether gestures or words brought about coordination between participants of intercultural encounters.

Nonetheless, gestures hold a great amount of promise for speakers who are either non-native speakers of a language they share with an interactional partner or use a third language to communicate. In a study of interactions between Korean graduate students and their American tutors, Belhiah (2018) documented how participants successfully used hand gestures for the purpose of accomplishing coordinated interaction. For example, a U.S. participant could manage orderly **turn-taking** by looking up to indicate that she was thinking and not ready to yield the **conversational floor**. A Korean participant touched his left cheek while listening and then touched his right cheek to indicate he was ready to speak. When talking about fishing, the U.S. tutor began performing "casting the line," and the Korean student joined him in coproducing the emblematic gesture, signaling he understood what the tutor meant.

In a study of international couples who used English as a lingua franca to understand one another, Pietikäinen (2018) documented how couples used combinations of words, sounds, and gestures to coordinate their actions. For example, while making a cake, a Norwegian man (Kjetil) wanted to explain to his Mexican partner (Carmen) that he wanted to dust the cake with sugar. Neither one of them, however, knew the words for "icing sugar" or "sieve," yet they managed to accomplish mutual understanding and what needed to be done to decorate the cake:

EXCERPT 11.1. (from Pietikäinen, 2018, p. 204, simplified)

1	Kjetil	We ... I was feeling like, say like like *melis* [icing sugar in Norwegian] like shh
2	Carmen	We could put a little bit ... just a little bit to make it like as a decoration not as a ...
3	Kjetil	Yeah but we need the ... one of these ...
4	Carmen	Do we?
5	Kjetil	Make ... If want to make like uh, shh shh
6	Carmen	Like a sprinkles?
7	Kjetil	Yeah.

Kjetil doesn't expect Carmen to understand what *melis* means, so he uses a type of paralanguage, **phonomimesis** (the imitation of a sound associated with an object) when he says "shh" (line 1) and "shh shh" (line 5). (Although the transcript is based on a sound recording, it is quite likely that Kjetil is also imitating shaking a sieve filled with icing sugar.) On lines 2, 4, and 6, Carmen uses language to clarify that the sugar Kjetil wants to use is for decorative purposes only. As a result of their shared efforts, by line 7, they are clear on what Kjetil wants (dusting the cake) and what they need to do to get there. The combination of words, gestures, and sounds allows them to understand "a sprinkles" (line 6) as "dusting" ("sprinkling icing sugar"), even though that is not the dictionary meaning of the word.

BARRIERS TO COORDINATED INTERACTION

1. **Overlooking meaningful embodied actions.** A basic challenge for the intercultural practitioner is understanding when a body movement has interactional function. This type of **local knowledge** will help you distinguish the twitch of an eye from a wink, a stretch from an attempt to get someone's attention, and accidental physical contact from an expressive touch.

2. **Misunderstanding the interactional meaning of embodied actions.** Eman's and Kyle's rich point narratives at the beginning of this chapter provide good examples of a participant not understanding what a particular type of gesture or a particular use of gaze means in interaction with another participant. As an intercultural practitioner, you need to reconstruct the **cultural norms of interaction and interpretation** pertaining to embodied communication in a given speech community.

3. **Misconstruing the type of embodied actions or their relationship to speech.** Correctly categorizing types of embodied actions in a speech community will

help you establish their meanings, not only relative to one another (e.g., distinguishing a tracing gesture from sensuous touch) but also relative to speech (e.g., a chopping movement can be used to bring emphasis to speech or to imitate the act of chopping).

4. **Missing the social meaning of embodied actions.** As an intercultural practitioner, you should also keep in mind that embodied actions very often (if not always) enact particular types of relationships between you and speakers. To follow these social meanings, you need to keep track of what types of embodied actions are considered locally appropriate in what types of relationships.

REFLECTION QUESTIONS

1. Think of a body movement that can take on interactional meaning. Now try combining it with other body movements and/or words. How many kinds of communicative actions can you perform with these combinations?

2. Try this experiment: make an attempt to carry on a conversation with someone while holding your body (including your gaze, face, head, neck, upper and lower body) perfectly still. What do you notice about how the conversation progresses and about your partner's reactions to your conduct?

3. How would you explain to a cultural outsider why it's inappropriate to sit down next to someone in a café where there are plenty of other seats available?

4. Review the 10 most recent online or text messages you sent to others. Did you use emojis that derive from embodied communication (facial expressions, gaze, gestures, etc.)? If you did, what were you "saying" with them? Why didn't you use words instead? If you did not, why did you chose to use text instead of emojis?

5. In a cultural group you consider your own, what types of norms and rules apply to physical contact with strangers? How do these norms and rules vary across gender and age groups?

12

"How Does This Make Sense to Them?"

Cultural Meanings of Communication

GABRIEL: I was in week 3 of a 6-week program of studying Incan architecture at a local university in Cusco, Peru. While school was my reason for travel, I took full advantage of my time in South America. At one point, I found myself in a hostel with some local men. We were sitting in a circle drinking a form of tea known as *mate*—an extremely popular drink in South America. When the man pouring the tea passed me my first cup, I drank its contents, passed the cup back, and said, "Thank you" to my gracious host. The whole circle looked at me funny, and the man with the tea said, "Are you sure? You have only had one cup." This confused me, for in my head all I had done was expressed my gratitude towards my host's generosity. What I did not realize is that, in Peru, *mate* circles are a ceremonial tradition. One does not say "thank you" until he has had as much *mate* as he pleases. Saying "thank you" tells the host that the cup you are drinking is your last desired cup. They explained to me their confusion, and I continued in the circle until I had drunk my fill of *mate*.

FRANCES: One particular rich point that comes to mind happened when my friends and I attended our first FC Barcelona (known

In this chapter, you will learn:

- about how cultural meaning is present in interaction

- to distinguish different types and layers of cultural meaning

- how speech communities offer their members a sense of belonging

locally as Barca) football game in Barcelona, Spain. Gazing around the massive stadium, it was mesmerizing to see the enormous crowd. Our nosebleed seats were located directly next to the away team's section. The sections were divided by a 6-foot-tall glass wall on each side. As if the glass wasn't enough, there were policemen with bulletproof vests and machine guns guarding and blocking off the visitors' sections from coming into Barca territory. The Atlético Madrid fans were aggressively chanting and pushing against the glass dividers. During the middle of the game, my friends and I got up to go get refreshments and check out the food stands. As we were leaving our seats, the three rows behind us started screaming at us to sit down. We didn't initially understand what they were yelling or why they were yelling. We scurried to the food stand to get some beers and hot dogs. To our surprise, we found out that the beer was nonalcoholic and that they did not serve alcohol at all in the stadium. The man at the concession stand looked at us and aggressively said, "Chicas, this isn't America … here in España, we take *futból* very seriously. We sit in our seats and watch the entire game. Now go back to your seats and show respect to FC Barca." We quickly returned to our seats to watch the rest of the game.

CULTURAL PRAGMATICS SAYS

Not everything we do has a culturally distinctive meaning. In other words, culture is not relevant to everything we do. It is up to the cultural investigator or the **intercultural practitioner** to discover whether a particular action or practice is culturally meaningful.

I began to think about what the concessions stand man said to us. At first, I was a little irritated that he pulled the classic "this isn't America" on us, but at the same time I was curious where he was coming from and interested in understanding the culture around the FC Barcelona team and their immense fan base. Later I learned that for Barca fans, the majority of whom are Catalonian, supporting the team is a sign of regional pride and a political statement of support for independence from Spain.

What makes meaning "cultural"? When members of cultural groups other than our own do something that doesn't make immediate sense to us, we are often quick to jump to the conclusion that when they acted in that way they were following the lead of "their culture." Therefore, we reason, what they did must have some sort of cultural meaning. This, however, is not always the case. Culture is not always the reason—or not the primary reason—for the breakdown of coordinated interaction. As an intercultural practitioner, be careful not to explain away interactional problems with "culture."

> *Culture* is supposed to be a solution, not a label that hides the real problems. Problems in task performance might be due to differences in personality or power, or circumstances, or goals, not to differences in culture. (Agar, 1994, p. 235)

This is not to say you shouldn't try to build culture when you encounter an unpleasant **rich point**. However, as you do so, keep in mind that the other speaker may simply be pursuing goals and interests different from yours in the context of the ongoing encounter. They may also be motivated to act by things other than culture, such as unique habits or preferences, fatigue, boredom, or even malice.

Generally speaking, the meaning of a (confusing) action or practice is "cultural" when you find there is at least some degree of consensus in the social group that the action or practice is normal (intelligible, appropriate, or even downright creative), you conclude you are dealing with misaligned **interactional frames** and/or **scripts**, and you feel the need to construct an **intercultural frame** that allows you to determine the act's meaning and move toward coordinated interaction.

The rich point narratives at the beginning of this chapter illustrate that in intercultural encounters, we are often made aware of what is "normal"

when we are called out for acting in ways that go against the grain of what is locally considered "normal" conduct. The cultural outsider senses they have just done something wrong or made a mistake, but what they did and why that was the wrong thing to do isn't obvious to them. In such moments, the focus of intercultural communication is holding the cultural outsider **accountable**—that is, alerting them that they engaged in some form of action that violated local expectations for normal conduct and calling upon them to mend their ways. The intercultural practitioner being held accountable is confronted with three broad questions, all of which point to aspects of cultural meaning:

1. HOW? – How are participants expected to act in this situation?

2. WHY? – On what cultural grounds are they expected to act in that way?

3. WHO? – What social group is holding me accountable, and what is at stake for them?

Both rich point narratives illustrate the violation of local expectations about appropriate conduct. In the first one, there is a disconnect between Gabriel's and the Peruvian participants' sense of the meaning of saying "thank you" after consuming *mate*. Below, we will discuss this type of norm as a **rule of interpretation**. In the second, other fans and the man at the concession stand are holding Frances and her friends accountable for disengaging from the ongoing game and disrespecting the club by doing so. In addition to disciplining the young women accountable, the concession stand employee also casts them as outsiders ("this isn't America") and **positions himself** as a cultural insider and as a member of a larger community ("here in España, we take *futból* very seriously"). Both students felt compelled to investigate the cultural grounds on which they were held accountable: Gabriel discovered a **communication ritual** as an element of a ceremonial event, while Frances discovered the political and communal aspect of soccer fandom in Catalonia.

In this chapter, we will review the "how," the "why," and the "who" of cultural meanings. We begin with a discussion of cultural norms and rules that shape how participants produce and interpret acts of communication. Next, we discuss cultural ideologies on the basis of which communicative action appears coherent, appropriate, and "natural." Then we look at social groups' view of, and deep investment in, certain forms of communication as expressions of shared communal identity.

THE "HOW": COMPETENT USE

One key observation intercultural practitioners have made many times before is that members of social or cultural groups are not very good at explaining the communicative rules and norms they follow in their daily lives. If I asked you to give me a list of the communicative rules and norms in a speech community of which you are a member, I assume you would not be able to just rattle off a definitive list. The reason for this difficulty is that, generally speaking, we are not aware of our social groups' norms and rules until someone—a cultural insider or outsider—violates or breaks one and other group members invoke the norm or rule to hold them accountable. Rules and norms don't exist in our heads or minds, ready to be recalled at will. They exist in communication: group members cite them to keep other members (or outsiders) in line, and they pass them on to others in the processes of **language socialization, such as** gossip. Gossip, or "evaluative talk about absent others" (Goldsmith, 1989/1990) is one of the most commonly used **speech genres** around the world for the purpose of telling stories about how people we know violated a norm or broke a rule.

The distinction between norms and rules is subtle. A particularly useful piece of teaching advice I got from someone when I started teaching in the United States was

A Practical Question

"If norms and rules are not readily available to cultural outsiders, how do I avoid making mistakes that invite negative criticism from group members?"

The short answer is: you don't. The long answer is that, precisely because rules and norms are communication resources to hold others accountable, a great way to find out about them is to make mistakes and ask group members to explain to you what rule you broke or what norm you violated. The mistakes you make will become rich points, and rich points are the first step toward building culture. Intercultural practice requires a certain degree of humility on the part of the practitioner: you should be prepared to lose face to gain local knowledge.

to set up ground rules and group norms at the beginning of the semester. "But how are those different?" I asked. "Don't rules and norms both tell us how to communicate in the classroom?" They do, but as I learned later, the way they work is a bit different, and the difference is a matter of degree:

- **Cultural norms** tend to be more widely shared and taken-for-granted expectations about how people should participate in social interaction. **Cultural rules** are relatively less widely shared and less taken for granted.

- Because **norms** are more taken for granted, group members find it harder to put them into words than **rules**.

- The authority behind the force of **norms** is usually a community. The authority behind the force of **rules** is often an individual (although the individual's authority and the force of rules are typically grounded in relevant communal norms).

- **Norms** usually apply across a broad range of speakers and contexts. **Rules** are often tied to particular contexts and to particular (groups of) speakers.

- When **norms** are violated, negative sanctions against the violator are not immediately obvious and are open to discussion and negotiation. When **rules** are broken, the negative sanctions are more obvious ("That's the rules!") and are more quickly implemented or threatened

To go back to the example of the classroom, "group norms" capture basic expectations about appropriate communicative conduct in the classroom that students and the instructor negotiate and formulate together. Ground rules are a list of expectations the instructor designs and presents to students, usually on the first day of class, along with the types of punishment students will receive if they break the rules.

The ability to recognize and act upon rules and norms that apply to **speech situations** (social situations in which speech is appropriate) and **speech events** (social situations organized around patterned forms of expression) is a fundamental requirement for **culturally competent** speakers.

Norms

As a cultural analyst, you are in the best position to formulate unfamiliar cultural norms. In order to do so, you will need to capture three elements of a norm: (1) the context or situation to which the norm applies, (2) the social goals participants are typically working toward, and (3) what types of action participants should or should not engage in.

- Context. Norms may refer to situations featuring particular types of participants (e.g., friend, stranger, family member, etc.) and/or types of physical settings (e.g., public, classroom, dorm room, etc.) and/or types of ongoing activity (e.g., date, meeting during office hours, band practice, encounter between strangers, etc.) and/or types of timing (e.g., morning, afternoon, night, etc.). The norm you are formulating may refer to some, but not all, of these features.

- Social goals or accomplishments are the goal(s) participants are working toward as they interact with one another (e.g., gaining information, maintaining a relationship or identity, financial gain, etc.). When we say participants are working toward social goals, we are not implying they are always manipulative or that they are never spontaneous. What we are implying is that meaningful interaction, no matter how friendly or casual, is strategic.

- Actions are observable communicative "doings" (e.g., asking, engaging in conversation, keeping silent, laughing, etc.).

We can put these three elements together into a model (Carbaugh, 1990) you can use to capture norms:

In context C, when pursuing social goal X, one should (not) do Y.

To use the second rich point narrative about attending an FC Barcelona game as an example, Frances appears to have discovered this norm:

Norm 1: In the context of an ongoing FC Barca soccer game, in order to show respect to the club and the game, all spectators (including fans and visitors) should stay engaged in the game.

Judging from her narrative, a complementary norm that calls for keeping misbehaving fans and visitors in line also seems to be relevant to FC Barca games:

Norm 2: In the context of an ongoing FC Barca soccer game, in order to make sure everyone respects the club and the game, all spectators are entitled to directly admonish other spectators who fail to stay engaged in the game.

The first norm applies to spectator conduct in a more general sense. The second is clearly a communication norm, one that belong to the category of **norms of interaction—** that is, norms that shape the ways in which participants are expected to participate in interaction. Another type of cultural communication norm, **norms of interpretation**, shape the ways in which a participant is expected to interpret what another participant says in the context of ongoing interaction.

Rules

As I discussed above, rules are relatively less widely shared, more easily articulated, and more narrowly applied than norms, and they prescribe relatively more obvious sanctions. The authority behind the force of rules can be an individual, a group of any size, or a community. To give you an example, while raising our three kids, my wife and I shared a concern with what in popular culture is often referred to as the "middle child syndrome." We were worried that our second child, Mira, would feel excluded as a result of having to fight for our attention harder than our oldest, Anna, who was already quite articulate, and our youngest, Adam, who was still a toddler. We decided to come up with a communication rule for our family:

> In the Boromisza-Habashi family, when the five of us are engaged in a conversation, in order to protect Mira from feeling excluded, no one is allowed to interrupt her when she speaks.

Simple, straightforward, easily applicable. When Mira speaks, no one else does, and siblings who violate the rule will be shushed. Following the distinction between the two types of norms, this rule falls into the category of **rules of interaction,** as it pertains to how participants engage in speech. The (more communally shared) rule the student in the first rich point narrative discovered is a **rule of interpretation**:

> In a *mate* circle, in order be a proper host, when a guest says "thank you," the host should interpret that as a request to stop serving them *mate*.

Gabriel's story also suggests that when a guest says "thank you" after their first serving of *mate,* the host has the right to question their appetite or their competence. In contrast to the Peruvian participants, Gabriel implies he was following a **rule of interaction** that was not appropriate for a *mate* circle:

> In the role of a guest, in order to show generosity to the host, one should thank the host when being served a beverage.

The Peruvian rule prompts Gabriel to reevaluate what sort of **speech act** saying "thank you" constitutes. In the American context, saying "thank you" performs a display of appreciation and gratitude; in the context of the *mate* circle, saying "thank you" performs a request for ending service.

In Frances's rich point narrative, the man at the concession stand "translates" the local norm of staying engaged in the game into a rule:

> In the context of an ongoing FC Barca soccer game, in order to show respect to the game and the club, spectators should sit in their seats and watch the entire game.

To the cultural outsider, this rule is more easily followed than the more general norm of staying engaged in the game.

As you think about cultural norms and rules, keep in mind that we humans are not cultural robots who follow norms and rules blindly. Don't imagine norms and rules as an operating system that determines how you act. Although we tend to follow them, we also break norms and rules in meaningful ways (Philipsen, Coutu, & Covarrubias, 2005). For example, when we break a rule, we sometimes communicate to the authority who enforces it that we disagree with their rules of conduct. Going against a communal norm can be a resource for claiming the identity of the rebel or the agent of social change.

Norms in Intercultural Practice

Norms and rules often feed into stereotyping and/or intercultural miscommunication. For example, Leonardi and Rodriguez-Lluesma (2013) documented how U.S. American and Indian engineers violated Mexican engineers' expectations about appropriate forms of consultation, collaboration, and innovation at a large engineering firm they called International Automobile Corporation (IAC). Mexican engineers expected to be in constant communication with one another, to share files, passwords, best practices, and procedures with one another during collaboration, and to follow guidelines closely during processes of innovation. Their adherence to these norms fed into stereotypes their counterparts from India and the United States had about them. As a Mexican engineer explained:

> According to the Americans and the Indians, we're all a little bit lazy because we don't start things from scratch and we spend all day talking because we're always working together on things. We're also not smart enough to come up with new ways of doing things. At least that's what they think. I've started to realize that they have these conceptions about us through little things they say and do when we talk to each other. (p. 488)

In another study, Kotani (2016) described how Japanese and American speakers followed incompatible rules for apologies. The Japanese rule for apologies calls for saying "sorry" and offering no or minimal **excuses** of **justifications** for the act. From the Japanese perspective, saying "sorry" is the admission of having caused someone discomfort or trouble and not necessarily the admission of being at fault. As a result, U.S. apologies that feature detailed explanations of why the offender did the offensive act sound excessive to Japanese speakers. By contrast, U.S. speakers see their explanations as an important way to service the relationship that is threatened by the offensive act. Excuses and justifications are designed to **interactionally frame** the offense as forgivable. When Japanese speakers don't offer such explanations or seem reluctant to listen, U.S. speakers see them as not invested enough in the relationship.

THE "WHY": CULTURAL IDEOLOGIES

Cultural ideology is a system of beliefs about communication (Philipsen, 1992) active in, and sometimes across, **speech communities**. Cultural ideologies answer the question: *What do these speakers have to believe to speak, or to evaluate speech, in this way?* Much like norms and rules, such beliefs don't exist in individual people's heads; rather, they are shared by, and available to, speakers who can invoke them when they see the need. They can also be reconstructed by cultural outsiders to explain local communicative conduct.

One aspect of life in the United States with which I had to come to terms when I moved to the country is the widely shared belief that communication, in general, is a good thing. I often heard people encourage others to "talk about their feelings" and to solve conflicts by "talking things out." I also heard people share words of wisdom like "Communication is key to a good relationship." "Communication" in the United States (Katriel & Philipsen, 1981) and the English-speaking world in general (Cameron, 2000) is seen as a solution to a wide variety of personal and social problems. Some communication scholars (Craig, 2005, 2013), including myself (Boromisza-Habashi, 2016), even talk about the existence of a **communication culture,** a globally available cultural ideology made up of

> the idea that communication is important, the idea that human problems are caused by bad communication and can be solved by better communication, the idea that communication is a technical skill that can be improved by applying principles and techniques disseminated by communication experts, the idea, in short, that it is "good to talk." (2005, p. 660)

To claim that *all* of the United States shares in communication culture is, of course, a generalization. The belief that communication is the lifeblood of social life and silence is nothing but the absence of communication is most widely shared in Anglo, White speech communities. Blackfeet speakers in the state of Montana, for example, typically assign more cultural significance to silence than speech (Carbaugh, 2005).

A Practical Question

"Is it possible that the group for which I'm building culture will be using cultural ideologies that will be completely unlike mine?"

The answer to this question depends on what you mean by "completely unlike." In a sense, if another group's cultural meanings are entirely unlike yours, they will not make sense to you at all. They will be simply unintelligible. This hardly, if ever, happens. More likely, you will encounter groups who have a different but recognizable cultural "take" on the world. Remember: the practice of building culture invites you to use similarities between your group and the other to bridge real differences.

Beyond the United States, Finnish speakers, who are also relatively more comfortable with silence in the context of interpersonal contact than US speakers and *much* less comfortable with small talk, follow these communication norms when conversing with people they don't know very well:

1. one should not state what is obvious;
2. if speaking, one should say something worthy of everyone's attention;
3. one should not invoke topics or themes that are contentious or conflictual (or more positively, one should keep present relations on harmonious ground);
4. one should be personally committed to or invested in what one says;
5. what you say properly—the unobvious, socially worthwhile, noncontentious, personally involving statements—forms a basis for subsequent interactions and social relations. (Carbaugh, 2005, p. 43)

In very simple terms, we could phrase the cultural ideology informing these norms as "communication is commitment." When you speak, your words commit you to not only the contents of what you say—you say what you mean and you mean what you say—but also to who you are and to the relationship with your conversational partner that begins to take shape as a result of your conversation. When American speakers engage in small talk or say things like "I'm just spitballing here" or "Let me just throw this idea out there," they strike Finns as bad stewards of their own words.

The Finnish example teaches us three things. First, we learn that culturally variable communication norms in the United States, Finland, or elsewhere are grounded in distinct cultural ideologies. Second, these ideologies tell us important things about how speech communities believe the world works. From the Finnish cultural perspective, talking to a relative stranger creates an interpersonal expectation that the next time participants meet they will talk to each other again. (In the United States, this expectation is either not there or is a lot less clear.) Third, cultural ideologies also contain hierarchies of value assigned to particular types of communication. In the example above, the **speech genre** known as small talk has relatively lower value—that is, it is a less desirable form of communication—in Finland than in the United States—although, as the *Wall Street Journal* reported, lately globalization has been forcing Finns to take lessons in small talk (MacDonald, 2019).

Cultural Premises

Let's take a look at cultural beliefs and values in greater detail. Cultural beliefs can be expressed as cultural **premises** that inform the ways we communicate. Much like logical premises, cultural premises are fundamental, taken-for-granted assumptions about the world, including communication. There are six types of cultural premises that pertain to communication (Carbaugh, 2007; Katriel & Livio, 2019). I will apply each to my own informal cultural interpretation of small talk, which I crafted over the years through trial and error.

1. *Premises about personhood* ("Who are we as we communicate in this way? What are our individual identities?")

   Example: Any type of person can engage in small talk with any other type of person, as long as the situation can be described as relatively informal. (Small talk is less likely to occur in formal situations such as a military exercise or a religious ceremony.)

2. *Premises about relationships* ("What kinds of relationships exist among us as we communicate in this way?")

   Example: Small talk between strangers doesn't necessarily indicate equal status or commitment to future interactions or a relationship. Longer episodes of small talk usually indicate that participants aren't close; shorter episodes of small talk before participants move on to more personal topics tend to indicate a closer interpersonal relationship.

3. *Premises about action* ("When we communicate with one another in this way, what are we doing? What are we accomplishing?")

   Example: Small talk is casual and therefore avoids "heavy" topics like sex, religion, and politics. The purpose of small talk between strangers is the polite recognition of the other's presence, perhaps the expression of curiosity in the other. In and of itself, small talk doesn't accomplish a relationship or an expectation of future interaction, even if participants state such an intent ("We should have lunch sometime!").

4. *Premises about emotion* ("What kinds of feelings do, or should, we experience when we communicate in this way?")

   Example: People participating in small talk feel at ease, perhaps curious, depending on the context. (Participants who don't feel at ease pretend they do.)

5. *Premises about place* ("When we communicate in this way, what are we saying about the place or the environment in which we are communicating?")

   Example: When participants engage in small talk, they are signaling they are in a place where talk between individual speakers is appropriate.

6. *Premises about time* ("What is our view of the connection between past, present, and future as we communicate in this way?")

Example: When participants engage in small talk with relative strangers in a situation where there is a possibility of a lasting (friendly, romantic, professional) relationship, they signal to each other that they are open, but not committed, to building that future relationship with one another.

Thanks to these premises, U.S. American speakers are rarely surprised when someone engages them in small talk. They also have a sense of how to engage in small talk in a recognizable way. But what's equally important is that, as they engage in small talk, U.S. speakers affirm these premises about humans, their speech, relationships, feelings, and connections to places. Conversations exist in culture, but culture also exists in conversations (Carbaugh, 2005).

Cultural Value

Some forms or styles of expression, or linguistic varieties, have greater **cultural value** than others—that is, a speech community regards them as appropriate objects of desire. Typically, speakers ascribe value to language: because of its utility in social interaction (use value), because it is taught in exchange for money or can be exchanged for gainful employment (exchange value), or because learners experience positive self-transformation in the process of learning it (acquisitive value) (Boromisza-Habashi & Fang, 2020).

African American speakers in the United States, for example, are well aware that African American English (AAE) carries less use value outside the African American speech community than Standard American English (SAE), the dominant variety (Alim & Smitherman, 2012). Speakers of SAE evaluate that variety as "better English" and consider it "more professional" as a result. By contrast, AAE is evaluated as "slang" or "broken English" in spite of the fact that AAE is as systematic, coherent, and useful in social interaction as SAE. African American parents recognize SAE's use value: the ability to competently use SAE is key to gaining respect in the world outside the speech community. As a result, they often advocate for the use of SAE in public schools and against giving AAE official status in the curriculum, even though education experts have shown that acknowledging the linguistic varieties kids speak at home facilitates learning (Morgan, 2014). The desire for education in a prestigious language (or linguistic variety) as opposed to the language of the home is not a uniquely U.S. phenomenon. Upper-class Xhosa parents in South Africa who speak Xhosa at home also prefer their children to be educated in English, which they see as the language of success and upward social mobility (de Klerk, 2000).

One easily recognizable feature of globalization is that some forms of expression carry high value across languages and speech communities. To give you an example, for years now, I have been studying the surprisingly high use, exchange, and acquisitive value of Anglo-American public speaking around the world. These days, you can take public speaking classes in most countries around the world, thanks to organizations like Toastmasters, self-help programs like the Dale Carnegie method, a global network of corporate public speaking trainers, and internationally popular TED talks. Wherever public speaking is taught, learners seem to reach the same conclusion: learning public speaking is valuable not only because it helps you become a better public speaker (use value) but also because the process of learning turns you into a better (more confident, relatable, successful) person (acquisitive value; Boromisza-Habashi & Reinig, 2018). In some cases, the value of public speaking can also be expressed in monetary terms, as learners are willing to pay good money to learn Anglo-American public speaking from well-credentialed instructors (exchange value).

Sometimes tensions develop between multiple valued forms of expression that coexist in the same context. Take the example of biracial and bicultural families where the parents were **linguistically socialized** in different speech communities. A study of Asian Caucasian families (Toomey, Dorjee, & Ting-Toomey, 2013) showed that the children of Asian and Caucasian parents experienced a tension between forms of expression with a high use value in their fathers' and mothers' speech communities. Oliver, the son of a White British father and a Korean mother, explained the tension in this way:

> My dad from my White side always taught me to be very assertive and speak up about what I wanted. My Korean mom, though, was always telling me how important family is and how I should respect my grandparents and that they always know what's best for the family. So I felt like there was some conflict there: if I didn't agree with my other family members or relatives, I was expected to *stay quiet* even though I wanted to *speak out*. (p.121)

Ideally, children in families like Oliver's become competent **code-switchers** who know how to move between valued forms of expression—such as "staying quiet" and "speaking out" in conflict situations—depending on the racial/cultural identities of their interactional partners.

THE "WHO": COMMUNAL IDENTITY

Growing up in Hungary, when I said something inappropriate, my parents would often stop me and say, "That's not how we talk in this family." As a teenager, I found this statement even more irritating than most other things I heard from my parents. "What if I don't want to talk like everyone else in this family? After all, I'm not my family. I am an individual human being free to make my own choices! Convince me that what I said was inappropriate instead of simply asking me to conform!" These days, as the parent of teenagers, I understand my own reaction to my parents' admonishments better, but I also appreciate their perspective more. In particular, I have a clearer sense of the human desire to belong and how that desire informs our communication choices. Yes, my parents were asking me to align my speech with the expectations of my immediate family and the larger network of our family relations, but they were not demanding that I conform for the sake of conformity. They wanted me to know that I belonged somewhere.

Communication Forms

The ways we speak to others contain implicit **metasocial commentary**—that is, information about the social group(s) with which we (don't) want to be associated (Carbaugh, 2005). In some cases, the very purpose of communication is to provide a particular type of metasocial commentary that transforms our experience of membership in a social unit of any size (group, family, organization, institution, nation, etc.) into an experience of belonging to a community. Speakers around the world use three typical **communication forms** for this purpose: myth, ritual, and social drama (Philipsen, 1987).

A Practical Question

"How do I know if the member of a group for which I'm currently building culture is simply mad at me for something I did or if they are trying to include me in a social drama?"

You can answer this question for yourself by trying to determine whether the cultural other you are interacting with sees you as a member of their community or an outsider. In the former case, there is a good chance they are initiating a social drama; in the latter, it is less likely they are.

Having said that, keep in mind that people initiate social dramas for the purpose of including outsiders in their community ("We are angry at you because we care about you/count you as one of us."). This applies to myths and rituals as well: you may hear them because someone is trying to include you, not because you are already "in."

Myths are stories we tell about a social unit in which we have membership in a way that captures our imagination and helps us see ourselves as belonging to a community with a continuous history. Linde (2003) found that employees at a company she called MidWest Insurance regularly told each other stories about the founding of the company and the careers of legendary sales agents for the purpose of building a shared sense of communal belonging.

Communication rituals are communication act sequences (or acts sequences involving communication) that, when participants perform them in the correct order, celebrate something that matters to everyone in the social unit. Russian toasting and drinking is such a communication ritual that affirms communal belonging (Nuciforo, 2013). The ritual consist of four types of acts: (1) announcing a drink; (2) making sure everyone is ready to have a drink; (3) proposing a toast; and (4) drinking together. When performed correctly, the ritual celebrates *ponimanie* ("understanding"), a shared sense of "soulful" interaction and togetherness.

Social dramas occur when a social unit tries to hold one of its members accountable by invoking a norm. As the norm is invoked, as its relevance is negotiated among members of the social unit, and as the offender either admits wrongdoing or not, participants experience a sense of belonging to a community built around shared norms. In the example at the beginning of this section, my parents invoked a norm to initiate a small-scale social drama and to bring me back into the fold, so to speak. Social dramas can be much more elaborate. Hastings (2001) reported a long-term social drama that took place on the campus of a U.S. public university where Asian Indian international students performed a public skit to make fun of their peers who appeared "too American" by not interacting with other Indians, imitating an "American" accent, and excessively criticizing India.

Speech Communities

The importance of rituals, myths, and social dramas is that they help us experience membership in **speech communities**, communities enacted and experienced through communication choices. Any social unit can become a speech community as long as its members recognize particular ways of engaging in social interaction as markers of community identity and membership. Morgan (2014) identified six features of speech communities: Members

1. share a communal identity and have a label for that identity;

2. share common activities, views, and/or beliefs;

3. attribute the same social meanings to local communication practices (verbal or embodied);

4. overtly distinguish the community's ways of speaking ("the way we speak") from those of others ("the ways others speak");

5. socialize novice members (their young or outsiders) into the community's ways of speaking; and

6. take pride in shared ways of speaking and use that pride to maintain a communal identity.

Many kinds of communities become speech communities through sharing and taking pride in an **expressive system** and policing their own social boundaries through policing appropriate (intelligible, acceptable, artful) forms of expression.

I have to add three caveats to our discussion of speech communities. First, while all speech communities are communities, not all communities are speech communities.

Not all communities rely on local ways of speaking to sustain their status as communities. The technical term "speech community" foregrounds the significance of speech in a community's formation and the experience of its members.

Second, as you build culture for particular social groups (which may or may not be speech communities), keep in mind that, in spite of the positive connotations of the word "community" in the English language, some social groups resist the "community" label because it symbolically sets them apart from ordinary people. While studying the relationship between queer Latin@ bilingual speakers and other social groups in Phoenix, AZ, Cashman (2015) noticed his research participants expressed discomfort with being identified as a "community." As one of her respondents put it in an interview:

> I don't know if I consider … if I'd like to call it a gay community. It almost sounds like we are part of a colony or something [laughs] and we're out there and you have to go find us and you know look at all these people. I don't know. I just don't feel comfortable calling it a community. I feel like if this is who we are and we're here living. We're here like anyone else who is straight or gay. We belong here. We don't need to be called a community. (p. 432, simplified transcript)

Lastly, some speech communities view the boundaries separating them from other communities of speakers less positively than others. In a study of Hmong students in a California high school, Findlay (1994) found one of the key reasons why these students stuck together was their limited English proficiency. With a few exceptions, these students avoided contact with English-speaking classmates for fear of being laughed at for their limited command of English.

BARRIERS TO COORDINATED INTERACTION

1. **Misjudging the scope of norms and rules.** As you build culture for a specific group, take your time determining how widely shared a norm or a rule is in that group. A number of norms can be contested within the same group, meaning that some members might question the legitimacy of a norm other members follow. The practical implication of this is that if you begin following a contested norm, you might end up inadvertently aligning yourself with a faction within the group and against another. Also, some members of the group may follow (and enforce) idiosyncratic rules that only apply to them and not to the whole group.

2. **Exaggerating the uniqueness of cultural meanings.** Even if the cultural meanings you encounter in a social group strike you as strange and unfamiliar, remain open to the possibility that there is a set of meanings you share with the other group. Try to identify those shared meanings and use them as a starting point toward building intercultural frames.

3. **Assuming the existence of a (speech) community.** U.S. speakers attribute many positive associations and emotional power to the term "community." We also talk with relative ease about ethnic and racial communities, gender and sexual communities, religious communities, urban vs. rural communities, and so on. Don't look for community where there is none. Some groups are just groups, and not all communities are speech communities. Mischaracterizing a social group can lead you to assume the existence of social relations in the group that simply aren't there.

REFLECTION QUESTIONS

1. Think about your favorite sport. What's a specific rule players are expected to follow? What general norm may have led to the creation of that rule?

2. When was the last time you broke a rule or violated a norm? Whose norm did you violate, or whose rule did you break? Why did you do it? Were there any negative sanctions? Whose sanctions did you have to face?

3. In the chapter, I mention that U.S.-style small talk can be found in most physical places. Can you think of places where U.S.-style small talk is inappropriate?

4. Review the U.S. cultural premises related to small talk I formulated based on my personal experience. Do you agree with my formulation? If not, why not?

5. Name a group, a community, and a speech community you count yourself as a member of. Does the way you interact with others help you maintain your membership? If so, how?

13

"Is This Normal to Them?"

When Our Sense of Normality is Disrupted

LASHAWN: The summer of 2015 was hot. As of February 2016, it was the hottest Northern Hemisphere summer on record. It was also an incredibly hot summer politically in the United States. On the heels of numerous high-profile murders of African -Americans at the hands of law enforcement officers, the Black Lives Matter movement was in full swing. On June 17, nine members of Emmanuel African Methodist Episcopal Church in Charleston, South Carolina, were murdered by a white supremacist, and there was an intense debate across the South about removing the Confederate flag from public places. On June 27, I was riding my bike to babysit and passed a parking lot near a shopping center on a major road in my hometown, Fayetteville, Arkansas. I saw several big pickup trucks parked next to one another with large Confederate flags waving high from the beds. I was taken aback. My heart started racing. I stopped riding to take in what I was observing. I wanted to engage the individuals in conversation to understand what, given the events surrounding the flag's controversy, encouraged them to fly it so prominently. I was late, however, and had to continue my ride, but I experienced a wave of intense emotion as I pedaled. I felt anger, fear, bewilderment, and sorrow.

In this chapter, you will learn:

- about how intercultural communication, or the lack thereof, threatens ontological security

- how the number-one mentality, cultural stereotyping, and relative social privilege can undermine the project of building culture

- the importance of being aware of your sense of what is "normal."

HARPER: I chose to study abroad in Granada, Spain. As I walked into my art history class on the first day of school, my art history teacher at la Universidad de Granada greeted me by saying, "Hola guapa!" which more or less translates to "Hello, hot stuff!" in English. When he first said this to me, I was taken back. I thought to myself, *Is that appropriate*? No teacher in the United States would ever say that to me when I walk into class. I responded with an awkward smile and then proceeded to sit at my desk. I knew that Granadans are typically stereotyped as dramatic and animated. However, I quickly came to learn that is how all Granadans greet each other. In Granada, when you see someone you know, both females and males will greet the other individual with "Hola guapo/a!" The individual receiving the greeting generally responds by giving a side kiss on the other person's cheek. This interaction is how people great each other no matter age, gender, or profession.

The majority of our interactions with others go smoothly. They feel routine, "business as usual." Most of the time, the expectations we bring to such interactions are met and we find we were able to reach the goals we set out to pursue. Nonetheless, throughout our communicative lives, we learn to expect the unexpected—that is, to be prepared for interactions in which others violate our expectations or keep us from reaching our goals. We have some plausible ready-made explanations for why our interactional partners might be acting in unexpected ways: "Yep, classic Margo!" "Brian is usually so cheerful … He must have gotten some bad news at work." "Okay, Mom, let's continue this conversation when you are not in a rush."

Sometimes, however, we sense that our conversational partner violated our expectations but we don't have an easy (or even a complicated) explanation for what happened. We step back from the flow of interaction and ask, "What is going on? What went wrong? Is someone at fault?" We feel that our sense of what is normal is disrupted. This is a bigger problem than it sounds: as humans, we are deeply invested in maintaining a sense of normalcy (order, meaning, and continuity) in our lives. In this chapter, I review possible responses to such disruptions, especially in the context of intercultural interactions in which you need to act as an **intercultural practitioner**. In particular, I contrast **building culture** with less practically useful responses that deny the richness of rich points (the **number-one mentality** and **cultural stereotyping**) or keep you from building culture altogether (**cognitive bias** and the lack of reflection on one's **relative social privilege**).

WHEN YOUR "NORMAL" IS DISRUPTED

There are multiple possible responses to the situation I describe above. One way to unravel the mystery of why a conversation derailed is to frame our interaction as "intercultural"—that is, as involving participants who are conceivably of different cultural backgrounds based on their race, nationality, gender, religion, region of origin, language or linguistic variety, and so on and to interpret our moment (or moments) of communicative confusion as a **rich point** (or a series of rich points).

As you respond to communication trouble in this way, five things happen:

1. You have just started **building culture** for your conversational partner(s).

2. By positing that your conversation is intercultural in nature, you have identified your partners as **cultural others**—that is, persons whose actions, you assume, are guided by a system of communicative actions and meanings different from yours.

3. You have just admitted that your conversational partner(s) doesn't seem to share your sense of what counts as "normal" interaction.

4. You have just opened up the possibility that you lack the **interactional frame** to interpret the meaning of something they had said or done, and, as a result, you may have said or done something that struck them as silly, inappropriate, or downright unacceptable and may now look like a fool to them.

5. Because you lack understanding of the frame for your conversational partner's actions, you also lack the **interactional script**: you can't think of an obvious way to go on interacting with them.

Moments in which all of the above are happening all of a sudden can be profoundly disorienting. We feel like we need to "fix" the situation, but we don't know how—in fact, we aren't even sure exactly what it is we are supposed to fix. We are thrown for a loop, and we often end up feeling confused, incompetent, or worse—angry, fearful, bewildered, and sad, like Lashawn in the first rich point narrative at the beginning of this chapter.

Threats to Ontological Security

Communication troubles—whether or not they are understood as intercultural—rich points, and the cultural othering with which they confront us can feel frightening because they undermine our sense of **ontological security** (Boromisza-Habashi & Xiong, 2019; Croft, 2012). We are ontologically secure when we feel like our individual selves, our lives, and the world around us form a continuous and orderly story line. The term "ontology" points to a sense of being; "ontological security" signals the human desire for a secure, uninterrupted sense of being. In a state of ontological security, humans feel they are in a social setting where interaction is at least somewhat predictable, their relationships are reasonably stable, and everyone seems to be acting according to shared common sense. In other words, the social world appears coherent and "normal." Rich points are rich because we can't simply dismiss someone else's actions as incoherent or "crazy." Instead, we sense there is more going on in the moment than meets the eye: deeper meanings, subtle differences, and underlying systems are at work that we are unable to easily access. Someone else's "normal" intrudes on our "normal," and our sense of self and the world is called into question.

Rich points rarely shatter our overall sense of normalcy. Also, they aren't always tied to single interactions in which someone violates our expectations. We can experience rich points at the tail end of a series of interactions as we pick up on a strange pattern, and our emotional response can vary from surprise through annoyance to a full-blown identity crisis. What connects these experiences and responses is that we reach for "culture" as an explanatory device. We find ourselves asking the question: "Is it possible that what they did there made sense to them but not to me? Is it possible that their action is, in one way or another, 'cultural'?"

However, the threat rich points and cultural othering pose to our ontological security can have a sort of ripple effect: cultural othering itself can undermine the ontological security of those we have "othered." It's not just our sense of what's "normal" that is disrupted by someone we now see as a cultural "other"; it is not just we who feel a need to restore a sense of normalcy without which we simply can't go on interacting. Our cultural other's ontological security may have also been disrupted as they see us suddenly look at them through a different pair of eyes. They, too, sense they are no longer "just people" to us but "people with unfamiliar cultures." You can probably see how this can get very awkward, very fast.

DISMISSING THE RICHNESS OF RICH POINTS

CULTURAL PRAGMATICS SAYS

You will know you have succeeded as an intercultural practitioner when you are able to restore coordinated interaction with a cultural other for the purpose of completing a task or set of tasks (e.g., explaining a task to, or organizing an event with, a coworker, organizing an event, communicating friendly intentions or mutual respect, providing the kind of help the other needs, etc.).

Once we acknowledge that we are forced to deal with cultural difference, we face a choice. You can accept the main argument of this book and assume that there are partially similar, partially different **expressive systems** at work, and we explore the possibility of not only different "normals" implied in and sustained by those systems but of a new, shared "normal" that can help us restore coordinated interaction.

However, this is not the only possible response to rich points. You are also free to *dismiss the richness of the rich point* that compels you to pursue systematic cultural differences and dismiss the other culture and the cultural other as inferior to us and our way of doing things.

The Number-One Mentality

A way of thinking that leads you to reduce the richness of rich points is what Agar (1994) calls the **number-one mentality.**

> There are two ways of looking at differences between you and somebody else. One way is to figure out that the differences are the tip of the iceberg, the signal that two different *systems* are at work. Another way is to notice all the things that the other person *lacks* when compared to you, the so-called *deficit theory* approach. Number-one types—American or any other—use the deficit theory. They're the best, anything else is less than the best, anyone who would call into question who they are when they're already the best is a fool or a masochist ... (p. 23, emphasis in the original)

The number-one mentality, which is a form of **ethnocentrism** (assuming your cultural group is the best one there is; Stewart & Bennett, 1991), offers you a deceptively easy solution to the disorienting experience of cultural difference: assume you are better than the other and expect them to either conform to your way of doing things or leave you alone. Noticing and explaining the breakdown of coordinated interaction as a mismatch between different expressive systems in intercultural interaction and then reconstructing and bridging elements of those systems requires more time, effort, and creativity. I say "deceptively easy" because although the number-one mentality produces quick results, it is much less likely to result in coordinated interaction than reconstructing and bridging expressive systems.

One expression of the number-one mentality is the expectation that all social groups in a given society—especially immigrants and minorities—assimilate into the majority society and its "culture." You might ask: "Why is expecting minorities and immigrants to assimilate a bad thing?" If you are indeed asking this question, chances are that you have, at a particular point or over years and years, internalized the **myth of assimilation or assimilationism**, the notion that each nation has a culture and that minorities and immigrants ought to earn the respect of the social majority by adopting the fundamental moral principles of that culture. Let me explain.

In the United States, we find a particular version of the myth of assimilation (Flores, 2001). This liberal, multiculturalist version claims the following:

- America's culture is multiculturalism.

- In America, similarities among social (racial, ethnic) groups matter more than differences.

- Everyone in America is a member of the human race and should treat others as members of the human race.

- America is a multicultural society and, as such, a melting pot of cultures.

- Too much emphasis on cultural difference (as opposed to similarity) feeds cultural fragmentation.

- Cultural fragmentation undermines the formation of the ideal American society united in social harmony and similarity.

- Everyone in America needs to find a way to fit into, and to promote, the harmonious society. Luckily, fitting in brings rewards, such as social and career success.

This message of universal humanity may sound agreeable, even exciting. Keep in mind, though, that all ideals, even supposedly universal ones, are conceived on someone's terms. The principles of U.S. assimilationism have a dual function: they can be held up as a (universal) ideal, but they can also be invoked to admonish groups or their members who aren't willing to completely and unconditionally join the project of building a harmonious society and nation. From the perspective of marginalized social groups, this—seemingly universal—social project was initiated and is sustained by a culturally, socially, and economically dominant (White, middle-class, genteel, English-speaking) majority. Hence, it is members of that majority who stand to benefit the most from it and who get to say how much difference is too much. This logic can be particularly alienating for members of marginalized groups (e.g., racial, ethnic, and sexual minorities and working-class citizens) who don't feel at home in the majority society, who feel like they have to give up too much to belong, who don't experience the social or economic benefits of the melting pot, or all of the above. Consider the example of the Chicana scholar Emma Pérez, who

> explains that as a young child she felt alienated and ridiculed in the largely White school she attended and that coming home to her mother after school restored a sense of calmness and tranquility. Talking with her mother in Spanish and singing songs with her mother in Spanish reconstructed cultural pride and location. (Flores, 2001, p. 32)

Assimilationism, if you take it to its logical conclusion, can lead you to evaluate Pérez's reaction to her experiences in the majority White school as a failure to assimilate rather than as the expression of a perfectly normal human desire for ontological security.

Another drawback of the type of assimilationism I describe here is that it can take on what the linguist Jonathan Rosa (2019) called a "postmulticultural" quality. In the context of the contemporary United States, **postmulticulturalism** applies especially often to Latinx people, whom an increasing number of U.S. citizens see as incorrigible and incapable of assimilation into majority society. Signs of postmulticulturalism include mass deportation, mass detention, and militarizing the country's southern border. In the context of intercultural interactions, postmulticulturalism gives speakers the license to automatically dismiss Latinx speakers who don't speak "proper English" or who "fail" to express themselves according to the expectations of dominant (majority White) society in other ways.

Some racial minority groups in the United States respond to postmulticulturalism by trying to mitigate being seen as a racial minority and to play into the expectations of multiculturalist assimilationism. **Model minorities** such as affluent Indian Americans in North Carolina seek to cast themselves as a cultural instead of a racial minority in order to avoid the stigma of being seen as a problem minority (Piller, 2017). Professional Indian Americans living in the region present themselves as hardworking patriots who speak "good English" and restrict their cultural identity to maintaining cultural institutions, national organizations, and film and music festivals. Model minorities sustain assimilationism in U.S. society, which, as we have seen before, can place linguistic, racial, and other types of minorities in positions of disadvantage.

A Practical Question

"Should we fault model minorities, Indian American or others, for doing the hard work of assimilating into U.S. society? Fitting in is a *huge* accomplishment for ethnic and racial minorities."

I am not advocating for morally faulting any of these minorities for the admittedly hard work of assimilation. I am simply pointing out that their efforts feed into expectations of assimilation toward minorities for whom it is less possible to "fit in." Also, as a **pluralist**, I believe in the possibility of a society that can accommodate those who don't accept the logic of assimilationism.

Cultural Stereotyping

Another common response to rich points that takes away from their richness is **cultural stereotyping**. In the context of social interaction, stereotyping involves naming groups of people ("Mexicans," "women," "millennials," "the one percent," etc.) and associating them with some essential quality—that is, a quality that defines them as a group. We rely on stereotypes for the purpose of accomplishing practical actions.

We invoke stereotypes explicitly (Robles & Kurylo, 2017) or implicitly to quickly devise an interpretation or a course of action when we are feeling stumped. In intercultural interaction, you may feel compelled to interact with cultural others on the basis of cultural stereotypes you hold to be at least partially accurate. Unlike cultural generalizations, cultural stereotypes contain an element of negative or positive judgment, they are often applied to individual members of stereotyped groups, they rarely allow exceptions, and they are supported by little to no evidence.

Unfortunately, stereotypes have two major disadvantages. First, they are only rarely, if ever, accurate representations of the expressive systems speakers rely on to interact with others. This is what Harper (in the second narrative at the beginning of this chapter) learned about greetings in Granada, Spain. After initially interpreting "Hola guapa!" as evidence that the people of Granada were indeed "dramatic and animated," she found out that this type of greeting was simply a convention. Second, the invocation of stereotypes can be the source of rich points for others, especially for those being stereotyped. Let's review examples of both of these disadvantages.

Carbaugh (2005) gives us three cultural stereotypes speakers invoke to explain unfamiliar or strange communicative actions that say nothing about what members of the stereotyped groups are attempting to do communicatively:

- In public areas, many Finns refrain from engaging in casual conversations with strangers. From a Finnish cultural perspective, casual conversation involves too much unnecessary talk (stating the obvious, no discussion of worthy topics, etc.). U.S. speakers interpret this as evidence of Finns' shyness and social reserve.

- Russian speakers often refrain from talking about sex in public. From a Russian cultural perspective, discussing sex in public takes away from its value. U.S. speakers interpret this as evidence that decades of oppression have taught Russians not to speak their minds in public.

- Many American speakers use talk to fill silences in interpersonal interactions with others they don't know very well. From a U.S. cultural perspective, silence is the lack of talk, which indicates lack of engagement and/or social distance. Silence should therefore be avoided. Finns (and other Europeans) interpret this as evidence that Americans are superficial.

CULTURAL PRAGMATICS SAYS

No language, linguistic variety, or speech style has inherent value. Think of them as different (although some-times overlapping) expressive systems, all of which can be used for the purpose of accomplishing coordinated interaction.

We don't just stereotype speakers: we often stereotype their speech as well. No language, linguistic variety, or regional speech style is "better" or "worse" than others by definition. Speakers nonetheless continue to distinguish more and less valued forms of speech and their more and less valued speakers. Stereotypes about people and their speech mutually reinforce one another in interaction: the qualities of a people are transferred to their speech, and vice versa. Consider these examples (Saville-Troike, 2003):

In Iran, Tehrani is reportedly prestigious because it is spoken in the capital, where life is to be enjoyed "and there are opportunities for everything and everybody"; Shirazi is good-sounding because it has a great literary heritage and has been the native dialect of many poets and musicians.

In Saudi Arabia, speakers of the Najdi variety are perceived as strong and pure because it is associated with the highly valued desert life. Additionally, it is the dialect spoken by the royal family.

In Indonesia, speakers of Hoakiau (Chinese) Malay are perceived as money-minded and hardworking because of their traditional role as businessmen in the economy.

In the United States, a southern "drawl" is associated by northerners with slow movement and laziness in men, though it is often admired in women. (pp. 190–191)

In intercultural encounters, cultural stereotypes are a resource for mitigating the unsettling experience of a rich point and the related threat to one's ontological security. However, the danger of invoking cultural stereotypes is not only that they tell you very little, if anything, about your conversational partner's expressive system: it can also lead someone else to experience a rich point and a threat to their sense of self. Consider, for example, the global cultural stereotype that native English speakers are White (Ramjattan, 2019). As a result of this stereotype, non-White teachers of English often find their own competence questioned either by students who travel to majority English-speaking countries to learn English as a foreign language or by their representatives. Maria, an ethnically Japanese English teacher employed at a private English language school in Toronto reported this encounter:

It was actually lunchtime, and I came to my class 5 minutes prior to teaching. I had some students in my room having lunch, and this Japanese student was just eyeing me. When she saw me going through materials, she realized that I was a teacher. She turned to me and was like, "Are you Japanese?" And I said, "'No, I'm not." And she was like, "Oh, okay." It was very awkward. … It seemed that she did not want to be taught by a Japanese person. (p. 135)

Encountering a non-White teacher in the classroom can disappoint students who feel they made a considerable investment into being taught English by an "actual" (read: White) native speaker of English. They sometimes communicate their dissatisfaction through representatives or intermediaries. Yun, an ethnically Chinese teacher working at the same school, reported the following:

My Saudi students have a cultural bureau that sponsors them. So the bureau apparently called our students up and asked if any of our teachers at Transnational School had an accent. My boss told this to me and seemed to imply that they were asking about me. I was like, "Do I have an accent?" And he replied,

"No, I don't think you have an accent blah blah blah." But in my head, I'm like, "Why are you bringing this up to me?" Like he brought it up not only once, but two or three times after that, which made it more hurtful for me. (p. 134)

In these examples, a cultural stereotype poses a threat to the ontological security of two non-White English teachers who were qualified enough to be hired by the Canadian language school. As I'm sure you can imagine, having your professional abilities questioned on the basis of your race is a major blow to one's self-worth.

Cultural stereotyping, which more or less completely disregards the expressive systems cultural others bring to intercultural encounters, can also have material consequences. Instructors at U.S. colleges and universities regularly stereotype Chinese international students as socially, linguistically, and academically incompetent (Heng, 2018). As a result of these stereotypes, Chinese students have a difficult time succeeding in some university courses—especially in the social sciences and the humanities, where there is a heavy emphasis on language skills—and their grades and career opportunities often suffer as a result. Chinese students' disappointing performance in the U.S. college classroom, Heng argues, has very little to do with their academic potential or intelligence and much more to do with the educational system into which they were socialized as kids and young adults and the ways of speaking they learned in the process. As the Chinese educational system places heavy emphasis on standardized testing, Chinese students arrive in the United States without knowledge of the type of classroom culture U.S. instructors take for granted and the language skills necessary to participate in that culture. They are confused by the learner-centered classroom where students share their thoughts and opinions and are rewarded for it with high participation scores. They are not used to challenging teachers and displaying critical thinking. They are well trained to take tests on English vocabulary and grammar but not to join a classroom discussion or to make an argument on the fly. Fortunately, most of them are resilient and creative enough to learn the expectations of the U.S. college classroom, but the learning curve is steep, institutional support is minimal, and instructors' discouraging feedback about their performance and abilities is not helping.

In some cases, culturally stereotyped speakers can turn stereotyping to their advantage. In the excerpt below, the president (P) of an Asian American Chamber of Commerce (AACC) located in Texas tells an interviewer (IR) about how their organization came to be as a result of local White politicians' desire to secure "the Asian vote" (Shrikant, 2018).

EXCERPT 13.1. (from Shrikant, 2018, p. 291, simplified)

P   The politicians challenged us: "Hey, what are you doing, Asians?" What Asians? There's no such … Strictly speaking, there's no such thing as Asian.

IR   Yeah …

P   There's only Indian, Chinese, Pakistani, Korean … But those are different! You cannot!

IR   So …

P   The language …

IR   The politicians were who? The mayor or …

P   Senators.

IR   Senators …

P   Yeah. "Hey guys, why don't you form yourselves? We need your votes."

IR   Oh okay, so these White senators, and they wanted … Okay.

P   Yeah, yeah. Well, there is somehow a connection because one White senator, [name], his wife is Asian.

IR   Oh

P   It started there. So [the idea spread to] [names two other senators] and all the different … Yeah, so they challenged us: "Hey, we need your votes. Can you fund my campaign?" "How do you do that?" "Well why don't you form yourself among yourselves?" That was the beginning, and I was the first. I was one of the many who sat down to form the group [the Asian American Voters' Coalition, which started registering voters]. … So they were thinking how to get that vote. The Asian vote. So we formed the voters' coalition. It was successful. So they said, now it's time. You have the politics. You need business. Why don't you form a chamber of commerce? So they formed the chamber of commerce.

The AACC's president clearly disagrees with White politicians' stereotypical talk about "Asians" as a homogenous racial category. However, he also narrates how immigrants from India, China, Pakistan, Korea, and other countries lumped together into the category of "Asian" countries were able to turn this stereotype into political power and networking opportunities with the willing collaboration of local White political and business elites who also benefited from the existence of "Asian" organizations. This win-win outcome, however, doesn't mean stereotyped minorities can always use stereotypes to their advantage. Notice that the "Asians" in this example were in a position to accumulate political and business influence and, as a result, became "useful" partners for Whites. The "Asian" teachers in the previous example had to face cultural stereotypes as individuals within an organization in which they were at the mercy of their employers and their "clients," the students. In addition, the political influence "Asians" in Texas accomplished did not dissolve the "Asian" stereotype. To this day, AACC members have to keep reminding outsiders of the linguistic, cultural, ethnic, and national diversity of "Asians" (Shrikant, 2018).

Both the number-one mentality and cultural stereotyping are strategies for restoring our sense of normality when we experience rich points. Both strategies involve forcing our own sense of what is "normal" on a cultural "other" for the sake of restoring our sense of ontological security. Both strategies have the potential to undermine our conversational partners' ontological security. In addition, they are simply impractical: they distract us from the uniqueness and complexity of expressive systems other than our own and thus keep us from building **intercultural frames** for the purpose of restoring coordinated interaction and getting things done with others.

These strategies, which speakers rely on much too often in intercultural encounters, remind us that our "normal" is not necessarily someone else's "normal." Situations in which we find ourselves interacting with, and depending on the collaboration of, cultural others for the sake of completing a task confront us with the fact that we live in a world where there isn't one "normal": rather, there are multiple "normals" we need to find ways to reconcile, at least momentarily.

AVOIDING BUILDING CULTURE

Let's turn to another way your "normal" can interfere with building culture: by *keeping you from considering the role of culture at all*. In this section, I will briefly discuss cognitive biases and then spend more time on relative social privilege, as it is a bit harder to grasp.

Cognitive Biases

A key reason for beginning to exercise reflexivity even before you experience a rich point is that our habitual ways of thinking can distract us from the necessity, possibility, and utility of building culture. When we find ourselves in situations in which we can't easily explain someone's conduct, we can easily fall back onto blaming others on the basis of their personality, their weak grasp on reality, or our commitment to being right. You should reflect on your own biases that fall into the following categories:

- **fundamental attribution error**: the tendency to overestimate the importance of individuals' personality and underestimate the role of context in their actions (Ross, 1977);

- **naïve realism**: the belief that only you see objective reality and your conversational partner doesn't (Ross & Ward, 1995); and

- **confirmation bias**: the tendency to pay attention only to information that confirms our personal theories about others and the world and to disregard information that conflicts with our assumptions (Wason, 1960).

Relative Social Privilege

My students often use the term "privilege," but they use it to mean different things. Some associate privilege with wealth, others with race, and yet others with being an American citizen. All of these interpretations of privilege have a kernel of truth in them, but they are too narrow and fixed to be useful. For the purpose of this discussion, let's define **relative social privilege** by identifying five of its characteristics:

> First, privilege is a special advantage; it is neither common nor universal. Second, it is granted, not earned or brought into being by one's individual effort or talent. Third, privilege is a right or entitlement that is related to a preferred status or rank. Fourth, privilege is exercised for the benefit of the recipient and to the exclusion or detriment of others. Finally, a privileged status is often outside of the awareness of the person possessing it ... (Black & Stone, 2005, p. 244)

Social privilege is easier to imagine if you tie it to particular contexts. Interaction with government agencies is a context that often serves as a stark reminder of one's social privilege or lack thereof. Joëlle Cruz, a communication scholar of African descent, gives us a visceral poetic description of her experience going through immigration control at an international airport in the United States as non-U.S. citizen:

> The brown body noticeably shrinks at immigration control upon entering the United States. Correction: the body starts to shrink as soon as the plane lands. The title (PhD) and all achievements do not matter anymore. The brown body becomes deferent and folds itself into a square: that of the desirable immigrant. I maintain what the body thinks is a polite facial expression: do not make too much eye contact as if to appear defiant, remain calm, and only answer questions you are asked. The brown body is irremediably scared of the uniforms at immigration control. It fears it always looks suspicious.

> To help, the body has traveled with more documents than necessary for the past 10 years. There are all the I-20s, which came attached to each student visa at all institutions where the body has been. There is the OPT card, or card for optional practical training, a 1-year work card that has long expired. There is the old passport as well as the new one. There is a special folder where all documents have been neatly contained, each piece painstakingly archived, each letter of support kept. The body carries the old passport because it contains multiple visas. "You never know, you simply never know" is what the body keeps telling itself.

> It is always a relief when the brown body crosses the invisible line after immigration control and is now in the U.S. It can now relax a bit, shop at airport stores for magazines and imagine tomorrow, next week, and maybe next month. Yet the

body lives in suspension still awaiting regularization in the form of permanent residency or a green card. The body holds privileged status as a professor on the tenure track but somehow exists in waiting. How much more time? How many more years? (Cruz, McDonald, Broadfoot, Chuang, & Ganesh, 2018, p. 5)

Contrast her experience with Canadian communication scholar Jamie McDonald's encounter with an agent of the Department of Motor Vehicles in Texas:

> I am a foreign national living in the U.S.
>
> But in my everyday life, I feel that I am largely read as "American."
>
> My foreignness is closeted to others who don't see a White male who speaks English with a North American accent as a foreigner.
>
> I also identify as gay.
>
> And I feel that I am read as gay most places that I go.
>
> Through my demeanor. Mannerisms. Clothes.
>
> It's not my gay identity that I feel is closeted to others.
>
> It's my foreignness.
>
> This becomes particularly clear when I arrive at a Texas Department of Motor Vehicles office in San Antonio to renew my driver's license during the summer of 2014.
>
> I fill out the renewal application and respond "no" to the question: "Are you a U.S. citizen?"
>
> I give the form to the agent and wait.
>
> After a few minutes, a confused look comes upon his face.
>
> "You're not an American citizen?" he asks.
>
> "Nope," I say. "I am on a temporary worker visa."
>
> He looks up at me again.
>
> "You look American to me!" he states. (Cruz, McDonald, Broadfoot, Chuang, & Ganesh, 2018, p. 7)

There are clear differences between the contexts of Cruz's and McDonald's experiences: one took place at the airport, the other at a DMV; Cruz was dealing with U.S. immigration, McDonald with a DMV agent. However, notice the important similarities: neither one of them is a U.S. citizen, both of them are involved in situations where a representative of a government agency determines their immigration status, and both of them have all of their paperwork in order. Once you consider these similarities, you will see the difference between the two cases that is the most important for the purpose of the discussion of social privilege—namely, that McDonald is White—and, in addition, speaks Standard American English—while Cruz isn't. Being White and speaking English without a noticeable "accent" affords McDonald the psychological comfort of passing as a "normal" citizen in the eyes of U.S. authorities, a luxury Cruz doesn't get to enjoy. McDonald enjoyed the social privilege of being seen as "normal" due to his race and language; Cruz didn't.

You may find yourself asking, "What was Cruz worried about if all of her paperwork was in order? Also, weren't Cruz's PhD and tenure track professor status sources of social privilege?" Let's take these questions one by one. The first question, ironically, comes from a place of social privilege because it calls into question someone's right to her own experience—in particular, the experience of a significant threat to ontological security. Also, if you assume U.S. immigration is a simple matter of documentation, you are disregarding the historical and psychological burden of the negative immigration experience all non-White people and/or non-native speakers of English entering the United States carry with them. Even if non-White and/or non-native speaker immigrants don't personally experience discrimination, disbelief, or suspicion from immigration officers, the example of others (e.g., family, friends, ancestors, immigrants, and refugees in the media) before them weighs heavily on their psyche as they approach U.S. immigration.

The answer to the second question is: not in this situation. Social privilege is context bound in the sense that what is the source of privilege in one type of social encounter is not one in another. Having a PhD can certainly be the source of privilege in an encounter with an undergraduate or graduate student. However, in an encounter with immigration, it has no such function. In fact, a PhD degree can work against one's social privilege. For example, people with PhD degrees often have to hide their credentials when they seek employment outside academia in order not to appear overqualified.

Social privilege is always relative to the social privilege of others with whom you are interacting. Also, multiple sources of privilege—such as being White and a competent speaker of Standard American English—can combine to give you, or your interactional partner, a greater amount of social privilege. The flip side of combined sources of social privilege is **intersectionality**, belonging in multiple social categories marked by the lack of social privilege, which in turn reinforces social hierarchies and systemic discrimination.

Linguistic Privilege

In the United States and beyond, we can distinguish the following widely recognized sources of social privilege (Black & Stone, 2005):

- Racial privilege

- Gender privilege

- Privilege derived from sexual orientation

- Privilege derived from socioeconomic status

- Privilege derived from age

- Privilege derived from physical or mental ability

- Privilege derived from religious affiliation

To this list, we must add **linguistic privilege**—that is, social privilege derived from one's ability to competently speak a linguistic variety or style valued in a particular social context. Speakers who are not fully (or not at all) competent in valued ways of speaking are acutely aware of this form of privilege and are sometimes harshly reminded of it. Consider the example of Dr. Bamidele Adeagbo, a medical doctor of Nigerian descent, who was called to testify in a court case in Alberta, Canada (Ogunyemi, 2019). The case involved two parents charged with failing to seek appropriate medical help for their son (who suffered from fatal bacterial meningitis) and instead trying to treat him with herbal remedies. Dr. Adeagbo performed the autopsy on the son. Justice Terry Clarkson acquitted the parents after questioning the credibility of Dr. Adagbo's testimony based on his accent:

> "His ability to articulate his thoughts in an understandable fashion was severely compromised by: his garbled enunciation; his failure to use appropriate endings for plurals and past tenses; his failure to use the appropriate definite and indefinite articles; his repeated emphasis on the wrong syllables; dropping his Hs; mispronouncing his vowels; and the speed of his responses," Clackson wrote [in his decision]. (para 6)

As this example shows, the lack of linguistic privilege combined with a lack of racial privilege is not only a moral but a practical issue as well. We can certainly fault the judge for dismissing the doctor's testimony on the basis of **accentism**—discrimination against people who speak a language with a perceived, nonvalued accent. However, we should also recognize the harm done to the professional credibility, reputation, and ontological security of Dr. Adeagbo and, by extension, the other hundreds of doctors of Nigerian descent working in Canada today.

Another way in which linguistic privilege shapes intercultural interactions is when relatively privileged speakers consider the use of particular forms and channels of speaking as the most valued forms of participation. Privileging language use over other forms of participation puts those members who are less competent or willing speakers at a disadvantage because they have fewer opportunities to shape the social life of the group or organization. While conducting research in an LGBT activist organization in southern Arizona, the communication scholar Karma Chávez (2012) interviewed the only queer woman of color in the organization. In the interview, the woman, Geovanna, contrasted "talking" and "acting" as two possible modes of doing activism. As she explained:

I'm surrounded by these smart people, and my perception is that they talk too much with these big-ass words and go in circles, and there's never a point where they act. Mexicans, Latinos, Native Americans, we tend to be more timid and to the point, but we perform action after that. (p. 31)

You can hear in Geovanna's words (being "surrounded by smart people" and their "big-ass words") that her involvement in the organization threatens her sense of ontological security. Chávez noticed that White activists tended to prefer meetings, emails, and strategy sessions as forms of participation—all forms of language use with which Geovanna was less familiar or comfortable. Unfortunately, the perfectly well-intentioned White members set the agenda of the organization using these forms and channels of language, effectively marginalizing Geovanna and failing to build successful alliances with non-White LGBT activists in the region.

A Practical Question

"How can you expect a judge to reflect on the expressive systems of all kinds of people who testify in the courtroom? Judges in most justice systems are already overworked."

You make a valid point about how overburdened justice systems tend to be around the world. However, this is not a good argument against finding solutions to the problem of cultural (including linguistic) difference in courtrooms. I would argue that government authorities ought to fund services that can help judges deal with cases like Dr. Adeagbo's.

From the perspective of the intercultural practitioner, the key issue with relative social privilege is that it prevents those with privilege from building culture, which requires treating one's conversational partner as a cultural other and carefully reconstructing the expressive system they bring to an interaction for the purpose of (re)establishing coordinated interaction. Instead, those with privilege often treat their conversational partners as the source of the interactional problem, at best, or deficient (less than, incompetent, uneducated, unmotivated, etc.) people, at worst. It is the responsibility of intercultural practitioners with social privilege to identify that privilege in the context of social interaction and to understand how it leads them to disregard cultural difference and to prevent the construction of intercultural frames and scripts.

BARRIERS TO COORDINATED INTERACTION

1. **Dismissing (underestimating, denying) the richness of rich points**. The number-one mentality and cultural stereotyping distract from the complexity of the culturally variable expressive systems that inform how speakers participate in social interaction. The more limited sense you have of relevant features of

misaligned expressive systems (i.e., systems of communication practices and their meanings), the less effective intercultural practitioner you are likely to be.

2. **Failure to identify relative social privilege.** Your relative social privilege in the context of a given interaction may give you license to avoid cultural reflection (i.e., building culture) altogether. In order to work toward restoring coordinated interaction with a cultural other, you will need to understand your privilege and how it is preventing you from building culture. The next step is carefully listening to relatively less privileged participants and tracking systematic similarities and differences between your expressive systems. Let me offer you a very simple rule of thumb: the more relative social privilege you have in a particular context, the more responsibility you have to listen, as opposed to forcing your "normal" on your conversational partner.

REFLECTION QUESTIONS

The reflection questions and prompts I list here are especially difficult. Try to be as honest as possible. Remember: your answers to these questions will help you see what sense of normalcy you are bringing to intercultural encounters.

1. Think of a time when you felt you were stereotyped. Who stereotyped you, and how? Now, think about when you might have (intentionally or unintentionally) stereotyped someone else. Who did you stereotype, and on what basis?

2. Do you agree with any/all of the tenets of liberal multiculturalist assimilationism? Why or why not?

3. Can you recall a time when you (explicitly or implicitly) invoked a cultural stereotype to make sense of a rich point?

4. Can you think of a cultural group or community who you think often act "too sensitive"? In what types of contexts do they seem to act "sensitive"? Once you identify a group, do a quick thought experiment: What if, when they are acting "sensitive," they are trying to tell you something important about what they believe?

5. Think about the classroom in which you are using this book. Who has relative social privilege in this context? What sort of privilege do they have? By comparison, who lacks relative social privilege?

14

"What Does an Intercultural Practitioner Actually Do?"

A Guide to Building Culture

JIAN: My family currently lives in a big city in southern China called Guangzhou. My younger brother and I were born and raised in Guangzhou, but my parents moved to the city from a small county called Pingyuan. We often travel back to Pingyuan to visit my parents' relatives. Two years ago, I traveled back to Pingyuan with my family for Chinese New Year. My father took me and my younger brother to my Grandfather's cousin's home. He was an old man with an elementary school education who lived in Pingyuan his whole life. My father asked the old man about his health and introduced me and my younger brother to him. He asked my father where I worked, and my father explained that I wasn't working yet and that I was going to study abroad that summer. When he heard this, he seemed angry and said to my father, "You spend too much on your daughter, it is useless for a girl to study that much!" His words made me angry, but I could not reply to him in a rude manner because he was older than me.

OAKLEY: As an infantryman in the United States Army, I had the opportunity to take part in training events with members of allied militaries. In the summer of 2007, my company was ordered to

In this chapter, you will learn:

- the process of building culture

- what happens before and after you build culture

- that building culture is not going to solve all your problems

train alongside a company from the *Armée de terre*, the French Army. Once all the logistics were worked out, we moved out on a simulated foot patrol, armed with empty weapons, with no simulated enemy to fight. We found communication not to be an issue, as hand signals translate relatively well regardless of language. The issue arose when we made our first security halt. Security halts are made for a variety of reasons, such as the leadership needing to check the map, radio higher command, or communicate instructions to the unit. The point of a security halt is to get moving quickly, but this fact seemed to be lost on the French. To our mild dismay, every time we stopped walking, all of them, officers included, would take off their rucksacks, sit, and start eating, regardless of how long it had been since their last meal. This was naturally frustrating to my unit due to the fact that our standard operating procedure (SOP) dictated that there are specific times and places to eat. This led us to believe that the French soldiers were lazy and not taking the training seriously. Our officers attempted to explain to their French counterparts how things were going to work, but they were having no part of it.

E very semester, on the first day of teaching intercultural communication, I tell my students that what I want to teach them is to run toward cultural difference instead of running away from it. Having better—that is, coordinated—intercultural interactions requires confronting cultural difference. This is, of course, much easier said than done. Encountering cultural difference can be upsetting or disorienting, to which the natural human response is flight. Also, even if you decide to confront cultural difference in social interaction, it is not obvious how best to confront and move past the experience of confusion, **misunderstanding**, or **miscommunication**.

In this chapter, I summarize insights from the rest of the book and present them to you in the form of a guide that will help you know what to do once you decide to run toward culture. I offer you a guide for discovering *cultural* differences in the ways you and a cultural other (or others) communicate, differences that may explain why your conversations or your relationship with a cultural other suddenly feels strange. In particular, this guide contains descriptions of the stages of the process of **building culture** and questions you can productively ask before, during, and after you have built culture. In order to make the discussion a bit less abstract and more easily adaptable to your situation, I will list questions relevant to two types of context in which building culture often becomes a necessity: interpersonal relationships, as in Jian's rich point narrative above, and relationships specific to the workplace, as in Oakley's.

FOUR DISCLAIMERS

Before we begin, let me make four disclaimers about the guide for building culture:

Building Culture Is a Nonlinear Process

The way I lay out the stages of building culture may lead you to believe the process is neat and linear. As you follow the stages, keep in mind that your particular situation or process may force you to circle back to earlier stages. Much of building culture consists of observation, creating hypotheses (creating possible explanations for why a cultural other is communicating the way they do), and hypothesis testing (asking speech community members for feedback on your hypothesis and acting on your hypotheses to see if they help you achieve **coordinated interaction** with a cultural other). When a hypothesis fails the ultimate test of participation in social interaction, you have to go back to the drawing board to figure out why and how you made a mistake in interpreting a type of communicative action. Going back to the drawing board involves making new observations, rethinking your hypothesis.

> ### A Practical Question
>
> "Is it possible that my hypothesis was correct, but the people with whom I was interacting weren't playing by the (cultural) rules of their social group?"
>
> Yes, that is possible. People may break the rules of their communities a couple of times, or consistently. This is why it's unwise to draw broad conclusions about a cultural group's ways of speaking on the basis of observing a single member.

Culture Is Not Always the Best Explanation

It is possible that the communication problem you experience in an intercultural encounter may not require a cultural explanation. Not all communication trouble has its roots in cultural differences, even if the participants are members of different **speech communities**. Sometimes coordinated interaction derails because participants have different interests, are working toward different goals, are not invested enough in the interaction, or lack necessary language proficiency. In addition, due to the inevitable threat to their **ontological security**, some participants might resist you treating them as cultural others. In such cases, building culture for the other participant(s) can be a waste of time and effort.

Building Culture Won't Automatically Solve Your Interpersonal Problems

There is a good reason why this book promises to help you accomplish better interactions and not better relationships. Yes, in some cases, coordinating your interactions with a significant other or a coworker from another speech community will also save your relationship with them. However, coordinating interactions can have the opposite effect as well. Imagine that understanding the cultural meaning of what a cultural other is telling you also means understanding that they are breaking up with you. Or imagine that you figure out something about the **expressive system** your coworker is using only to learn that they think of you as incompetent and want to make sure you don't get a promotion. Building culture will help you accomplish a common frame of cultural reference and action with your cultural other, but it will not guarantee interpersonal harmony.

How You Use the Guide Is Ultimately Up to You

Because social interaction is complex and context bound, it is only partially predictable. No guide can prepare you for every possible interaction, intercultural or otherwise. The same goes for the guide presented in this chapter: it offers you a basic structure for discovering cultural difference in social interaction, but it can't prepare you for encounters with particular others from particular speech communities under particular (social, political, historical, institutional, economic, etc.) circumstances. This is the reason you will find lots of questions in addition to recommendations for action in this guide for building culture. By answering relevant questions, you can identify your own way toward establishing coordinated interaction with a cultural other. *You* will need to creatively adapt the guide and its insights to your particular circumstances.

With these disclaimers in mind, let's turn to the guide for building culture. The process begins even before you come face-to-face with cultural different in interaction. You can begin laying the groundwork, so to speak, for building culture by exercising **reflexivity**. After discussing reflexivity, I turn to the seven stages of building culture. I end this chapter with reflections for the period after you will have built culture.

BEFORE YOU BEGIN BUILDING CULTURE

Reflexivity is an ongoing process you should be mindful of, and pursue, throughout your life. In a broad sense, reflexivity means keeping track of your place in the world, including your worldview, opinions, attitudes, preferences, likes and dislikes, commitments, and principles. For the purpose of building culture, reflexivity prompts you to ask the question: "What is normal to me?" Intercultural encounters can be disorienting and confusing because they violate your expectations about normalcy, and they force you to come to terms with the simple fact that your "normal" is not the only one out there and that your "normal" may be more complicated or contradictory than you thought.

Let me give you an example from one of my own attempts to build culture. As I was getting to know the Egyptian side of my wife, Nora's, family, I heard them say *insh'allah* a lot, especially when they were discussing future plans. ("We will see you next year, *insh'allah*.") The closest English translation of the phrase, I learned, was "God willing." This practice partially resonated with my understanding of Egypt as a society where being religious was the norm, but it didn't dovetail with my impression of my wife's immediate family as agnostic at best. (They would tell me that they are Coptic Christians in ethnic heritage but not in faith.) I later figured out that the *use* of the term said something fundamentally important about the Egyptian worldview: believing that you are in control of your future is an act of conceit. *Insh'allah* is a routine but humble admission that we live in a big and unpredictable world, and therefore we need to leave room for the unexpected in our lives. This outlook on life initially struck me as overly defeatist and thus led me to experience a rich point. Later, however, as I began to understand the local logic of *insh'allah*, I realized it was my optimistic, can-do, enterprising American sense of "normal" that set me up to assume I was in control of my life. It also set me up to feel a certain sense of shame in response to losing control. The tiny voice of this "normal" quietly tells me temporary loss of control over my life as a result of an unexpected and bad turn of events is evidence that I just wasn't adequately prepared. By contrast, the philosophy of *insh'allah* made perfect sense within my much more pessimistic Hungarian sense of "normal," which tells me to always expect the worst. To this day, I am grateful for *insh'allah* because it helped me understand my "normal," an understanding I can carry with me into other intercultural encounters.

The sense of "normal" you bring to intercultural encounters includes more than expectations about the future. They also include other sources of normality of which you should be aware, as much as possible, in order to manage the threat to your sense of ontological security in intercultural encounters. Typically, you become aware of your sense of "normal" when it is unexpectedly called into question by something you either directly experience or by the experiences of others who matter to you.

Below, I list categories of questions that should help you exercise day-to-day reflexivity. The questions are intentionally broad and open-ended, and they are addressed to the widest possible range of readers. The list is obviously incomplete, in particular because they are not tied to specific types of situations. Think of this list as a reflexivity "starter pack."

Views of culture:

- In what cultures do you think you have membership? How did you become a member?

- In what ways do these cultures shape your worldview, beliefs, actions, and relationships?

- How would you describe the most recent history of these cultures?

- Would you describe these cultures as relatively dominant, powerful, or influential compared to others? Which others?

Views of language and communication:

- What languages and/or dialects do you speak?

- Do you see yourself belonging to a speech community?

- Do you regard any language(s) as your native language(s)?

- Do you speak a standard language? How do you know it's a standard language?

- Do you think there are languages and/or dialects that are more important than others? Why?

- Are you worried about the way people (or some groups of people) speak today? Do you think speech is deteriorating in some way?

- Do you see yourself as someone who interacts easily with others?

- What communication technologies do you use? Do you think these technologies improve human communication and human lives?

Moral principles:

- What moral principles are important to you?

- What moral principles do you think are under threat in contemporary life?

- How far would you go in enforcing these moral principles in your social network, in your society, or in the world?

Social and political views:

- What worries you the most about the way your social group(s) or society is changing?

- How would you describe the ideal society? Is the society you live in close to that ideal?

- Do you assign more value to progress and social change or to tradition and the status quo?

- Do you think the needs and views of the majority or the needs and views of minorities should shape society? Either? Both?

- What do you think should be the basis of good governance (e.g., liberal democracy, a strong and just ruler, human rights, economic prosperity, environmental responsibility, etc.)?

- Do you think a world without countries and borders is something humanity should strive for?

- How would you describe your own racial, ethnic, gender, sexual, national, and class identities? How do you feel about these identities?

- How do you think societies should deal with social and political diversity? What types of institutions (should) help societies deal with diversity?

- Who/what do you think has (or should have) rights (e.g., humans, minorities, refugees, the natural environment, animals, corporations, etc.)?

Religious views:

- Would you describe yourself as religious? Spiritual? Agnostic?

- What does your religious, spiritual, or secular worldview say about those who don't share your worldview?

- How do you see the role of religion in society?

Sources of social privilege:

- Do you experience enjoying unearned advantages over others? What kinds of advantages?

- What is the source of these advantages? (Who do you have to thank for them?)

Intersectionality:

- What kinds of oppression do you experience in your life? Who or what are the source(s) of those kinds of oppression?

- How is that oppression tied to your identity?

- Do you experience multiple forms of oppression tied to multiple identities you call your own?

Cultural stereotypes:

- What social groups do you think of as "cultures"?

- How do you expect members of these groups to look? How do you expect them to act? How do you expect them to communicate?

- How do you expect them to see you? How do you expect them to evaluate the way you look, act, and communicate?

Ethnocentrism:

- Of which cultural group(s) do you consider yourself a member?

- Do you believe your group is "better" than others? In what sense?

- Do you think your group is closer to your ideal society than others? Why?

Cognitive biases (fundamental attribution error, naïve realism, confirmation bias):

- Do you think people's actions are shaped more by their personalities than by their circumstances?

- Do you think you have a better grasp on reality than others? Which others?

- Do you often find yourself "tuning out" information that challenges or undermines your views and beliefs about the world?

I am sure some of these questions will sound more relevant to you than others and you will think of other questions that shape your sense of normality that are not represented on the above list. Feel free to add questions to the list, individually or with others, that help you develop a better grasp on the "normal" you bring to the table as you interact with cultural others—or that keep you from recognizing cultural difference.

THE STAGES OF BUILDING CULTURE

Building culture begins with the decision to respond to an unfamiliar situation with thought. The American philosopher John Dewey (1910) said:

> Thinking begins in what may fairly enough be called a *forked-road* situation, a situation which is ambiguous, which presents a dilemma, which proposes alternatives. As long as our activity glides smoothly along from one thing to another or as long as we permit our imagination to entertain fancies at pleasure, there

is no call for reflection. Difficulty or obstruction in the way of reaching a belief brings us, however, to a pause. In the suspense of uncertainty, we metaphorically climb a tree; we try to find some standpoint from which we may survey additional facts and, getting a more commanding view of the situation, may decide how the facts stand related to one another. (p. 11; emphasis in original)

Disruptions in the flow of communication with others force you to choose among three possible ways forward:

1. You can hold on to your sense of what is normal, disregard the disruption, and go on like nothing happened. This choice tends to be informed by relative social privilege or cognitive biases that prevent you from recognizing the need for reflection and building culture.

2. Given a reason to believe your interactional partner is the member of a cultural group different from yours, you can entertain the possibility that cultural difference may have something to do with the disruption. However, you opt for quick solutions (such as the number-one mentality or cultural stereotyping) rather than sustained reflection.

3. You can respond to the disruption, as Dewey suggests, with thinking: you pause, assume the relevance of cultural differences, and climb that metaphorical tree to get a bird's-eye view of how your interaction with the cultural other led to the disruption. This choice allows you to proceed to the first stage of building culture: experiencing the disruption as a rich point.

Choosing the third option puts you on a path toward building culture.

Stage 1: Experiencing a Rich Point

Rich points happen unexpectedly. You can't do anything to prevent them from happening, but you do quite a bit in response to them. When you experience a disruption to the "normal" flow of communication between you and a cultural other, don't panic: prepare to learn something. Remember: rich points are not necessarily single occurrences of a cultural other saying something unexpected that sparks in you the combined feeling of confusion and intrigue. You can also arrive at the same gut-level reaction in the wake of a series of disruptions that you hadn't recognized as disruptions to the "normal" flow of interaction before.

Stage 2: Suspending Interaction

Your next task is to withdraw from interaction. This may not be immediately possible: some interactions are easier to withdraw from than others. What matters is that you

You can only investigate an unfamiliar expressive system from your own perspective. The fact that you bring a perspective (or a set of perspectives, if you are proficient in more than one expressive system) to building culture means that you may not be able to notice cultural practices or meanings that matter a lot to another cultural group, even when they are right in front of you.

find time to catch your breath and begin to think about the *interaction* that led to your rich point. Try to recall who said what, in what order. Or, if the source of your rich point is not a particular instance but a *type* of interaction, think about the contexts in which that interaction tends to happen: where it happens, who is there, and who says what.

As you begin to reflect and reconstruct *interaction* (as opposed to personalities, who is right and wrong, who has a firm grasp on reality and who doesn't, etc.) and you start to guess the cultural other's meanings and motivation, there is an important rule of thumb you should follow: "You don't know what you don't know" (Agar, 2019, p. 106). You haven't yet climbed that metaphorical tree Dewey talked about; you don't yet have evidence to back up your own hypotheses about the other's communication conduct. Remember: you are not *inventing* culture, you are *building* it from relevant, useful pieces of information about differences between your expressive system and someone else's.

Another point of consideration at this point of building culture is whether you are in a position to conduct cultural inquiry, either in the moment of experiencing the rich point or at all. Are you on equal footing with your conversational partner? Do you have the freedom to conduct cultural inquiry? Is the other doing something that violates your moral principles? If your answer to any of these questions is "no" (e.g., your physical safety, mental health, or freedom of movement is under threat, you are being coerced or exploited, you are risking losing your livelihood, etc.), you may not have the luxury to think deeply about cultural differences on the spot. You will need to disengage and retreat. Again, try to find the time to think about what happened and make a determination about whether or not cultural inquiry would require you to sacrifice your safety.

At this stage of building culture, you can ask the following questions in order to get a better sense of your particular intercultural communication encounter:

Context 1: Interpersonal relationships

- What is the nature of the relationship between you and the cultural other? Are you socially close or distant? Are you equals, or does one of you have power or authority over the other?

- What would be the social significance and the social consequence of your withdrawal from the conversation?

- Would staying engaged in the conversation threaten your physical safety, safe passage, or mental health? Would withdrawal from the conversation threaten your physical safety or mental health?

- Is it possible or preferable to wait until the conversation is over to find time to reflect on your rich point?

- Is this rich point related to a single event or to a repeated occurrence of confusing but intriguing conduct? If the latter, in what context does the conduct tend to occur?

Context 2: Workplace relationships

- What is the nature of the relationship between you and the cultural other in the context of the organization? What are your organizational roles? Are you socially close or distant (that is, do you see yourselves as similar, different, or somewhere in between)? Are you equals, or does one of you have power over the other due to your different positions in the organizational hierarchy?

- What would be the social significance and the social consequence of your withdrawal from the conversation? What would be the meaning and consequence of your withdrawal from the perspective of the organization?

- Would staying engaged in, or withdrawing from, the conversation threaten your physical safety, mental health, position, or livelihood?

- Is it possible or preferable to wait until the conversation is over to find time to reflect on your rich point?

- Is this rich point related to a single event or to a repeated occurrence of confusing but intriguing conduct?

- If the latter, in what context does the conduct tend to occur?

A Practical Question

"I have never had a formal "job" but I have been a member of formal organizations (e.g., schools, churches, political movements, etc.). Do these questions apply to other types of organizations beyond one's workplace?"

Yes, they do. These questions will help you reflect on how any relevant organization might shape your intercultural encounters.

Stage 3: Establishing a Communication Pattern

Your next task is figuring out whether the odd bit of communication you encountered during your rich point is part of a communication pattern. Is this bit of communication

A Practical Question

"How can I collect more in-depth data if I have the opportunity to carry out an extensive ethnographic project in an unfamiliar speech community?"

You can experiment with taking field-notes or conducting ethnographic interviews. There are many guides to data collection out there, so you might as well start with the classics: Emerson, Fretz and Shaw's *Writing ethnographic fieldnotes* (2011), and Spradley's *The ethnographic interview* (1979/2016). Keep in mind, though, that you can build culture without conducting extensive ethnographic research.

typical or generic in some way? Making this determination requires two things: carefully reconstructing what the cultural other said that threw you for a loop and observation. The rule of thumb to follow at this stage is to find at least three instances of the same unit of communicative conduct across speakers you categorize as belonging to the same culture. A single occurrence of the bit of communication related to your rich point can be a random incident; two occurrences, a random coincidence. Also, if you can't see other members of the same group engage in the same conduct as the speaker involved in your rich point, it's quite likely you are dealing with an individual's quirk.

This is a great time to note your observations in a **field journal** and to start informally **interviewing** others familiar with the social group you are starting to treat as a cultural group, including members of the group. You can start asking some early exploratory questions, such as "Is this a typical way to say *X* in this group?" "Does saying *X* strike you as odd?" "Do people in your group say or do *X* a lot, or is it just this person?" Answers to these questions may confirm that you are dealing with a type of communicative conduct that is cultural, but they may also push you to identify groups within groups (e.g., "It looks like not all Hungarians talk like this, only people from the capital city, Budapest." "It seems that not only Coptic Christians say *insh'allah* but Muslims do too."). Or, again, it is possible you've just encountered someone with an idiosyncratic manner of speaking.

At this stage of building culture, you can ask the following questions in order to get a better sense of the communication pattern whose cultural meaning you are trying to unravel:

Context 1: Interpersonal relationships

- Is the odd bit of communication peculiar to the cultural other with whom you were interacting when you experienced a rich point? Or is it typical within their cultural group? If not the whole cultural group, is it typical in a smaller social group (e.g., immediate or extended family, circle or friends, neighborhood, fan club, religious community, etc.)? Does the pattern stretch beyond the boundaries of the group?

- If it is typical in their cultural group, a smaller group within the larger group, or beyond the larger group, is it typical in the type of relationship you have with this person?

Context 2: Workplace relationships

- Is the odd bit of communication peculiar to the cultural other with whom you were interacting when you experienced a rich point? Or is it typical in their cultural group? Or is it typical in the organization in which both of you work or a group within that organization? If the pattern extends beyond the organization, how far does it extend?

- If it is typical in their cultural group, in the organization (or a group within the organization), or beyond, is it restricted to particular types of workplace relationships (e.g., friends, relationship between people of equal rank, relationships between supervisors and supervisees, etc.)?

Stage 4: Labeling the Communication Pattern

Once you have established that you are dealing with a communication pattern, it's time to identify what type of pattern you are looking at. More precisely, you need to find out what type of communication *practice* you are dealing with. Identifying the type of communication practice at the heart of your rich point will help you ask better questions of members of the cultural group you are studying, make better observations, and collect more relevant information for the purpose of understanding local **interactional frames** and **scripts** and building **intercultural frames**.

You have two sources of labels at your disposal: **practical** and **academic metadiscourse**. Labels derived from practical metadiscourse are cultural members' labels for types of communication practices; academic metadiscourse offers you labels crafted by communication scholars and researchers. It is quite possible that the social group you are treating as a culture has a metadiscursive label for the practice or the context in which it is typically used. You may hear your informants do the labeling for you:

"That's not an *insult*, that's a *compliment!*"

"Yeah, Tyler really needs to stop *swearing* around Grandma."

"Oh wow, she totally *spilled the tea!*"

"Hey man, why are you bringing up work? We're just *hanging out.*"

In addition to practical metadiscourse, this book helps you identify a range of communication practices using academic metadiscourse. The list below contains academic labels for communication practices I discuss in this book. This list represents the types of communication practices my students came across most often in their intercultural encounters. Keep in mind that there are many other communication practices, which means you may need to find other labels for the purpose of building culture and accomplishing coordinated interaction.

- Words and cultural key terms

- Language selection

- Code-switching

- Code-mixing

- Address terms (pronouns, proper names, kinship terms)

- Speech acts and act sequences

- Speech genres

- Topic selection and topic management

- Humor

- Biased/prejudiced speech

- Silence

- The amount of talk

- Embodied (nonverbal) expression

- Myth

- Communication ritual

- Social drama

Using labels derived from practical and academic metadiscourse, you will be able to ask better questions of your informants and search for relevant research insights in this book and, if possible, communication scholarship. You will be able to combine the metadiscursive label with secondary search terms such as "communication," "discourse," or "[social] interaction" and the name of your target culture to find scholarly sources relevant to the project of building culture, provided you have easy access to them through your educational institution. Don't worry: not having access to scholarly sources will not undermine your ability to build culture. Work with what you have. Culture building is primarily a practical, not an academic, exercise, which means you have to use the information at your disposal. The ultimate test of the validity of the culture you build is not the academic literature but whether you are able to use the culture you built for a target group for the purpose of accomplishing coordinated interaction.

Below, I list terms you can use in online searches to identify relevant academic and nonacademic (e.g., online articles, videos, social media posts, etc.) information in addition to the search terms I mentioned above. Primary search terms are specific to the culture you are building; secondary search terms increase the likelihood that you will find sources that tell you something important about *cultural* variation in communication practices; tertiary search terms are likely to point you to sources that are specific to the two interactional contexts I highlight in this chapter (interpersonal and workplace relationships). Note that the two lists of tertiary terms are not mutually exclusive—some terms I list for interpersonal relationships may help you find materials related to workplace contexts, and vice versa. Try combining terms from these lists to find information that is useful to *you*. The terms in square brackets are optional; try searching with and without them.

Primary search terms: "[local/academic label for the communicative practice]," "[name of the culture]" (e.g., "*insh'allah* + Egypt" or "*insh'allah* + "key term" + Egypt")

Secondary search terms: "communication," "discourse," "[social] interaction," "culture," "ethnography," "anthropology," "speech community," "society"

Tertiary search terms (Context 1: Interpersonal relationships): "interpersonal communication," "family communication," "social role," "social skills," "interpersonal skills," "identity," "ethnic," "racial," "gender," "interracial [relationship]," "interethnic [relationship]," "relationship," "intimate relationship," "gender roles," "conflict," "[interpersonal] closeness," "[interpersonal] distance," "power," "love," "sex," "romance," "[interpersonal] tension," "[interpersonal] harmony," "relationship building," "relationship maintenance," "interpersonal history," "interpersonal ideology," "social media," "online interaction"

Tertiary search terms (Context 2: Workplace relationships): "professional relationship," "workplace relationship," "mentoring (relationship)," "[workplace] romance," "[workplace] diversity," "[workplace] conflict," "workplace culture," "organizational culture," "human resources," "socialization," "conflict [management]," "[workplace] bullying," "discrimination," "leadership," "decision-making," "collaboration," "[collaboration] technology," "teamwork," "group interaction," "group communication," "power," "resistance," "inclusivity," "globalization," "[transnational] corporation"

As you sort through the materials (articles, videos, social media, and blog posts, etc.) you have collected, evaluate your sources by asking questions like these:

- Is the source credible?

- On what grounds is it making claims about the form and meaning of the communication practice you are trying to understand (author's own firsthand experience or research, others' research or firsthand experience, etc.)?

- Is there reason to believe the source is willfully misrepresenting the practice (that is, give it an interpretation that goes against the local interpretation of the practice)?

Stage 5: Reconstructing Relevant Contexts

When people communicate, they act, and as they act in patterned, context-bound ways, their actions take on the character of practices. A key challenge of building culture is determining how communication practices take shape against the background of particular **contexts**. At this stage of building culture, you should already have a body of materials (notes of your observations, answers to informal interview questions, articles, blog posts, etc.) you can search for clues about how members of the target culture use the communication practice you are trying to interpret in particular contexts, for particular purposes. Understanding context takes you a step closer to not only understanding but also using the practice with members of the social group.

As you describe the typical contexts of your communication practice, remember that you are seeking to identify not one but four kinds of contexts: the physical (or virtual) and social **setting**, the **embodied** (nonverbal, nonvocal) **environment, language**, and the **extrasituational context** (frames of reference that apply across interactions; Goodwin & Duranti, 1992; Scollon & Scollon, 2001). Let's review the types of questions that will help you establish the relevance of each of these contexts. Remember: as you seek to identify *typical* and *relevant* contexts, you need to decide which questions below will be the most helpful for the culture you are building.

Setting

- Where is the practice used (physical and/or online spaces, public and/or private spaces, neighborhoods, farms, villages, small towns, cities, etc.)?

- Who is there when group members use this type of practice? Are human and/or nonhuman (deities, animals, etc.) participants involved?

- What sorts of social roles do they have (family members, strangers, friends, romantic partners, etc.)?

- What kinds of relationships exist among them (social distance, power relation)? Do social privilege and/or intersectionality shape participation?

- At what time(s) is the practice used (morning, afternoon, night, weekday and/or weekend, holidays, etc.)?

Embodied environment

- Does the practice consist of verbal/vocal or nonverbal/nonvocal actions? Does it have elements of both types of action (e.g., when group members say *X*, do they also use particular types of gesture, posture, physical distance, and/or gaze)?

- Is the practice prompted by/a response to nonverbal/nonvocal (embodied) actions?

- Do group members use their immediate physical environment (objects, furniture, stage, floorplan, etc.) and/or their bodies (clothing, make-up, accessories) meaningfully as they engage in this practice?

Language

- Do participants typically say or do something before or after they engage in this practice?

- Does the practice itself have a typical act sequence/purpose/topic/genre?

- Do participants use speech, writing, silence, or other media (video, overhead projection, PowerPoint slides, notes, amplification, recordings, etc.) to perform the practice?

- How transparent are participants about the practice or the sequence in which it is embedded (i.e., is there an agenda that's available to everyone, or do participants assume shared knowledge of the practice and its context)?

- Do members use a single or multiple languages and/or linguistic varieties and/or codes as they engage in this practice?

Extrasituational context

- What kinds of local knowledge (cultural background information) do participants rely on for meaningful participation?

- What kinds of historical relations among participants are relevant to the practice (interpersonal histories; the history of the group/society; racial/ethnic, gender, class, national, religious relations; histories of discrimination, exploitation, colonial relations, etc.)?

- What is the relative social prestige of the language/linguistic variety/code they use?

- In what kind(s) of institution does the practice occur? How, if at all, does the institution shape the practice and/or the contexts (setting, embodied environment, language) in which it occurs?

- Does the social group consider itself a speech community? Does the practice feed into the group's sense of speech community?

- What are the social consequences of participation in the practice for participants?

Interpersonal and workplace relationships are two particular types of contexts in which group members use communication practices. These two contexts will shape how you determine the relevance of other types of contexts.

Context 1: Interpersonal relationships

- This context may prompt you to begin your investigation of relevant contexts with reflection on various aspects of the relationship among participants (relational histories, social roles and identities, gender, racial, sexual relations, etc.). Make sure you don't lose sight of larger structural (historical, cultural, economic, political) relations that shape relationships among individuals.

Context 2: Workplace relationships

- This context may prompt you to begin your investigation of relevant contexts with reflection on the organization (its policies, hierarchies, conventions and traditions) and people's (professional) roles in it. Make sure you don't lose sight of interpersonal relations among participants that may exist outside/parallel to organizational structures and those larger structural (historical, cultural, economic, political) relations that shape relationships among individuals

Stage 6: Establishing Connections to Local Systems of Meaning

At this stage of building culture, you make the move from *description* to *interpretation*. You move from describing local acts, patterns, practices, and contexts to the "how" (competent use), the "why" (cultural ideologies), and the "who" (communal identity) of communication. To return to the example of *insh'allah*, figuring out that it is appropriate to say the term at the beginning or end of stating future plans answered my "how" question, while answering "why" entailed investigating the cultural reasons (many) Egyptians felt compelled to use *insh'allah* the way they did. For me, answering the "why" question required asking questions such as: Does the use of the term have religious connotations? Does using the term cast you as a religious person? What does the use of the term say about how Egyptians see persons relative to their personal histories and the passage of time? Why don't Egyptians see people as being in full control of their futures, and why do they see those who assume they are in complete control as foolish? As to the "who," I learned *insh'allah* is a shared practice all across Egypt, regardless of religion, class, and ethnicity. (In fact, saying *insh'allah* as a practice stretches beyond the borders of Egypt into the Muslim world, but I have not yet figured out how far.)

Answering "how," "why," and "who" questions will necessitate drawing on everything you know about the culture you are building, including cultural insights about other local communication practices in particular and the target group in general. No, I'm not saying you need to have thorough, complete, and holistic knowledge of the group's culture. Let me assure you: such knowledge doesn't exist. Social groups and their perspectives on the world are complex, diverse, and ever-changing. No group holds still for someone to study all of their ways, which is why not even the best-trained, most seasoned ethnographer is able to produce a description of a culture that will account for everything a cultural group's members say, do, think, and believe. In fact, today it would be the best-trained, most seasoned ethnographers who would say that any account of a culture is created from an observer's perspective. This doesn't mean the culture you build is "subjective." It only means that, no matter how rigorous your approach and no matter how efficiently you work toward the ultimate goal of coordinated interaction with group members, the culture you build will be grounded in your activities, movements, social network, experiences, needs, trials and errors, and successes. This is what makes you an intercultural practitioner, as opposed to an omnipresent, omniscient cultural sage—which doesn't exist.

Criteria for the competent use of communication practices, cultural ideologies, and communal identity mutually inform one another. As you seek to unearth the "how," the "why," and the "who" relevant to the practice you are interpreting, these are the interpretive devices you can rely on:

"How": **Norms (of interpretation and action) and rules (of interpretation and action)**

- Formulate norms/rules of action as: "In context *C*, when pursuing social goal *X*, one should (not) do *Y*."

- Formulate norms/rules of interpretation as: "In context *C*, when pursuing social goal *X*, one should (not) interpret when someone does *Y* as *Z*."

"Why": **Cultural ideologies**

- Formulate cultural ideologies as **cultural premises** about personhood, relationships, action, emotion, place, and time.

- Formulate cultural ideologies as **cultural value** (use value, exchange value, acquisitive value).

"Who": Communal identity

- Formulate **communication forms** a group uses to foster a communal identity by identifying **myths, rituals, social dramas.**

- Use the following criteria to identity **speech communities:** (1) shared communal identity; (2) common activities, views, beliefs; (3) shared social meanings attributed to communication practices; (4) shared awareness of "our way of using language" vs. "the ways others speak"; (5) socialization of novice members; (6) taking pride in local ways of speaking.

Now that you have advanced to this stage of building culture, try seeking answers to following context-specific questions.

Context 1: Interpersonal relationships

- Where do the norms and/or rules that shape your conversational partner's expectations about this practice come from? Are they specific to your immediate relationship? Your conversational partner's family, social network, or group/society? Who will sanction you if you break relevant norms and/or rules, and how? What is your (social) reward for following norms/rules?

- What does this practice say (as **metacultural commentary**) about your conversation partner's views about who you are, your relationship to your conversational partner, the utility and meaning your partner attributes to this practice, the feelings and sense of place associated with this practice, and the past, present, and future of your relationship?

- How, if at all, does this practice contribute to your conversational partner's sense of communal identity (**metasocial commentary**)? Is there a sense that an incompetent performance of the practice will violate that communal identity or a sense of belonging?

Context 2: Workplace relationships

- Do the norms/rules that shape your conversational partner's expectations about this practice

CULTURAL PRAGMATICS SAYS

Keep in mind that once you begin to reconstruct cultural meanings you may find that the information you gather directly from your local informants becomes less and less helpful. More often than not, this has to do with the fact that cultural meanings are so taken for granted that they are beyond group members' limits of awareness.

come from the organization? If not, what is their origin? Will the organization sanction or reward you for successfully following relevant norms/rules? Are there other sources of sanctions and rewards?

- Does this practice say anything about how the organization where you work "sees" you, your relationships to others in and beyond the organization (including your conversational partner), the utility and meaning of the practice, the feelings and sense of place attributed to this practice, and your past, present and future in the organization?

- How, if at all, does the practice contribute to the organization's sense of its own communal identity? Is there a sense that an incompetent performance of the practice will violate the communal identity of the organization or the organization's sense of you as a communal member?

Stage 7: Attempting Coordinated Interaction

The last stage of building culture invites you to follow the following time-honored rule of thumb: the proof of the pudding is in the eating. You are now ready to put your interpretation of the communication practice that constituted, or contributed to, your rich point to use. This is not as easy as it sounds. The first time I used *insh'allah* in an English sentence with a member of my Egyptian family, I was not feeling comfortable, to say the least. I wanted to get the pronunciation, the rhythm, the placement, and the meaning of the phrase just right. Fortunately, the family tends to accept my often misplaced efforts to incorporate Egyptian Arabic phrases into my speech with grace and mild amusement, so after a few tries, I got it right. I became able to not just say the phrase but also to communicate that I, like my Egyptian friends and family, were prepared to expect the unexpected and be fine with things not turning out the way I had planned.

There is more to this personal example than "I learned to talk like an Egyptian." In truth, I didn't. I learned to use a single phrase for a particular purpose in one locally recognizable way. As my wife reminded me recently, there is much more to learn about all the different identities people present when they use the phrase, the different **speech genres** in which the phrase takes on meaning, and other phrases that have the same or similar functions as *insh'allah*. But this doesn't change the fact that I have built culture. I moved past a rich point, I built an **intercultural frame** within which I make sense to my conversational partners on their terms and mine in spite of the fact that I am speaking English, and I have the **interactional script** for saying *insh'allah* at appropriate times, in appropriate conversational places. I have also learned something about Egyptian cultural meanings in the process. My understanding of Egyptian ways of speaking is still extremely limited, but what I can say does work in interaction, and I know why. *That's* the most you can hope to get out of building culture.

I was lucky, of course. I had access to a big group of helpful, kind, and friendly informants, and the practice I set out to interpret is widely used and widely documented. You may be trying to tackle a much more complex and elusive practice, and you may be receiving a lot less help than I did. Nonetheless, I encourage you to stick to the guide I presented here and not to be afraid to fail, assuming you have the luxury of engaging in extended cultural inquiry and multiple rounds of trial and error. Not everyone has these privileges: just think about the asylum seeker being questioned by immigration officers in their second (or third, or fourth) language, the tourist being threatened with physical violence in an unfamiliar land, or the low-level employee at a company that was just overtaken by a foreign corporation and is going through downsizing.

AFTER YOU HAVE BUILT CULTURE

As long as you interact with members of a group you have decided to treat as a culture, the process of building culture never ends. True, you may experience fewer and fewer rich points over time, and going through the seven stages of building culture may take less effort, but you should remain open to the possibility of having to build culture. Expressive systems are more complex and change more quickly than any cultural outsider (or even insiders) can imagine. This is especially true in a world of hybrids (Agar, 2019) in which social groups and their expressive systems are more likely to mix and mingle than ever before.

As I mentioned at the beginning of this chapter, another possibility you should always be mindful of is that building culture is not always the right solution to the communication trouble you are experiencing with someone you are treating as a cultural other. In the process of building culture, you may come to realize the conversational partner involved in your rich point is not using an expressive form different from yours; rather, they may be simply unfriendly or uncooperative, or they may be pursuing interests that are different from, or in conflict with, yours at the moment. "Culture" will not work in such encounters.

However, few experiences are as empowering in intercultural encounters as when you get the "culture" you built to work. Finding a way to coordinate your interaction with a cultural other is a reminder of communication's potential to facilitate getting tasks done, whether that task is as small as ordering food in a restaurant or as big as starting, affirming, transforming, or ending a relationship.

REFLECTION QUESTIONS

1. Based on what you have read in this chapter, how would you advise Jian, the author of the first rich point narrative at the beginning of this chapter, to build

culture? As you read her narrative, do you see her making early moves toward building culture for her grandfather's cousin? Is she moving in the right direction? How should she proceed?

2. How would you advise Oakley, the author of the second rich point narrative, to build culture? Is he already moving toward building culture? Is he moving in the right direction? How should he proceed?

3. Imagine an intercultural practitioner entering your cultural group and trying to figure out how to interact with its members. Can you think of someone you know who would be either a lousy informant or not a very good person for this practitioner to observe? Why do you think that?

4. Can you think of an intercultural encounter in which you experienced an interpersonal challenge that was not based on "cultural" differences? What type of difference caused the challenge? How do you know that was the case?

5. Can you recall an intercultural encounter where someone said something that struck you as "not normal"? What expectation about normalcy did the person violate?

Glossary

abduction the cyclical process of identifying the local meanings of communicative conduct in the process of interacting with members of a cultural group

academic metadiscourse communication scholars' and researchers' professional talk about communication practices

accentism discrimination against people who speak a language with a perceived, nonvalued accent

accountability (in social interaction) the notion that a speaker's language use can be subjected to evaluation by local standards of appropriate conduct

act sequence a locally recognizable sequence of speech acts

altercasting the practice of casting a conversational partner as having particular qualities or identities through the strategic selection of appropriate communication styles and resources

autonomous organization of topics the practice of individual meeting participants raising relatively few topics and then discussing them for extended periods of time, resulting in a monological communication style

building culture the well-informed, rigorous reconstruction of the form and local meaning of unfamiliar communicative conduct in an unfamiliar social group or community in the process of interacting with its members

centering institution an institution with the authority to decide what meanings of communicative conduct will be considered normal and valuable

chronemics interaction by the allocation of time

civil inattention the practice of respecting strangers' negative face wants in public

code norms, rules, and expectations about communicative conduct specific to particular languages and linguistic varieties

code-mixing the fusion of formerly distinct codes into a new code

code-switching the practice of switching between codes as speakers switch between audiences or interactional partners in order to index meanings, hierarchies, values

cognitive bias a gap between a subjective and a rational interpretation of the world

Communication Accommodation Theory (CAT) a theory predicting that speakers will adjust their speech patterns according to whether they seek to increase, decrease, or maintain social distance between themselves and others

communication culture a globally available cultural ideology that suggests communication is important, human problems are caused by bad communication and can be solved by better communication, and communication is a technical skill that can be acquired from communication experts

communication form a type of communication sequence that serves the specific purpose of highlighting and enacting community boundaries and membership; includes myth, communication ritual, and social drama

communicative action the things we do with words, phrases, syntax, pauses, intonation, and so on in the context of social interaction

communication practice patterned sequences of context-bound, culturally meaningful, and accountable communicative actions

communication resource any (set of) linguistic or nonlinguistic (nonverbal, visual, material, etc.) objects speakers can use for the purpose of meaningful communication

communication ritual a type of communication form that, when correctly performed, pays homage to a sacred object

confirmation bias a type of cognitive bias involving the tendency to pay attention only to information that confirms your personal theories about others and the world and to disregard information that conflicts with your assumptions

contact culture a cultural group in which members frequently engage in, and facilitate, physical touch

context any feature of the situation that acts as a background to communicative actions relative to which those actions take on meaning for the participants involved; includes physical and social setting, embodied environment, language, and cultural background knowledge

conversational floor speakers who hold the conversational floor claim to speak continuously without interruption by other participants of social interaction

conversational topic subject matters introduced into conversation

coordinated interaction social interaction in which participants share a sense of (1) the interactional frame and script and (2) the interactional goals they are working toward

cultural ideology a system of beliefs about communication

cultural norm culturally variable expectations for appropriate action across situations

cultural norm of interaction a cultural norm that guides how speech ought to be produced in interaction

cultural norm of interpretation a cultural norm that guides how speech ought to be interpreted in interaction

cultural other a speaker whose actions the intercultural practitioner assumes to be guided by an expressive system different from their own

cultural pragmatics an approach to intercultural communication concerned with (1) how people who find themselves in intercultural communication encounters can produce knowledge about unfamiliar context-bound uses of language and the social and cultural meanings of those uses and (2) how they can act on that knowledge for the sake of coordinating their communication with cultural others

cultural premise culturally variable beliefs and assumptions about the world (including but not limited to communication) that serve as the basis for communicative action

cultural rule culturally variable guidelines for action in particular types of situations

cultural rule of interaction a cultural rule that guides how speech ought to be produced in interaction

cultural rule of interpretation a cultural rule that guides how speech ought to be interpreted in interaction

cultural stereotyping naming groups of people (e.g., "Mexicans," "women," "millennials," "the one percent," etc.) and associating them with some essential quality that defines them as a group

cultural taboo actions social groups forbid of their members on the basis of cultural beliefs and values

cultural value a cultural group's regard for something as an object of desire relative to processes of use, exchange, and acquisition

culture as process an approach to culture that regards culture initially as a working assumption and later as the product of cultural inquiry that is a form of translation and is fundamentally relational, partial, and plural

culture as thing an approach to culture that regards culture as something groups of people or individuals possess

culture shock the psychological state of mild to severe anxiety and disorientation common among people who find themselves transplanted to other countries and suddenly encounter cultural difference

cyclical inquiry a type of inquiry or research the person conducting the inquiry may need to repeat in light of new experiences or evidence

deductive argument patter a sequence of argument in which the speaker introduces the argument first and then provides evidence in support of it

diaspora a group of people from the same home country relocating to, and maintaining social ties in, a different country, within or across generations

direct style a communication style that makes the speaker's meaning and intention relatively obvious

discrimination the unfair or prejudiced treatment of people belonging to marginalized social categories

Duchenne smile a "genuine smile" featuring exposed teeth, raised corners of the mouth, raised cheeks, crow's feet in the corners of the eyes, slightly lowered eyelids, and arched eyebrows

elaborated code a set of principles for planning, organizing, and regulating communication that values the use of complex vocabulary and grammar to produce speech that can be understood without shared background information and without access to nonverbal cues

emblem a nonverbal gesture that is translatable into particular words or phrases

ethnic humor humor centered on interethnic and interracial relations

ethnocentrism the assumption that one's cultural group is the best one there is

ethnography a qualitative research methodology designed to study the life of social groups from the perspective of, and in interaction with, group members

excuse the practice of admitting a problematic past act was inappropriate but denying full responsibility for committing it

expressive system a system of locally recognized, culturally meaningful communicative conduct

face a speaker's desired self-image, presented to others and managed in the process of social interaction

face threat an act that runs the risk of damaging someone's face

field journal a journal in which someone engaged in participant observation can write down a day's events and begin to keep track of communication patterns

for-anyone-anywhere genre a speech genre designed to be, or conceived as, available to everyone around the world

functional load (of speech) the culturally variable social meaning of the choice to speak, as opposed to staying silent

gatekeeping encounter interaction where there is a clear distinction between participants who possess the authority to set conversational rules and expectations and participants who are required to conform to them

fundamental attribution error a type of cognitive bias involving the tendency to overestimate the importance of the role of individuals' personalities and to underestimate the role of context in their actions

haptics interaction by touch

heteroglossia the use of two or more languages or varieties of languages in a speech community, where the use of each language is considered appropriate for particular social functions, occasions, or institutions

high-context culture a type of cultural group in which speakers can lean heavily on shared frames of reference and say a lot with very few words

humor the use of language for comic effect

hybridization combining local and nonlocal styles of expression

iconic gesture a gesture with a natural resemblance to what it denotes

indexicality the function of human action (including language use) to point to elements of various contexts of social interaction and thereby take on meaning

indirect style a communication style that requires the audience to infer a speaker's meaning and intention

inductive argument sequence a sequence of argument in which the speaker provides evidence in support of an argument and then produces the argument itself

inferencing interpreting another speaker's intended meanings

interactional frame participants' shared sense of the type of social situation in which the interaction takes place

interactional script participants' shared sense of how interaction should unfold in a given interactional frame

intercultural frame a new interactional frame intercultural practitioners construct from elements of participants' mismatched interactional frames for the purpose of restoring coordinated interaction in intercultural encounters

intercultural practitioner someone engaged in the practice of building culture for practical purposes (e.g., maintaining a relationship, collaboration, persuasion, etc.)

interdependent organization of topics the practice of meeting participants raising a relatively high number of topics and discussing them for limited periods of time, resulting in a dialogic style of communication

intersectionality a concept calling attention to how sorting people into intersecting and interacting social categories of race, class, gender, sexuality, ability, and so on can reinforce social hierarchies and relationships of discrimination

interviewing a method of cultural inquiry that involves focused conversations with informants about local communication practices and their local meanings

iterative inquiry a type of inquiry or research where certain stages of the process may have to be repeated before the person conducting the inquiry can move on to the next stage

joking relationship a type of social relationship where tension and conflict are common and thus participants use ritualized forms of humor to maintain social harmony

justification the practice of accepting full responsibility for a problematic past act but denying that it was inappropriate

key terms/key words terms or words that carry especially significant meanings for a social group; meanings that "unlock" other important cultural meanings for those engaged in cultural inquiry

kinesics interaction by body movement

kinship terms terms that mark one's family relation with the addressee

language complex widely used languages, including all of their varieties

language death the death of a language's last speaker

language ideology a set of cultural beliefs about the function and value of various languages and linguistic varieties and about the value (social standing, prestige) of those who speak them

language socialization the process of cultivating culturally appropriate ways of speaking among novice speakers (primary language socialization) or adult speakers (secondary language socialization)

lingua franca a shared communication resource among speakers who speak different languages

linguistic privilege a type of relative social privilege derived from one's ability to competently speak a linguistic variety or style valued in a particular social context (typically the standard variety of a dominant language)

linguistic taxonomy the systematic classification of words and concepts that map relationships among their referential meanings

local genre a speech genre unique to a particular speech community

local knowledge a culturally specific system of meanings that renders local communicative conduct meaningful for cultural groups members

localized ethic a culturally specific system of moral beliefs that shapes action

low-context culture a type of cultural group in which speakers have less shared knowledge to draw on and therefore need to rely more on spoken words

meaning (of a communicative action) a communicative action's function for participants in a given moment of interaction, relative to contexts indexed by the action

member check a method of cultural inquiry that involves asking informants for feedback on one's interpretations of local communication practices and their meanings

metacultural commentary information implied in a speaker's speech about cultural beliefs and values in their social group

metasocial commentary information implied in a speaker's speech about their social group's view of itself as a community

miscommunication (in intercultural communication) a communication problem that participants recognize as a culturally based misunderstanding with social consequences

misunderstanding the failure to understand language use in context

model minority a social minority whose members pride themselves on the ability to assimilate into majority society and cast themselves as a cultural instead of a racial minority in order to avoid the stigma of being seen as a problem minority

monolingualism (1) the ability to speak only one language; (2) a language ideology that values standard varieties of languages (and their speakers) over more marginal varieties (and their speakers)

myth a type of communication form made up of stories speech community members tell in a way that captures the imagination and helps members see themselves as belonging to a community with a continuous history

myth of assimilation/assimilationism an ideology suggesting that each nation has a culture and that minorities and immigrants ought to earn the respect of the social majority by adapting to the fundamental moral principles of that culture

multilingual speaker a speaker who speaks more than one language or linguistic variety

naïve realism a type of cognitive bias based on the belief that only you see objective reality and your conversational partner doesn't

negative face a speaker's self-image as a person whose autonomy ought to be respected

noncontact culture a cultural group in which physical touch is neither sought out nor facilitated

number-one mentality the assumption that (1) all other cultural groups are less valuable than one's own and (2) anyone who belongs to the most valuable cultural group and denies they are the most valuable is misguided

ontological security the feeling that your individual self, your life, and the world around you forms a continuous and orderly story line

paralanguage interaction by nonlinguistic vocal behavior

participant observation a method of cultural inquiry that involves observing a social group while interacting with its members

participants of social interaction everyone physically or virtually co-present in the immediate situation and implicated in the ongoing communication activity, including speakers, silent participants, and bystanders who overhear the interaction

patronymic convention in naming the tradition of children receiving their fathers' last name at birth

personal address a speaker's use of locally available terms to refer to other persons in interaction with them

person referencing a set of practices designed to identify persons, whether or not they are present in the interaction

phonomimesis the imitation of a sound associated with an object

pluralism a philosophical approach that acknowledges diversity of perspectives, beliefs, values, and practices in society and embraces the notion that such diversity cannot be fully resolved, only managed through democratic forms of communication

positive face a speaker's self-image as a person worthy of appreciation, presented to others in interaction

positive politeness the communication strategy of appealing to someone's positive attributes in order to avoid offending them (e.g., with criticism)

postmulticulturalism an ideology according to which some minority groups are incorrigible and incapable of assimilation

practical metadiscourse cultural members' lay (nonacademic) talk about communication practices

pragmatic meaning a type of meaning linguistic elements take on as they become actions in the context of social interaction

primary genre a type of speech genre in everyday communication, such as rejoinders or personal letters

referential meaning a type of meaning most commonly attributed to particular linguistic elements such as words, abstracted from their everyday use, commonly found in dictionaries

reflexivity the intercultural practitioner's effort to reflect on their place in the world, including their worldview, opinions, attitudes, preferences, likes and dislikes, commitments, and principles

relational inquiry an approach to research that sees knowledge as necessarily resulting from interactions between researchers and research participants

relative social privilege a special, unearned advantage given to people of preferred social status or rank at the exclusion or detriment of others

research paradigm a system of basic theoretical assumptions about how the world (including intercultural communication) works and about how the world (including intercultural communication) should be studied

restricted code a set of principles for planning, organizing, and regulating communication that shifts emphasis from verbal expression toward nonverbal communication and the indexing of shared, taken-for-granted knowledge

rich point the combined experience of intense surprise, confusion, and fascination when confronted with an unfamiliar cultural practice

secondary genre a type of speech genre derived from everyday communication, such as novels and speeches

social drama a type of communication form that occurs when a social group attempts to hold one of its members accountable by invoking a norm

social interaction the sequence of meaningful communicative actions between two or more participants that are meaningful relative to a set of contexts

speech act the use of speech in a social situation to perform an action with social consequences

speech community community enacted and experienced through members' communication choices

speech event a social event with a locally recognized beginning and end governed by the norms inherent in the speech acts that constitute it

speech genre a locally recognized and named generic form of language use

speech situation a type of social situation in which speech is appropriate and to be expected

stance a speaker's evaluative position toward an object (e.g., event, person, idea, issue, etc.) expressed in social interaction

terms of endearment terms of address one uses with intimate others

topic-delayed organization (of talk) the practice of explicitly naming the topic of the conversation relatively late in the course of the conversation

topic-first organization (of talk) the practice of explicitly naming the topic of the conversation at the beginning of, or early in, the course of the conversation

topic selection the act of identifying a particular subject matter as an appropriate conversational topic and introducing it into an ongoing conversation

topic management the conversational actions speakers perform with topics

translocal genre a speech genre that circulates across cultural boundaries

turn at talk a participant's utterance in the course of social interaction

turn-taking participants of social interaction taking alternating turns-at-talk in an orderly, sequential fashion

upgrader linguistic elements (especially words) that intensify an utterance and make it more direct

verbal hygiene a set of practices directed at preserving the "purity" of a language (particularly vocabulary and grammar) from external corruption and thereby affirming the value and unity of the community that calls that language its own

World Englishes systematically different varieties of English around the world

References

Adult Swim. (2010, April 12). Death Star yo mama | Robot Chicken | Adult Swim [Video file]. https://www.youtube.com/watch?v=V4n0F9R90F0

Agar, M. (1994). *Language shock: Understanding the culture of conversation.* William Morrow.

Agar, M. (1994). The intercultural frame. *International Journal of Intercultural Relations, 18*(2), 221–237. https://doi.org/10.1016/0147-1767(94)90029-9

Agar, M. (1999). How to ask for a study in qualitatisch. *Qualitative Health Research, 9*(5), 684–697. doi: 10.1177/104973299129122162

Agar, M. (2006). Culture: Can you take it anywhere? Invited lecture presented at the Gevirtz Graduate School of Education, University of California at Santa Barbara. *International Journal of Qualitative Methods, 5*(2), 1–16.

Agar, M. H. (2019). *Culture: How to make it work in a world of hybrids.* Rowman & Littlefield.

Akiyama, Y. (2017). Vicious vs. virtuous cycles of turn negotiation in American-Japanese telecollaboration: Is silence a virtue? *Language and Intercultural Communication, 17*(2), 190–209. doi:10.1080/14708477.2016.1277231

Albert, R. & Ha, A. (2004). Latino/Anglo-American differences in attributions to situations involving touch and silence. *International Journal of Intercultural Relations, 28* (3–4), 253–280. doi:10.1016/j.ijintrel.2004.06.003

Alim, H. S., & Smitherman, G. (2012). *Articulate while Black: Barack Obama, language and race in the U. S.* Oxford University Press.

Allen, B. J. (2011). *Difference matters: Communicating social identity.* Waveland Press.

Arató, A. (2018, September). Waking up as a meme-hero [Video file]. https://www.ted.com/talks/andras_arato_waking_up_as_a_meme_hero

Austin, J. L. (1962/2014). How to do things with words. In A. Jaworski & N. Coupland (Eds.), *The discourse reader*, 3rd. ed. (pp. 51–61). Routledge.

Bailey, B. (2000). Communicative behavior and conflict between African American customers and Korean immigrant retailers in Los Angeles. *Discourse & Society, 11*(1), 86–108. doi:10.1177/0957926500011001004

Bailey, B. (2000). Language and negotiation of ethnic/racial identity among Dominican Americans. *Language in Society 29*, 555–582.

Bailey, B. (2004). Misunderstanding. In A. Duranti (Ed.), *A companion to linguistic anthropology* (pp. 395–413). Blackwell Publishing.

Bailey, B. (2007). Heteroglossia and boundaries. In M. Heller (Ed.), *Bilingualism: A social approach* (pp. 257–274). Palgrave Macmillan.

Bailey, B. (2017). *Piropo* [amorous flattery] as a cultural term for talk in the Spanish-speaking world. In D. Carbaugh (Ed.), *The handbook of communication in cross-cultural perspective* (pp. 195–207). Routledge.

Bakhtin, M. M. (1986). *Speech genres and other late essays.* Translated by V. W. McGee. University of Texas Press.

Banks, S. P., Ge, G., & Baker, J. (1991). Intercultural encounters and miscommunication. In N. Coupland, H. Giles, & J. M. Wiemann (Eds.), *"Miscommunication" and problematic talk* (pp. 103–120). SAGE.

Bardhan, N., & Zhang, B. (2017). A post/decolonial view of race and identity through the narratives of U.S. international students from the Global South. *Communication Quarterly, 65*(3), 285–306. doi:10.1080/01463373.2016.1237981

Basso, K. H. (1972). "To give up on words": Silence in Western Apache culture. In P. Giglioli (Ed.), *Language and social context* (p. 67–86.). Penguin Books.

Basso, K. H. (1979). *Portraits of "the Whiteman": Linguistic play and cultural symbols among the Western Apache.* Cambridge University Press.

Beaulieu, C. M. J. (2004). Intercultural study of personal space: A case study. *Journal of Applied Social Psychology, 34*(4), 794–805. doi:10.1111/j.1559-1816.2004.tb02571.x

Belhiah, H. (2013). Gesture as a resource for intersubjectivity in second-language learning situations. *Classroom Discourse, 4*(2), 111–129. doi:10.1080/19463014.2012.671273

Bell, N., & Attardo, S. (2010). Failed humor: Issues in non-native speakers' appreciation and understanding of humor. *Intercultural Pragmatics, 7*(3), 423–447. https://doi.org/10.1515/IPRG.2010.019

Bernstein, B. (1964). Elaborated and restricted codes: Their social origins and some consequences. *American Anthropologist, 66*(6), 55–69. doi:10.1525/aa.1964.66.suppl_3.02a00030

Billig, M. (2006). Political rhetorics of discrimination. In K. Brown (Editor-in-Chief), *Encyclopedia of language and linguistics* (2nd ed.), *Vol. 9.* (pp. 697–699). Elsevier.

Black, L. L., & Stone, D. (2005). Expanding the definition of privilege: The concept of social privilege. *Journal of Multicultural Counseling and Development, 33*(4), 243–255. doi:10.1002/j.2161-1912.2005.tb00020.x

Blackledge, A., & Creese, A. (2017). Translanguaging and the body. *International Journal of Multilingualism, 14*(3), 250–268. doi:10.1080/14790718.2017.1315809

Blommaert, J. (2001). Investigating narrative inequality: African asylum seekers' stories in Belgium. *Discourse & Society, 12*, 413–449. doi: 10.1177/0957926501012004002

Blommaert, J. (2005). *Discourse: A critical introduction.* Cambridge University Press.

Bonilla-Silva, E., & Forman, T. A. (2000). "I am not a racist but ...": Mapping White college students' racial ideology in the USA. *Discourse & Society, 11*(1), 50–85. doi: 10.1177/0957926500011001003

Boromisza-Habashi, D. (2010). How are political concepts "essentially" contested? *Language & Communication, 30*(4), 276–284. doi:10.1016/j.langcom.2010.04.002

Boromisza-Habashi, D. (2013). *Speaking hatefully: Culture, communication, and political action in Hungary*. Pennsylvania State University Press.

Boromisza-Habashi, D. (2016). What we need is good communication: Vernacular globalization in some Hungarian speech. *International Journal of Communication, 10,* 4600–4619. http://ijoc.org/index.php/ijoc/article/view/4110/1788

Boromisza-Habashi, D., & Fang, Y. (2020). Rethinking the ethnography of communication's conception of value in the context of globalization. *Communication Theory.* doi:10.1093/ct/qtz042

Boromisza-Habashi, D., & Martínez-Guillem, S. (2012). Comparing language and social interaction. In F. Esser & T. Hanitzsch (Eds.), *Handbook of comparative communication research* (pp. 134–147). Routledge.

Boromisza-Habashi, D., & Reinig, L. (2018). Speech genres and cultural value in the Anglo-American public speaking course as a site of language socialization. *Journal of International and Intercultural Communication, 11*(2), 117–135. doi:10.1080/17513057.2018.1428765

Boromisza-Habashi, D., & Xiong, B. (2019). Intercultural communication and security. In B. C. Taylor & H. Bean (Eds.), *The handbook of communication and security* (pp. 121–135). Routledge.

Braithwaite, C. (1990). Communicative silence: A cross-cultural study of Basso's hypothesis. In D. Carbaugh (Ed.), *Cultural communication and intercultural contact* (pp. 321–327). Lawrence Erlbaum Associates.

Briggs, C. L. (1986). *Learning how to ask: A sociolinguistic appraisal of the role of the interview in social science research*. Cambridge University Press.

Burke, K. (1945). *A grammar of motives*. Prentice Hall.

Cameron, D. (1995). *Verbal hygiene*. Routledge

Cameron, D. (2000). *Good to talk? Living and working in a communication culture*. SAGE.

Cameron, D. (2003). Globalizing "communication." In J. Aitchison & D. M. Lewis (Eds.), *New media language* (pp. 27–35). Routledge.

Carbaugh, D. (1990). Communication rules in Donahue discourse. In D. Carbaugh (Ed.), *Cultural communication and intercultural contact* (pp. 119–149). Lawrence Erlbaum Associates.

Carbaugh, D. (1993). Cultural pragmatics and intercultural competence. In L. Löfman, L. Kurki-Suonio, S. Pellinen, & J. Lehtonen (Eds.), *The competent intercultural communicator.* AFinLA Yearbook 1993. Publications de L'Association Finlandaise de Linguistique Appliquée, 51 (pp. 117–129).

Carbaugh, D. (2005). *Cultures in conversation*. Lawrence Erlbaum Associates.

Carbaugh, D. (2007). Cultural discourse analysis: Communication practices and intercultural encounters. *Journal of Intercultural Communication Research, 36*(3), 167–182. doi:10.1080/17475750701737090

Carbaugh, D., & Wolf, K. (1999). Situating rhetoric in cultural discourses. In A. González & D. V. Tanno (Eds.), *Rhetoric in intercultural contexts* (pp. 19–30). SAGE.

Carbaugh, D., Berry, M., & Nurmikari-Berry, M. (2006). Coding personhood through cultural terms and practices: Silence and quietude as a Finnish "natural way of being." *Journal of Language and Social Psychology, 25*(3), 203–220. doi:10.1177/0261927X06289422

Cashman, H. (2015). Intersecting communities, interwoven identities: Questioning boundaries, testing bridges, and forging a queer *latinidad* in the U.S. Southwest. *Language and Intercultural Communication, 15*(3), 424–440. doi:10.1080/14708477.2015.1015344

Chávez, K. R. (2012). Doing intersectionality: Power, privilege, and identities in political activist communities. In N. Bradhan & M. P. Orbe (Eds.), *Identity research and communication: Intercultural reflections and future directions* (pp. 21–32). Lexington Books.

Connell, C. (2010). Doing, undoing, or redoing gender? Learning from the workplace experiences of transpeople. *Gender & Society, 24*(1), 31–55. doi:10.1177/0891243209356429

Connolly, W. E. (2005). *Pluralism.* Duke University Press.

Covarrubias, P. (2000). Of endearment and other terms of address: A Mexican perspective. In M. Lustig & J. Koester (Eds.), *AmongUS: Essays on identity, belonging, and intercultural competence* (pp. 9–17). Addison Wesley Longman.

Covarrubias, P. O. (2008). Masked silence sequences: Hearing discrimination in the college classroom. Communication, Culture & Critique, 1(3), 227–252. https://doi.org/10.1111/j.1753-9137.2008.00021.x

Covarrubias, P., Kvam, D., & Saito, M. (2019). Symbolic agonistics: Stressing emotion and relation in Mexican, Mexican@, and Japanese discourses. In M. Scollo & T. Milburn (Eds.), *Engaging and transforming global communication through cultural discourse analysis: A tribute to Donal Carbaugh* (pp. 179–194). Rowman & Littlefield.

Craig, R. T. (2005). 2004 ICA Presidential Address. How we talk about how we talk: Communication theory in the public interest. *Journal of Communication, 55*(4), 659–667. doi:10.1111/j.1460-2466.2005.tb03015.x

Craig, R. T. (2013). Communication theory and social change. *Communication & Social Change, 1*(1), 5–18. doi:10.4471/csc.2013.01

Croft, S. (2012). Constructing ontological insecurity: The insecuritization of Britain's Muslims. *Contemporary Security Policy, 33*(2), 219–235. doi: 10.1080/13523260.2012.693776

Cruz, J., McDonald, J., Broadfoot, K., Chuang, A. K., & Ganesh, S. (2018). "Aliens" in the United States: A collaborative autoethnography of foreign-born faculty. *Journal of Management Inquiry.* doi:10.1177/1056492618796561

Danesi, M. (2017). *The semiotics of emoji.* Bloomsbury.

Davies, C. E. (2004). Developing awareness of crosscultural pragmatics: The case of American/German sociable interaction. *Multilingua, 23*(3), 207–231. https://doi.org/10.1515/mult.2004.010

de Klerk, V. (2000). To be Xhosa or not to be Xhosa ... That is the question. *Journal of Multilingual and Multicultural Development, 21*(3), 198–215. doi:10.1080/01434630008666401

Dewey, J. (1910). *How we think.* D. C. Heath & Co.

Dewey, J. (1925/1958). *Experience and nature.* Dover.

Dewey, J. (1938). *Logic: The theory of inquiry.* Henry Holt & Co.

Du-Babcock, B. (1999). Top management and turn taking in professional communication: First-versus second-language strategies. *Management Communication Quarterly, 12*(4), 544–575. doi:10.1177/0893318999124003

Egner, I. (2006). Intercultural aspects of the speech act of promising: Western and African practices. *Intercultural Pragmatics, 3–4*, 443–464. doi:10.1515/IP.2006.027

Eltahawy, M. (2015). *Headscarves and hymens: Why the Middle East needs a sexual revolution.* Farrar, Starus and Giroux.

Emerson, R. M., Fretz, R. I., & Shaw, L. L. (2011). *Writing ethnographic fieldnotes* (2nd ed.). University of Chicago Press.

Feinberg, M., & Willer, R. (2015). From gulf to bridge: when do moral arguments facilitate political influence? *Personality and Social Psychology Bulletin, 41*(12), 1665–1681. doi:10.1177/0146167215607842

Findlay, S. (1994). Structure and process in speech subcommunities of Hmong students at a Northern California high school. *Linguistics and Education, 6*(3), 245–260. doi:10.1016/0898-5898(94)90013-2

Fitch, K. (1991). The interplay of linguistic universals and cultural knowledge in personal address: Colombian *madre* terms. *Communication Monographs, 58*, 254–272.

Fitch, K. (1998). A ritual for attempting leave-taking in Colombia. In J. N. Martin, T. K. Nakayama, & L. A. Flores (Eds.), *Readings in cultural contexts* (pp. 179–186). Mayfield.

Fitch, K. L. (1998). Speaking relationally: Culture, communication, and interpersonal connection. Guilford Press.

Flores, L. A. (2001). Challenging the myth of assimilation: A Chicana feminist response. In M. J. Collier (Ed.), *Constituting cultural difference through discourse* (pp. 26–46). SAGE.

French Embassy U.S. [@franceintheus]. (2018, July 18). On @TheDailyShow, @Trevornoah called the @FrenchTeam's World Cup win an "African victory." Read Ambassador @GerardAraud's response: [Tweet]. https://twitter.com/franceintheus/status/1019691552384352257

Fujio, M. (2004). Silence during intercultural communication: A case study. *Corporate Communications: An International Journal, 9*(4), 331–339. doi:10.1108/13563280410564066

García-Sánchez, I. (2010). Serious games: Code-switching and gendered identities in Moroccan girls' pretend play. *Pragmatics, 20*(4), 523–555. doi:10.1075/prag.20.4.03gar

Geertz, C. (2000). *The interpretation of cultures.* Basic Books.

Giles, H., & Ogay, T. (2007). Communication accommodation theory. In B. B. Whaley & W. Samter (Eds.), *Explaining communication: Contemporary theories and exemplars* (pp. 293–310). Lawrence Erlbaum Associates.

Goffman, E. (1981). *Forms of talk.* University of Pennsylvania Press.

Goldsmith, D. (1989/90). Gossip from the native's point of view: A comparative analysis. *Research on Language and Social Interaction, 23*(1–4), 163–194. doi: 10.1080/08351818909389320

Goodwin, C., & Duranti, A. (1992). Rethinking context: An introduction. In A. Duranti & C. Goodwin (Eds.), *Rethinking context: Language as an interactive phenomenon* (pp. 1–42). Cambridge University Press.

Guidi, A. (2017). Humor universals. In S. Attardo (Ed.), *The Routledge handbook of language and humor* (pp. 17–33). Routledge.

Gumperz, J. J. (1982). *Discourse strategies*. Cambridge University Press.

Hall, E. T. (1959). *The silent language*. Doubleday.

Hall, E. T. (1966). *The hidden dimension*. Doubleday.

Hall, E. T. (1976). *Beyond culture*. Anchor Press.

Hall, E. T. (1992). *An anthropology of everyday life: An autobiography*. Doubleday.

Halverson, C. B., & Tirmizi, S. A. (2008). *Effective multicultural teams: Theory and practice*. Springer.

Hart, T. (2016). Learning how to speak like a "native": Speech and culture in an online communication training program. *Journal of Business and Technical Communication, 30*(3), 285–321. doi: 10.1177/1050651916636363

Hasler, B., & Friedman, D. (2012). Sociocultural conventions in avatar-mediated nonverbal communication: A cross-cultural analysis of virtual proxemics. *Journal of Intercultural Communication Research, 41*(3), 238–259. doi:10.1080/17475759.2012.728764

Hastings, S. O. (2001). Social drama as a site for the communal construction and management of Asian Indian "stranger" identity. *Research on Language and Social Interaction, 34*(3), 309–335. doi: 10.1207/S15327973RLSI34-3_2

Haviland, J. B. (2007). Person reference in Tzotzil gossip: Referring dupliciter. In N. J. Enfield & T. Stivers (Eds.), *Person reference in interaction: Linguistic, cultural, and social perspectives* (pp. 226–252). Cambridge University Press.

Heng, T. T. (2018). Different is not deficient: Contradicting stereotypes of Chinese international students in U.S. higher education. *Studies in Higher Education, 43*(1), 22–36. doi: 10.1080/03075079.2016.1152466

Hochschield, A. R. (2016). *Strangers in their own land: Anger and mourning on the American right*. The New Press.

hooks, b. (2015). *Feminism is for everybody: Passionate politics*. Routledge.

Hua, Z. (2010). Language socialization and interculturality: Address terms in intergenerational talk in Chinese diasporic families. *Language and Intercultural Communication, 10*(3), 189–205. doi:10.1080/1470903348531

Hughes, J. M. F., & Tracy, K. (2015). Indexicality. In K. Tracy (Ed.), *The international encyclopedia of language and social interaction* (pp. 788–793). Wiley-Blackwell.

Hwang, H. C., & Matsumoto, D. (2013). Nonverbal behaviors and cross-cultural communication in the new era. In F. Sharifian & M. Jamarani (Eds.), *Language and intercultural communication in the new era* (pp. 116–137). Routledge.

Hymes, D. (1972). Models of the interaction of language and social life. In J. J. Gumperz & D. Hymes (Eds.), *Directions in sociolinguistics: The ethnography of communication* (pp. 35–71). Holt, Rinehart and Winston.

Iyengar, S. S. (2010, July). The art of choosing. https://www.ted.com/talks/sheena_iyengar_on_the_art_of_choosing

Jackson, J. P., & Weidman, N. M. (2006). *Race, racism, and science: Social impact and interaction*. Rutgers University Press.

Jones, T., & Hall, C. (2019). Grammatical reanalysis and the multiple *n-words* in African American English. *American Speech, 94*(4), 478–512. doi:10.1215/00031283-7611213.

Katriel, T. (1985). "Griping" as a verbal ritual in some Israeli discourse. In M. Dascal (Ed.), *Dialogue: An interdisciplinary approach* (pp. 367–381). John Benjamins.

Katriel, T., & Philipsen, G. (1981). "What we need is communication": "Communication" as a cultural category in some American speech. *Communication Monographs, 48*(4), 301–317. doi:10.1080/03637758109376064

Katriel, T., Livio, O. (2019). When discourse matters: Temporality in discursive action. In M. Scollo & T. Milburn (Eds.), *Engaging and transforming global communication through cultural discourse analysis: A tribute to Donal Carbaugh* (pp. 57–71). Rowman & Littlefield.

Keels, M. M., & Powers, R. S. (2013). Marital name changing: Delving deeper into women's reasons. *Advances in Applied Sociology, 3*(7), 301–306. doi:10.4236/aasoci.2013.37038

Kendon, A. (2004). *Gesture: Visible action as utterance.* Cambridge University Press.

Kiesling, S. F. (2004). Dude. *American Speech, 79*(3), 281–305. doi:10.1215/00031283-79-3-281

Kim, E. Y. A., & Brown, L. (2014). Negotiating pragmatic competence in computer mediated communication: The case of Korean address terms. *CALICO Journal, 31*(3), 264–284. doi: 10.1139/cj.31.3.264-284

Kissling, E. A. (1991). Street harassment: The language of sexual terrorism. *Discourse & Society, 2*(4), 451–460. doi:10.1177/0957926591002004006

Kosztolányi, D. (2011). *Kornél Esti: A novel* (B. Adams, Trans.). New Directions.

Kotani, M. (2016). Two codes for remedying problematic situations: Japanese and English speakers' views of explanations and apologies in the United States. *Journal of Intercultural Communication Research, 45*(2), 126–144. doi:10.1080/17475759.2015.1126756

Kotani, M. (2017). Dynamic nature of boundaries of speech communities: Learning and negotiating codes in intercultural communication. *Journal of Intercultural Communication Research, 46*(5), 463–477.

Kovats-Bernat, J. C. (2002). Negotiating dangerous fields: Pragmatic strategies for fieldwork amid violence and terror. *American Anthropologist, 104*, 1–15.

Kreiss, D. (2016). *Prototype politics: Technology-intensive campaigning and the data of democracy.* Oxford University Press.

Krøløkke, C. (2009). Intersectionality. In S. W. Littlejohn & K. Foss (Eds.), *The encyclopedia of communication theory* (p. 566). SAGE.

Lakoff, G. (2004). *Don't think of an elephant! Known your values and frame the debate: An essential guide for progressives.* Chelsea Green Publishing.

Leonardi, P., & Rodriguez-Lluesma, C. (2013). Occupational stereotypes, perceived status difference, and international communication in global organizations. *Communication Monographs, 80*(4), 478–502. doi:10.1080/03637751.2013.828155

Liberman, K. (1990). Intercultural communication in Central Australia. In D. Carbaugh (Ed.), *Cultural communication and intercultural contact* (pp. 177–183). Lawrence Erlbaum Associates.

Linde, C. (2003). Narrative in institutions. In D. Schiffrin, D. Tannen, & H. E. Hamilton (Eds.), *The handbook of discourse analysis* (pp. 518–535). Blackwell.

Little, K. B. (1968). Cultural variations in social schemata. *Journal of Personality and Social Psychology, 10*(1), 1–7. doi:10.1037/h0026381

Liu, J. (2002). Negotiating silence in American classrooms: Three Chinese cases. *Language and Intercultural Communication, 2*(1), 37–54. doi:10.1080/14708470208668074

Lyiscott, J. (2014). 3 ways to speak English. *TED.com.* https://www.ted.com/talks/jamila_lyiscott_3_ways_to_speak_english

MacDonald, A. (2019, May 28). Small talk is tough for Finns. So they're taking lessons. "I love your shirt." *The Wall Street Journal.* https://www.wsj.com/articles/small-talk-is-tough-for-finns-so-theyre-taking-lessons-i-love-your-shirt-11559061410

Martin, J. N., Nakayama, T. K., & Carbaugh, D. (2012). The history and development of the study of intercultural communication and applied linguistics. In J. Jackson (Ed.), *The Routledge handbook of language and intercultural communication* (pp. 17–36). Routledge.

Matsumoto, D., & Hwang, H. C. (2013). Culture and nonverbal communication. In J. A. Hall & M. L. Knapp (Eds.), *Nonverbal communication* (pp. 697–727). De Gruyter Mouton.

Matsumoto, D., & Kudoh, T. (1993). American-Japanese cultural differences in attributions of personality based on smiles. *Journal of Nonverbal Behavior, 17*(4), 231–243. doi:10.1007/BF00987239

Matwick, K., & Matwick, K. (2015). East meets West: The discourse of Japanese American cookbooks as intercultural communication. *Journal of Intercultural Communication, 39,* 1–12.

McArthur, T. (July 2005). Chinese, English, Spanish—and the rest. *English Today, 21*(3), 55–61. doi: 10.1017/S0266078405003123

McCulloch, G. (2019). *Because internet: Understanding the new rules of language.* Riverhead Books.

Meeuwis, M. (1994). Leniency and testiness in intercultural communication: Remarks on ideology and context in interactional sociolinguistics. *Pragmatics, 4,* 391–408.

Meyer, D. P. (Producer, Director). (2011). *You laugh but it's true* [Motion picture]. United States: Day 1 Films.

Meyer, J. (2015). *Whistled languages: A worldwide inquiry on human whistled speech.* Springer.

Miller, A. N. (2002). An exploration of Kenyan public speaking patterns with implications for the American introductory public speaking course. *Communication Education, 51*(2), 168–182. https://doi.org/10.1080/03634520216505

Miller, L. (1994). Japanese and American meetings and what goes on before them: A case study of co-worker misunderstanding. *Pragmatics, 4*(2), 221–238. https://doi.org/10.1075/prag.4.2.03mil

Morgan, M. H. (2014). *Speech communities.* Cambridge University Press.

Muñoz, K. L. (2014). *Transcribing silence: Culture, relationships, and communication.* Left Coast Press.

Murphy, L. (2018). *The prodigal tongue: The love-hate relationship between American and British English.* Penguin Books.

Nakane, I. (2006). Silence and politeness in intercultural communication in university seminars. *Journal of Pragmatics, 38*(11), 1811–1835. doi:10.1016/j.pragma.2006.01.005

National Communication Association. (2019, October 4). *NCA Concepts in Communication Video Series—Culture Shock* [Video file]. https://youtu.be/KRXZpegaBO0

Native American students. (2018, September 26). Postsecondary National Policy Institute (PNPI). https://pnpi.org/native-american-students/

Neuliep, J. W., & Johnson, M. (2016). A cross-cultural comparison of Ecuadorian and United States face, facework, and conflict styles during interpersonal conflict: An application of face-negotiation theory. *Journal of International and Intercultural Communication, 9*(1), 1–19. doi:10.1080/17513057.2016.1120844

Nielsen, L. B. (2004). *License to harass: Law, hierarchy, and offensive public speech.* Princeton University Press.

Nofsinger, R. E. (1990). Rethinking "topic." *Communication Reports, 3*(1), 45–47. https://doi.org/10.1080/08934219009367500

Nuciforo, E. V. (2013). Russian toasting and drinking as communication ritual. *Russian Journal of Communication, 5*(2), 161–175. doi:10.1080/19409419.2013.805670

Oberg, K. (1960). Cultural shock: Adjustment to new cultural environments. *Practical Anthropology, 7*(4), 177–182. https://doi.org/10.1177/009182966000700405

Ogunyemi, B. (2019, October 20). A doctor was mocked by a judge for his accent. I hope you can relate. *CBC News.* https://www.cbc.ca/news/about-cbc-news-1.1294364

Pan, Y., Scollon, S. W., & Scollon, R. (2002). *Professional communication in international settings.* Blackwell.

Patterson, C. J., & Farr, R. H. (2017). What shall we call ourselves? Last names among lesbian, gay, and heterosexual couples and their adopted children. *Journal of GLBT Family Studies, 13*(2), 97–113. doi:10.1080/1550428X.2016.1169239

Patterson, M. L. (2012). Nonverbal communication. In V. Ramachandran (Ed.), *Encyclopedia of human behavior (2nd ed.*; pp. 731–738). Elsevier/Academic Press.

Philips, S. U. (1972). Participant structures and communicative competence: Warm Springs children in community and classroom. In C. B. Cazden, V. P. John, & D. Hymes (Eds.), *Functions of language in the classroom* (pp. 370–394). Teachers College Press.

Philipsen, G. (1975). Speaking "like a man" in Teamsterville: Culture patterns of role enactment in an urban neighborhood. *Quarterly Journal of Speech, 61*(1), 13–22. doi:10.1080/00335637509383264

Philipsen, G. (1976). Places for speaking in Teamsterville. *Quarterly Journal of Speech, 62*(1), 15–25.doi: 10.1080/00335637609383314

Philipsen, G. (1987). The prospect for cultural communication. In L. Kincaid (Ed.), *Communication theory: Eastern and Western perspectives* (pp. 245–254). Academic Press.

Philipsen, G. (1992). *Speaking culturally: Explorations in social communication.* SUNY Press.

Philipsen, G., Coutu, L. M., and Covarrubias, P. (2005). Speech codes theory: Restatement, revisions, and response to criticisms. In W. B. Gudykunst (Ed.), *Theorizing about intercultural communication* (pp. 55–68). SAGE.

Pietikäinen, K. (2018). Misunderstandings and ensuring understanding in private ELF talk. *Applied Linguistics, 39*(2), 188–212. doi:10.1093/applin/amw005

Pilcher, J. (2017). Names and "doing gender": How forenames and surnames contribute to gender identities, difference, and inequalities. *Sex Roles, 77*(11–12), 812–822. doi:10.1007/s11199-017-0805-4

Piller, I. (2017). *Intercultural communication: A critical introduction* (2nd ed.). Edinburgh University Press.

Ramjattan, V. (2019). The White native speaker and inequality regimes in the private English language school. *Intercultural Education, 30*(2), 126–140. doi:10.1080/14675986.2018.1538043

Rapatahana, V. (2017). English language as thief. In. M. Borjian (Ed.), *Language and globalization: An autoethnographic approach* (pp. 64–76). Routledge.

Robles, J. S., & Kurylo, A. (2017). "Let's have the men clean up": Interpersonally communicated stereotypes as a resource for resisting gender-role prescribed activities. *Discourse Studies, 19*(6), 673–693. doi: 10.1177/1461445617727184

Rodríguez, L. (2019). "Time is *not* a line." Temporal gestures in Chol Mayan. *Journal of Pragmatics, 151,* 1–17. doi:10.1016/j.pragma.2019.07.003

Rogerson-Revell, P. (2010). "Can you spell that for us nonnative speakers?": Accommodation strategies in international business meetings. *Journal of Business Communication, 47*(4), 432–454. doi:10.1177/0021943610377304

Rosa, J. (2019). Looking like a language, sounding like a race: Raciolinguistic ideologies and the learning of *latinidad.* Oxford University Press.

Ross, L. (1977). The intuitive psychologist and his shortcomings: Distortions in the attribution process. In L. Berkowitz (Ed.), *Advances in experimental social psychology* (Vol. 10). Academic Press.

Ross, L., & Ward, A. (1995, May). *Naïve realism: Implications for social conflict and misunderstanding.* Working Paper No. 48. Stanford Center on Conflict and Negotiation.

Sandel, T. L., Buttny, R., & Varghese, M. (2019). Online interaction across three contexts: An analysis of culture and technological affordances. *Journal of Intercultural Communication Research, 48*(1), 52–71. doi: 10.1080/17475759.2018.1552616

Sarkar, M., & Winer, L. (2006). Multilingual codeswitching in Quebec rap: Poetry, pragmatics and performativity. *International Journal of Multilingualism, 3*(3), 173–192. doi:10.2167/ijm030.0

Saville-Troike, M. (2003). *The ethnography of communication: An introduction* (3rd ed.). Blackwell.

Scollon, R., & Scollon, S. W. (2001). *Intercultural communication: A discourse approach.* Blackwell.

Scott, K. D. (2017). *The language of strong black womanhood: Myths, models, messages, and new mandate for self-care.* Lexington Press.

Searle, J. (2008 [1965]). What is a speech act? In I. Hutchby (Ed.), *Methods in language and social interaction, Vol. 1* (pp. 8–23). SAGE.

Sharifian, F. (2014). World Englishes, intercultural communication and requisite competences. In J. Jackson (Ed.), *The Routledge handbook of language and intercultural communication* (pp. 310–322). Routledge.

Shrikant, N. (2018). "There's no such thing as Asian": A membership categorization analysis of cross-cultural adaptation in an Asian American business community. *Journal of International and Intercultural Communication, 11*(4), 286–303. doi:10.1080/17513057.2018.1478986

Sotirova, N. (2018). A cry and an outcry: Oplakvane (complaining) as a term for communication practice. *Journal of International and Intercultural Communication, 11*(4), 304–323. doi:10.1080/17513057.2018.1479439

Spradley, J. P. (1979/2016). *The ethnographic interview*. Waveland Press.

Stewart, E. C., & Bennett, M. J. (1991). *American cultural patterns: A cross-cultural perspective*. Intercultural Press.

Streeck, J. (2015). Embodiment in human communication. *Annual Review of Anthropology, 44,* 419–438. doi: 10.1146/annurev-anthro-102214-014045

Streeck, J., & Knapp, M. L. (1992). The interaction of visual and verbal features in human communication. In F. Poyatos (Ed.), *Advances in nonverbal communication: Sociocultural, clinical, esthetic and literary perspectives* (pp. 3–23). John Benjamins.

Tannen, D. (1985). Silence: Anything but. In D. Tannen & M. Saville-Troike (Eds.), *Perspectives on silence* (pp. 93–111). Ablex.

Tatar, S. (2005). Why keep silent? The classroom participation experiences of non-native-English-speaking students. *Language and Intercultural Communication, 5*(3–4), 284–293. doi:10.1080/1408470508668668902

Team Coco. (2018, January 23). *Ismo: Ass is the most complicated word in the English language—CONAN on TBS* [Video file]. https://www.youtube.com/watch?v=RAGcDi0DRtU

The Daily Show With Trevor Noah. (2018, July 18). *Trevor responds to criticism from the French ambassador—Between The Scenes | The Daily Show* [Video file]. https://www.youtube.com/watch?v=COD9hcTpGWQ

The Daily Show. [@TheDailyShow]. (2018, July 16). TONIGHT: Congratulations to Africa on winning the 2018 Men's World Cup! [Tweet]. https://twitter.com/TheDailyShow/status/1019012366082723840

The Official Steve Harvey. (2018, August 23). Steve Harvey: Chuuuuch vs. service—You do know there is a difference right? [Video file]. https://www.youtube.com/watch?v=DKOS5jdzzzU

Thurlow, C. (2006). From statistical panic to moral panic: The metadiscursive construction and popular exaggeration of new media language in the print media. *Journal of Computer-Mediated Communication, 11*(3), 667–701. doi:10.1111/j.1083-6101.2006.00031.x

Toomey, A., Dorjee, T., & Ting-Toomey, S. (2013). Bicultural identity negotiation, conflicts, and intergroup communication strategies. *Journal of Intercultural Communication Research, 42*(2), 112–134. doi:10.1080/17475759.2013.838984s

Tsang, W. K., & Wong, M. (2004). Constructing a shared "Hong Kong identity" in comic discourses. *Discourse and Society, 15*(6), 767–785. doi:10.1177/ 0957926504046504

Tufekci, Z. (2017). *Twitter and tear gas: The power and fragility of networked protest*. Yale University Press.

Vargas-Urpi, M. (2013). Coping with nonverbal communication in public service interpreting with Chinese immigrants. *Journal of Intercultural Communication Research, 42,* 340—360. doi:10.1080/17475759.2013.83895

Veit-Wild, F. (2009). "Zimbolicious"—the creative potential of linguistic innovation: The case of Shona-English in Zimbabwe. *Journal of Southern African Studies, 35*(3), 683–697. doi:10.1080/03057070903101896

Vismans, R. (2009). Advanced learners' use of Dutch second-person pronouns during residence abroad. *Journal of German Linguistics, 21*(2), 211—230. doi:10.1017/S1470542709000269

Wade, P. (2015). *Race: An introduction*. Cambridge University Press.

Wason, P. C. (1960). On the failure to eliminate hypotheses in a conceptual task. *The Quarterly Journal of Experimental Psychology, 12*, 129–140.

Watson, O. M. (1970). *Proxemic behavior: A cross-cultural study.* Mouton.

Wierzbicka, A. (1997). *Understanding cultures through their key words: English, Russian, Polish, German, and Japanese.* Oxford University Press.

Williams, T. (1985). The nature of miscommunication in the cross-cultural employment interview. In J. B. Pride (Ed.), *Cross-cultural encounters: Communication and mis-communication* (pp. 165–175). River Seine Publications.

Witteborn, S. (2010). The role of transnational NGOs in promoting global citizenship and globalizing communication practices. *Language and Intercultural Communication, 10*(4), 358–372. doi:10.1080/14708477.2010.497556

Woman who changed self to please boyfriend enjoying happy long-term relationship. (2012, June 13). *The Onion.* https://www.theonion.com/woman-who-changed-self-to-please-boyfriend-enjoying-hap-1819576600

Woolard, K. A. (1998). Language ideology as a field of inquiry. In B. B. Schieffelin, K. A. Woolard, & P. V. Kroskrity (Eds.), *Language ideologies: Practice and theory* (pp. 3–47). Oxford University Press.

Xiao, L., & Gao, Y. (2016). Intercultural *Taoci* email: New wine in an old bottle. In Y-S. Chen, D-H. V. Rau, & G. Rau (Eds.), *Email discourse among Chinese using English as a lingua franca* (pp. 135–162). Springer.

Yadete, N. N. (2017). A journey with English: Reexamining the pragmatic stance toward the language of globalization. In M. Borjian (Ed.), *Language and globalization: An autoethnographic approach* (pp. 50–63). Routledge.

Yamada, H. (1990). Topic management and turn distribution in business meetings: American versus Japanese strategies. *Text, 10*(3), 271–295. https://doi.org/10.1515/text.1.1990.10.3.271

Yoshida, T., Yashiro, K., & Suzuki, Y. (2013). Intercultural communication skills: What Japanese businesses today need. *International Journal of Intercultural Relations, 37*(1), 72–85. doi:10.1016/j.ijintrel.2012.04.013

Zentella, A. C. (1997). *Growing up bilingual: Puerto Rican children in New York.* Blackwell.

Image Credits

IMG 1.1: Source: https://pixabay.com/photos/pathway-walking-person-walking-1149550/.

IMG 2.1: Source: https://pixabay.com/photos/boardwalk-footpath-green-hike-21583/.

IMG 3.1: Source: https://pixabay.com/photos/misty-fog-walk-pathway-272587/.

IMG 4.1: Source: https://pixabay.com/photos/face-pathway-wall-graffiti-2675967/.

IMG 5.1: Source: https://pixabay.com/photos/greece-skopelos-glossa-village-2746940/.

IMG 6.1: Source: https://pixabay.com/photos/pathway-clouds-scenery-sky-3882061/.

IMG 7.1: Copyright © 2018 Depositphotos/dechevm.

IMG 8.1: Copyright © 2013 Depositphotos/DesignPicsInc.

IMG 9.1: Copyright © 2012 Depositphotos/Alan.

IMG 10.1: Copyright © 2013 Depositphotos/DesignPicsInc.

IMG 11.1: Source: https://pixabay.com/photos/mountain-bike-dolomites-bicycle-tour-4510246/.

Fig. 11.1: Copyright © Shutterstock Images LLC/StockLite.

IMG 12.1: Source: https://pixabay.com/photos/architecture-art-color-colour-1867934/.

IMG 13.1: Copyright © 2010 Depositphotos/alexhd57.

IMG 14.1: Copyright © 2011 Depositphotos/photography33.

Index

China, 69
Euro-English, 69
Indian, 69
Nigerian, 69
thief or a resource, 69–70
United Nations, 69
essentialist view, 10
essentially contested term, 57
ethnic humor, 116, 123–126
ethnocentrism, 201, 222–223
ethnography, 7–8, 31
Euro-English, 69
every "faith" matters, 132–133
excuses of justifications, 186
expanding circle countries, 68
expressive systems, 107, 162, 200
extrasituational context, 27–28, 230, 231

F

face, 30–31
face threat, 103
facial expressions/actions, 170–173
    as metacommunicative comments,
       170
    as narrative components, 170
    go online, 172–174
    of emotion, 170–171
    with pragmatic functions, 170
failed humor, 121–123
faith, 137–138
field journal, 37, 226–227
Findlay, S., 194
for-anyone-anywhere genres, 110
Foreign Service Institute (FSI), 21–22
Forman, T. A., 138
four disclaimers, 217–218
frame, 173
French culture, 3
Friedman, D., 169
functional load, 148
fundamental attribution error, 208, 222

G

gatekeeping encounters, 65–67
Geertz, C., 99
gender identity transition, 89
genres, 101–102, 108–110
Germany, 116
    culture, 3
gestures, 174–178. *See also* iconic gestures
getting cussed out, 153
globalization, 119–120, 175
    effects, 84–85
Goethe-Institut, 63
Goffman, E., 26, 137

H

Hall, E. T., 21–22
Halverson, C. B., 150
haptics, 166
Hart, T., 68
Harvey, S., 102
Hasler, B., 169
Hastings, S. O., 193
hate speech in Hungary, 56–57
heteroglossia, 71
heteroglossic, 72
The Hidden Dimension (Hall), 167, 169
high-context cultures, 149–150, 150
Hochschild, A., 140–141
Hopi cultures, 21
Humboldt, A., 3
humor and topic, 121–126
Hungary, 56–57
Hwang, H. C., 175
hybridized, 119
Hymes, D., 100–101

I

iconic gestures, 174
indeterminate situation, 7
indexicality, 50
index identities, 70
indexing, 149
Indian English, 69
indirect style, 116
inductive argument pattern, 118
inferencing, 123
inner circle countries, 68
inquiry, 7
insh'allah, 219, 233
interactional frames, 33, 181, 227
interactionally frame, 186
interactional script, 199, 235
intercultural communication
    approaches to, 17–20
    as social interaction, 25–29
    critical paradigm, 19–20
    general approach of, 20–22
    goal of, 24–25
    interpretivist paradigm, 18–19
    postpositivist paradigm, 17–18
    practical approach to, 34
    practical exercise, 23
intercultural encounters, 51–52
intercultural frames, 33, 208, 227
intercultural miscommunication, 46–47, 86,
    118–119
intercultural practitioners, 116
interdependence matters, 133
interdependent organization, 119

nonverbal communication
  defined, 165–166
  embodiment vs., 162–165
  types of, 165–167
norms, 183–184, 233
norms in intercultural practice, 186
norms of interaction, 184
norms of interpretation, 165, 184
northwestern China, 19
number-one mentality, 198, 201–203, 223

O

Oberg, K., 4
ontological security, 199–200, 217
oplakvane (rituals), 109
organizing topics, 118–119
outer circle countries, 68

P

paralanguage, 167
partial, 8
participant observation, 37
participants, 26
particular social situations, 147–148
patronymic convention, 88
personal address, 79–94
  address terms, 81–83
  barriers, 94
  kinship terms, 90–93
  proper names, 86–90
  second-person pronouns, 83–86
personal convictions matter, 133
personal distance, 167
personal introductions sequence, 105–107
person referencing, 81. *See also* personal
  address
Philipsen, G., 101, 148
phonomimesis, 177
Pietikäinen, K., 176
piropo, 43, 136–138
plural, 9
pluralism, 132–136
pluralist, 203
ponimanie, 193
positions himself, 181
positive face, 103, 138, 157
positive politeness, 90
positive social face, 126
postmulticulturalism, 202
postpositivist paradigm, 17–18
practical, 227
practical goal, 33–34
pragmatic meanings, 48
premises, 132–133. *See also* cultural
  premises
    about action, 189
    about emotion, 189
    about personhood, 189
    about place, 189

about relationships, 189
about time, 189
presentation, 109–110
primary genres, 108
product, 9
promise, 102–103
proper names, 81, 86–90, 89–90
proxemics, 166, 167–170
public distance, 168
public speaking, 110
public square, 141

Q

quotable gestures, 162

R

race relations, 138–140
Rapatahana, V., 69
reading scholarship, 38
real or desired interpersonal relationship, 91
reconstructing relevant context(s), 35,
  230–233
referential meaning, 47, 98
reflexivity, 40, 218–219
relational, 7, 8
relative social privilege, 198, 209–212, 223
research paradigms, 17
restricted code, 149
rich points, 3–6, 34, 130, 165, 199, 223
right-wing bias, 141
rituals, 234
Rodriguez-Lluesma, C., 186
Rogerson-Revell, P., 64
Rosa, J., 202
rule(s), 183, 185–186, 233
    of interaction, 185
    of interpretation, 181, 185

S

salsipuede, 9
Save the Children (STC), 19
Scollon, R., 86
Scollon, S. W., 86
scripts, 33, 181, 227
secondary genres, 108
second-person pronouns, 81, 83–86, 84
sense of normality, 197–214
    avoiding building culture, 208–214
    barriers, 213
    dismissing the richness of rich points,
      200–208
    disrupted, 198–200
setting, 27–28, 230
sexist speech, 136
simplistic, 10
The Silent Language (Hall), 21
"SoCal", 54
social control, 121